The Secrets to Ultimate Weight Loss

The Secrets to Ultimate Weight Loss

A REVOLUTIONARY APPROACH TO CONQUER CRAVINGS, OVERCOME
FOOD ADDICTION, AND LOSE WEIGHT WITHOUT GOING HUNGRY

Chef AJ with Glen Merzer

ISBN: 1979414254
ISBN 13: 9781979414258
Library of Congress Control Number: 2017917208
Hail to the Kale Publishing

Praise from M.D.s for THE SECRETS TO ULTIMATE WEIGHT LOSS

Chef AJ's larger than life personality will smooth the path to the diet you must follow to enjoy the health and happiness you deserve. Her personal and professional experiences have earned her the right to be considered the world expert on "Making the Change."—John McDougall, M.D., Co-founder of the McDougall Program

This book will save your life. Tackling food addictions and weight issues squarely and honestly, Chef AJ gives you everything you need to get healthy and stay that way. She is so warm, honest, encouraging, and understanding, you'll feel you have a new friend pulling for you every step of the way.—Neal D. Barnard, M.D., F.A.C.C., Adjunct Associate Professor of Medicine, George Washington University School of Medicine, President, Physicians Committee for Responsible Medicine, Washington, D.C.

As the New York Times Best-Selling Author of HOW NOT TO DIE, *if you merely add the Letter T to my book you will, in essence, learn everything you need to know on How Not to DieT by reading Chef AJ's book. The same dietary principles that saved my beloved grandmother's life are outlined in this book and just might save yours as well.*—Michael Greger, M.D., F.A.C.L.M. of NutritionFacts.org

Chef AJ's The Secrets to Ultimate Weight Loss is your prescription for a much healthier life. Chef AJ poignantly shares her personal struggles with food, and the incredibly practical and life-transforming insights she has gained. Her writing style is the style with which she approaches life—optimistic, playful, and inspirational. I know many of my patients will benefit from this book.—Robert Ostfeld, M.D., MSc, Director of Preventive Cardiology, Montefiore Health System

Chef AJ has written a simple logic-based approach to weight and health management. She is a living testimony to her work. She is a model of the living benefit of a plant-based way of eating. Follow her guide and her advice for a long, active, and radiant life. From a Public Health perspective, this is the population health approach.—Terry Mason, M.D., C.O.O., Cook County Department of Public Health

This book is a must-read for at least 70% of the US population. As a practicing cardiologist, I see many patients with obesity among many other co-morbid conditions that contribute to the progression of their heart disease. I have often said to many of my patients, "You don't need a cardiologist, you need a chef." Chef AJ is that chef. The words in this book are from the heart of a chef and are beneficial for the heart of the patient.— Baxter Montgomery, M.D., F.A.C.C., Clinical Assistant Professor of Medicine University of Texas Health Science Center, Houston, Founder, Montgomery Heart and Wellness

Chef AJ has whipped up the perfect recipe for healing and wholeness in The Secrets to Ultimate Weight Loss *with a generous pinch of wisdom, experience, transparency, hope, and fun. The creative and practical steps blended with delicious recipes infuse happiness to the taste buds, health to the body, and freedom to truly live.*—Scott Stoll, M.D., Co-Founder, Plantrician Project and International Plant Based Nutrition Healthcare Conference, 1994 Olympian, Best-selling author and inspirational educator

Chef AJ has simplified the answer to permanent weight loss and excellent health. She is a highly persuasive mentor and will soon become your friend; I recommend you give her book The Secrets to Ultimate Weight Loss *your utmost attention.*—Craig McDougall, M.D., Physician at Dr. McDougall's Health and Medical Center.

Food addiction is real, it can be harsh, it can be challenging, and it can be extremely painful...but it no longer needs to be. In her new book, Chef AJ shares the insights and strategies that will help you break the cycle and empower yourself towards better and long-lasting health. Her honesty and vulnerability in sharing her own experiences are commendable and will prove invaluable to anyone struggling with weight loss. And Chef AJ not only gives you a compelling reason why it is time for change but with over 100 mouthwatering recipes, some of which we have had the pleasure to taste, she shows you how to make that change an easy and delicious one for you and your loved ones!—Alona Pulde, M.D. and Matthew Lederman, M.D., New York Times Best-Selling Authors

This is a potentially life-changing book for the millions of Americans out there who struggle to lose weight and to overcome their food addictions despite trying diet after diet. Chef AJ offers a simple, inexpensive, and incredibly effective approach that does not involve yet another fad diet, but rather a healthy eating lifestyle based on whole, plant-based foods. Follow her advice and I am confident you will attain a healthy weight and maintain it!—Anthony Lim, M.D., J.D., Medical Director, The McDougall Program, Staff Physician, TrueNorth Health Center

Chef AJ is a real-life success story and a true motivator. Reading about her lifelong struggles and her eventual success will inspire anybody looking for a role model to follow. She provides such a common sense and easy pathway to success that you cannot go wrong following her sage advice.—Garth Davis, M.D. author, *Proteinaholic*

I have known Chef AJ's work for over a decade, and this book sums it all up delightfully and very usefully. By using her own story, she shows the difficulty of the problem and an approach that works. She blends together the soft emotional ingredient with the hard calories to form something that is digestible and healthy. It's a good read.—Roger L. Gould, M.D., author, *ShrinkYourself*

Chef AJ's done it again. Fueled by deep personal passion as well as her expert's knack for healthy cooking, AJ gifts us with not only more delicious recipes, but also simple wisdom that anyone can use to stay on their own wellness path.—Pam Peeke, M.D., M.P.H., F.A.C.P., F.A.C.S.M., Pew Foundation Scholar in Nutrition, University of Maryland, author of the NYT bestseller *The Hunger Fix: The 3 Stage Detox and Recovery Plan for Overeating and Food Addiction*

If you want to lose weight forever by eating when you are hungry and eating until you are full, read this book. Follow Chef AJ's plan and you will succeed. Her personal testimonial and professional experience are blended in this book in a way that is motivating, encouraging, relatable, and clear. I look forward to recommending it to my patients.—Thomas M. Campbell, M.D., co-author, *The China Study* and author, *The China Study Solution*

Having helped so many achieve better health as they reach their weight loss goals, Chef AJ deserves her renown for such accurate perception of what people need to succeed. Her delightful humor and incisive candor have once again been put together in an informative guide that is well worth the read.—Linda Carney, M.D., first medical director of Rip Esselstyn's Engine 2 Immersions

Praise from Health and Fitness Experts for
THE SECRETS TO ULTIMATE WEIGHT LOSS

It is one thing to listen to some "Diet Doctor" or read his book about some new weight loss gimmick. It is quite another to have a top-flight chef who has truly made the journey herself explain exactly how she remade her body and reclaimed her self-esteem. Chef AJ is a coach like no other in the plant-based world. Her passion for her craft is infectious and resilient—and can carry you along on a tidal wave of excitement and promise to a whole new you. There have been over 75,000 books written on the subject of weight loss. Forget them all. This is the one you want. Get it. Read it. Join AJ and live it. She will show you exactly how to earn the rebirth of your spirit, and the life you deserve.—Douglas J. Lisle, Ph.D., Founder of Esteem Dynamics, Esteemdynamics.com

In her new book, The Secrets to Ultimate Weight Loss, *Chef AJ bares her soul, giving the reader an insight into the challenges faced in trying to lose weight and keep it off. She details a struggle that is shared by many, and reveals a plan that actually has worked for her and will work for anyone who is willing to apply the strategies diligently. She has taken her skill as a professional chef and developed simple-to-make recipes that will ease the transition to healthy eating. I suggest you read this book, learn the secrets, and eat the food... What have YOU got to lose?*—Alan Goldhamer, D.C., Co-founder of the TrueNorth Health Center, co-author, *The Pleasure Trap*

This is a very important message, told by an author who knows what it is like to be overweight and what it is like to solve the problem. A great read, with a few smiles to enjoy along the way.—T. Colin Campbell, Jacob Gould Schulman Professor Emeritus of Nutritional Biochemistry, Cornell University

If you have ever struggled with overweight or obesity, you simply must read this book. Chef AJ tells a story of personal triumph over weight that will touch, inspire, and empower you. She shares secrets that will not only help you achieve permanent weight loss, but also exceptional health for life. Her system is simple, and it works brilliantly. With over 100 fabulous plant-based recipes, you are in for a delightful culinary adventure.—Brenda Davis, R.D., co-author, *Becoming Vegan: Comprehensive and Express Editions*

If you want to lose weight and — most importantly— keep it off for good, there is simply no better guide on Earth than Chef AJ. A formerly obese food addict, she gets it, and she gets you. A must read for anyone and everyone who has ever struggled with food, The Ultimate Weight Loss Program is your Eureka! moment. A step-by-step bible that will undoubtedly change your life!—Rich Roll, bestselling author, *Finding Ultra* and *The Plantpower Way*

Chef AJ is a gem, her information is pure gold, and her recipes are all crown jewels. That makes The Secrets to Ultimate Weight Loss...*priceless! Make it happen!*—Rip Esselstyn, author of the N.Y. Times bestseller, *The Engine 2 Diet* and the #1 bestseller *Plant-Strong.*

"As a fellow food addict in blissful recovery, I celebrate Chef AJ's valuable contribution to freeing others from the prison of food cravings, self-recrimination, and weight issues. So few books on weight loss get to the problem behind the problem. This one does—and solves it too."—Victoria Moran, author, The Love-Powered Diet and director, Main Street Vegan Academy

"As CEO of Whole Foods Markets for 39 years, I can say with confidence that few things affect our company's performance more than the health, and health costs, of our Team Members. I can also say with confidence that everyone, especially those with weight issues, would benefit from reading Chef AJ's The Secrets to Ultimate Weight Loss. *I would heartily recommend it to my Team and everyone else."*—John P. Mackey, CEO Whole Foods Markets

We are big fans of Chef AJ's recipes, which are easy to make, delicious, and always a winner with our readers.—Brian Wendel, president of Forks Over Knives, and Darshana Thacker, Forks Over Knives Chef

Chef AJ makes me excited to get into the kitchen to try her recipes. Her dishes will introduce many of you to new grains, such as quinoa and millet, and new ways to use familiar seasonings, such as chili powder, paprika, and garlic. Most important, she uses ingredients I can easily find at my local market.—Mary McDougall, Co-founder of the McDougall Program

In a field where most books are laced with dogma and impose baseless rules and restrictions, Chef AJ's The Secrets to Ultimate Weight Loss *cuts through the fat. AJ has built her program on a foundation of sound science while addressing the quintessential components of behavior change. With practical guidelines and simple yet mouthwatering recipes that I've personally followed and loved, this book offers the perfect balance of structure and flexibility to produce real results. I highly recommend it to anyone who seeks healthy, sustainable fat loss.*—David Goldman, M.S., R.D., C.S.C.S., Director of Research and Education, MealLogger

You don't have a weight problem; you have a math problem. That simple, profound insight is at the heart of Chef AJ's brilliant book, The Secrets to Ultimate Weight Loss. *And once you understand it, it will change your life.*

With her trademark humor, breathtaking vulnerability, and brisk common sense, Chef AJ shows us how the developed world's obesity problem need not exist. That we don't need to restrict or count calories or portion size or exercise until our heads fall off. That once you discover the vast array of foods that you and I and all humans were designed to eat, the pounds will fly off and you will feel the joy of once again controlling your health destiny.

Turn off the late-night infomercials selling thigh masters and fat burning doodads. Ignore the pseudo-experts who tell you to manipulate your digestion with dangerous fad protocols. Politely decline the offers of your multi-level marketing friends pushing exotic fat-busting superfoods from the jungles of Borneo at forty bucks per liter.

Read this book. Weep. Laugh. Discover. Do. Rejoice.

And then share this message with others.—Howard Jacobson, Ph.D., contributing author to *Whole: Rethinking the Science of Nutrition* and *Proteinaholic*, Host, the *Plant Yourself Podcast*, PlantYourself.com

The delicious, easy, surprising recipes in The Secrets to Ultimate Weight Loss *prove that plant-based eating AJ's way is miraculous not only for those who want to lose weight but also for those who want to transform their health.*—Ann Crile Esselstyn, author with Jane Esselstyn, *The Prevent and Reverse Heart Disease Cook Book*

Chef AJ eloquently articulates one of the most powerful and life-changing methods for achieving your ideal weight in The Secrets to Ultimate Weight Loss. *Let's face it, losing weight is hard. That's why most of us struggle with it. But Chef AJ explains how you can take control of your weight for good. Understanding nutrient density and calorie density is paramount, and nobody explains it better than Chef AJ. She also walks her talk with her own inspiring weight loss journey, and she shares her secrets with us. If you have not yet achieved your ideal weight, Chef AJ's* The Secrets to Ultimate Weight Loss *is an absolute must-read.*—Robert Cheeke, Founder/President, VeganBodybuilding.com, author, *Shred It!*

Chef AJ's The Secrets to Ultimate Weight Loss *definitely delivers. It details how to achieve your ideal weight—permanently. Three years ago, I used the principles AJ outlines in this entertaining and educational book to lose thirty pounds. AJ's recipes are simple, healthy, delicious, and fun to prepare. Anyone can do this; Chef AJ makes it so easy. Her book is a blueprint for recovering your youth, your vigor—and your waistline! Quite simply, AJ's program works.*—Jeff Nelson, Founder, vegsource.com and Healthy Lifestyle Expo

Whenever someone asks me about how to lose weight healthily on a plant-based diet, I always point them to Chef AJ. I've witnessed firsthand the life-changing power and real results of her approach—through her brilliantly simple treatment of the powerful calorie density concept, easy and delicious recipes, and genius techniques that make it practical and sustainable (even on the road!). AJ has done us all a service by truly taking the mystery out of healthy weight loss.—Matt Frazier, author, *No Meat Athlete* and *The No Meat Athlete Cookbook*

Chef AJ was my very first plant-based crush as well as my first in-person encounter in the movement. I met her at the NOLA VegFest in 2013 as I was just beginning my plant-based journey. Her first book, Unprocessed, *was an asset to my wife and me as we transitioned to the lifestyle. Since then, I've heard AJ speak and I've met her several more times. Not only has my crush deepened but so has my knowledge on caloric density, and how to finally successfully and confidently keep the weight off, as I have lost 230 pounds this time, with plants, with caloric density, and with Chef AJ's example and very straightforward approach to conveying what she has learned from the WFPB giants, especially Dr. McDougall. This book is a great addition to the tool box, and has further educated me and empowered me to feel confident that I finally have been clued in to the ultimate weight loss secret. I love being able to share that secret, and this book has really made that easy. And her recipes are always go-to crowd pleasers which is crucial for the advance of the plant-based movement. So get the book, and help her change the world.*—Joshua Dan LaJaunie, plant-based athlete

I've seen Chef AJ keep an audience in rapt attention with her humor and honesty. Now she speaks the truth again in engaging written form, sharing the ultimate story of overcoming food addiction that will keep you turning pages whether you want to lose weight or not.—Miyoko Schinner, entrepeneur, author

I met Chef AJ when she came to a cooking class I taught with my wife Sanae Suzuki at our house a long time ago. She was very enthusiastic and curious about healthy and delicious food. Her new book, The Secrets to Ultimate Weight Loss, *has over 100 recipes, and all of them are easy to make and devilishly tasty even though they are prepared with no oil, salt, nuts, seeds, soy, or gluten. If you wondered how veganism can bring new joy in cooking and eating, look no more.*—Eric Lechasseur, plant-based chef, author, *Love, Eric* cookbook

As a chef who makes a living cooking SOS free food, I know first-hand how difficult it is to make it taste good. Chef AJ does a wonderful job achieving this. Inside this book, you'll find losing weight a delicious journey.—Chef Ramses Bravo, Executive Chef TrueNorth, Health Center, author, *Bravo!*

For most of us, one emotion in particular hinders our transition from food addiction to lifelong healthy eating: Fear. We fear that health-promoting foods will not satisfy us, so why bother? But with Chef AJ as your guide, this fear can be put to rest once and for all. Her delicious and creative recipes do not sacrifice great flavor for health and weight loss. I am a true fan, and wholeheartedly recommend Chef AJ's The Secrets to Ultimate Weight Loss *to anyone striving to make lasting change in how they eat, look and feel.*—Cathy Fisher, author, *Straight Up Food: Delicious and Easy Plant-based Cooking without Salt, Oil or Sugar*

Chef AJ is a passionate and vibrant educator whose mission is to "make healthy taste delicious." In her new book, The Secrets to Ultimate Weight Loss, *AJ accomplishes just that with delectable recipes that follow the principles of calorie density and her very own 10 commandments for ultimate weight loss. Chef AJ's inspiring life story and her simple and easy-to-follow advice will change your life forever.*—Rosane Oliveira, D.V.M, Ph.D., Adjunct Assistant Professor, Public Health Sciences, University of California Davis School of Medicine, Founding Director, UC Davis Integrative Medicine.

Acknowledgments

Thank you to Dr. Alan Goldhamer, Dr. Doug Lisle, and Dr. John McDougall for teaching me everything I needed to know about losing weight the healthy way. Thank you to John Pierre, for teaching me to enjoy exercise and inspiring me to become a kinder, more compassionate person.

Thank you to Janell Parque for her superb editing, and thank you to my co-author Glen Merzer, without whose creative contributions this book would never had been completed.

Thank you to Ananda Prohs, my Reiki guru, and Bailey, my spirit animal, for filling me with light and love.

Thank you to all the participants of *The Ultimate Weight Loss Program* for their courage, perseverance, and support.

And to my husband Charles, who loved me fat and thin.

Dedication

This book is dedicated to everyone who has ever suffered because of their weight. And for my mother and brother: I wish I had known this information in time to help you.

Disclaimer

T his book is not a substitute for medical advice and should not be taken as such. Please consult with a medical professional before making any diet or lifestyle changes.

Table of Contents

Foreword

Presently, the United States is in an absolute quagmire over how to finance the escalating high costs of health care, now consuming 18% of the gross national product. Drug prices and interventional costs have skyrocketed, and there is no end in sight for this escalation.

It does not have to be doom and gloom, as we have at our fingertips the seismic revolution of health.

This revolution will never come about with the invention of another pill, procedure, or operation. This revolution will come about when health and nutritional organizations show the public the food literacy that can empower them to eliminate chronic disease.

The economists Topel and Murphy, reporting in the University of Chicago Press in 1999, estimated that the resolution of cardiovascular disease would generate over 40 trillion dollars in economic value.

The late Dr. William Connors studied hundreds of the Tarahumara Indians of Northern Mexico for hypertension and obesity and found none in this plant-based culture.

Other diseases which appear largely eliminated and resolved with whole food, plant-based nutrition include Type 2 Diabetes, strokes, vascular dementia, Crohn's disease, ulcerative colitis, rheumatoid arthritis, lupus, multiple sclerosis, allergies, and asthma, to mention a few. In short, the answer to the health care crisis is to eliminate disease safely and inexpensively.

The first step is to educate the public and the medical profession by scientific study, lecture format, internet presentations, books, and film. But mere health awareness is not enough. Without understanding how to acquire and prepare plant-based food, the public is lost.

Enter Chef AJ and her irrepressible personality. For decades, she has been at the frontier of creating healthful and tasty plant cuisine. Thousands have heard her captivating message in lectures, on the internet, and in her earlier book, *Unprocessed*. Her most recent book, *The Secrets to Ultimate Weight Loss*, solidifies her role as a leader in the evolution of plant-based eating.

Caldwell B. Esselstyn, Jr., M.D.
Author: *Prevent and Reverse Heart Disease*

Introduction

I was overweight from the age of five, obese by eleven, anorexic in my teens, bulimic and obese in my twenties, addicted to prescription diet pills in my thirties, and overweight and suffering from an addiction to processed and refined foods in my forties and early fifties. For the past six years, without the aid of pharmaceutical drugs, I have achieved and maintained what I consider my ideal weight of about 117 pounds, and enjoyed excellent health, feeling more energetic and productive than ever before in my life. I lost fifty pounds to reach that weight, and the pounds came off easily and effortlessly, while I enjoyed generous portions of healthy and delicious foods, without ever weighing my food, counting calories, or restricting my portions.

My struggles with food were always lonely and fraught with guilt and anxiety. Growing up, I felt that there was not a single person to whom I could talk who would truly understand what I was going through. Could anyone even comprehend how much I was suffering from my dysfunctional and discordant relationship with food, or how it was impacting every area of my life? It was affecting not just my physical health, but also my ability to hold a job, to have healthy personal relationships, and to nurture my spiritual and emotional well-being. Not realizing that from a very young age I was actually suffering from an addiction to refined carbohydrates (sugars and flours), I felt that I was somehow defective and that there was something seriously wrong with me. Addiction is a disease that thrives in isolation, and I felt completely and totally alone.

I have now had the opportunity to work with over two thousand people who have experienced similar, or even worse, struggles than my own. I have written this book so that you will know, if you suffer in a similar way, that you are not alone. Food addiction (more accurately, processed food addiction) is real. You are not lazy or weak-willed. You do not lack discipline or willpower. You have a biogenetic disease. Having that disease is not your fault.

But once you understand this, it becomes your responsibility to change the foods that you eat if you wish to recover. You will need to completely and permanently abstain from all the foods that you are addicted to, which for almost all food addicts are the refined sugars, flours, alcohol, and any foods that contain them as ingredients. For food addicts, powders like sugars and flours are drugs, not food. In their manufacture, they go through the same sort of refining process that drugs and alcohol do. Once you abstain from them, you can begin to stabilize your brain chemistry. For almost all the individuals with whom I have had the privilege to work, their excess weight was a direct result of their food addictions. As soon as they eliminated all sugars (real and artificial, caloric and non-caloric), all flours (even the so-called healthy, whole grain ones), dairy products, high-fat foods, and alcohol, and any other foods that were personal food triggers (foods that lead to bingeing or overeating) for them, and as soon as they began addressing as well the emotional reasons why they were using food as a drug to medicate in the first place, their brain chemistry began to stabilize, perhaps for the very first time in their lives. Once they treated their food addiction and they began to recover from it, the excess weight fell off.

Even if you feel that you do not suffer from food addiction, this book will help you if you wish to shed unwanted pounds. And if you are already at your ideal weight, understanding its lessons might help you help a friend or family member. It will also teach you the healthiest and easiest way to maintain your weight and prevent common diseases brought on by the Western diet.

Whether or not you believe that sugars, flours, and alcohol are addictive, the simple fact is that they are still not health-promoting foods and will not help to facilitate weight loss. They are highly processed foods that are not found in nature and have been stripped of their water, fiber, and vital nutrients, such as vitamins, minerals, phytochemicals, and antioxidants. They are very calorically dense when compared to whole, natural food. These are also the foods that many people in general, and overweight people in particular, simply cannot moderate their use of. These processed foods can cause many people to have food cravings and to overeat.

So, how do you know if you have a problem with a particular type of food or drink? Please ask yourself these ten questions and answer as honestly as possible:

1) Do you absolutely have to consume it daily, or perhaps even several times a day?
2) Do you feel bad if you are unable to get your fix?
3) Do you think about it often and can't wait until you are able to consume it again, even if you have just had it?
4) Is it difficult for you to moderate your use of it?
5) Do you often consume more of it than you intended to?
6) Do you often feel shame or regret after consuming it?
7) Do you have physical or emotional withdrawal symptoms when you try to abstain from it?
8) Is it difficult for you to get through even a single day without consuming this substance?
9) Does abstaining from it result in any physical or emotional discomfort?
10) Does the mere thought of abstaining from it bring on strong emotions, such as anxiety, sadness, anger, or grief?

If you answered yes to any of these questions, you may be suffering from an addiction. How does the thought of giving up these foods or beverages for even a day make you feel? How about for twenty-one days? What emotions come up when you consider the possibility of having to abstain from these substances forever?

Food addiction is not yet widely recognized in the larger medical community, but many doctors and scientific researchers are working very hard to broaden our understanding of it. There are thousands of articles in medical journals pertaining to food addiction, and several helpful books with a scientific bent have already been written on the subject. This book will touch on the science behind food addiction, but do not expect deep scientific analysis and documentation here. We are concerned with the experience of food addiction and obesity—what it has been like for you and me to suffer from it—and, far more importantly, with the best, healthiest way to overcome it. That is something I know both from my experience in recovering from these afflictions, and as a professional chef, health educator, and weight loss coach. I have helped well over two thousand people lose substantial amounts of weight and make profound improvements in their health.

Food addiction exists on a continuum, with people having varying degrees of vulnerability to these addictive substances. Whether or not you believe in food addiction, or believe that you may be a food addict, if you follow the dietary recommendations outlined in this book, you will most certainly lose weight. And you may also regain your sanity.

No matter how long or how deeply you have suffered, there is hope. But it starts with stabilizing your brain, and to do that, you first have to get the food right.

Even if every program you have tried has resulted in failure, *The Ultimate Weight Loss Program* can be the answer to your prayers, the only program you'll ever need. I truly believe that you absolutely can have the health, and the body, that you so richly deserve, and I would like to help you to achieve both.

CHAPTER 1

My Journey to Ultimate Weight Loss

There are countless diet books out there promising you that you will lose weight. Perhaps you've read some of them. But I'll bet some of the authors of those books never were overweight or struggled with emotional eating and food addiction, and so they simply may not understand the psychological and physiological issues that hold so many of us back. And, without naming names, a number of other diet book authors remain seriously overweight.

I spent most of my life suffering from being either overweight or obese, and battling emotional eating and an addiction to refined food until I discovered the one plan that will overcome all these afflictions. And it's not a diet because diets don't work. Did you know that ninety-eight percent of those who lose weight, usually through a great deal of suffering and deprivation, gain it all back within two years, and then some?

What I am proposing isn't the latest fad. There is no weighing, measuring, or counting of calories, points, or carbs. There are no superfoods that you have to eat or expensive pills, potions, or powders that you have to take. You eat as much food as you want, as often as you want, until you are comfortably full, but of the *right foods*. Foods that are not only familiar to you, but that are comfort foods that will fill you up without filling you out. Delicious foods that you already enjoy eating, many of which you've been mistakenly depriving yourself of for many years. The type of foods that our ancestors ate throughout most of human history, and that are still eaten today in many parts of the world that are largely free of the high rates of obesity, heart disease, and diabetes that plague the majority of Americans. But before I explain to you the details of this nutritionally sound and delicious plan, I would like to share my story so that you will understand that until I discovered *The Secrets to Ultimate Weight Loss*, nothing truly ever worked for me, at least not for very long.

If you are overweight or obese, or even if you are slender but suffering from emotional eating or food addiction, I genuinely understand your pain and how these diseases may affect virtually every area of your life. I truly know what it's like to walk in your shoes, because I walked in them for over fifty years, nearly my entire life. I often think of myself as "*nouveau* thin" because the majority of my life was lived in a fat body.

I want you to know that wherever you are in your journey, there is hope. As long as you are still breathing, there is always hope. Recovery is possible and you can heal. But it has to start with getting the food right.

For most of my life, I would do things like stockpile packages of cookies, boxes of pastries from the bakery, and bars of candy. I would "hide" them in the freezer so that I wouldn't be constantly tempted by them, promising myself that I would "be good" and not eat them, or perhaps "eat just one." (If you can "eat just one" of any hyper-palatable food, then you are not a food addict.) I would open and close the freezer door numerous times a day. I tried to walk away, truly I did, but the urge to eat these foods overpowered me and I completely lost control. I simply could not stop myself from eating them. The power that they had over me was just too great, and no amount of willpower that I could muster was a match for them. It was a constant battle and one that I always lost. And the story always had the same ending—empty bags full of crumbs. When I would finally wake up from the food coma, full of shame, disgust, and self-hatred, I would promise myself that I would never do it again. I would keep that promise. Until the next time. And there was always a next time. Sound familiar?

I had a very tumultuous childhood. I distinctly remember being an emotional eater from the age of five, when I first became fat. When I learned to eat the diet that was consistent with our species' natural history, and address the reasons why, since early childhood, I was using food as a drug to soothe myself, all three of my conditions—the emotional eating, the food addiction, and the obesity—were addressed and began to heal. But the foods that healed me were not the foods that I ate for the first fifty years of my life, the foods that were responsible for making me fat and sick. While getting a handle on your emotions is extraordinarily helpful, unless you get the food right, any weight loss you may achieve is likely to be temporary.

I was born in Chicago in 1960 to a morbidly obese mother who had struggled with her weight, food addictions, and emotional eating her entire life. Statistics show that if one of your parents is obese, you have a forty percent chance of becoming obese.[1] If both of your parents are obese, that chance increases to eighty percent, whereas lean parents have only a seven percent chance of having an obese child. My mother was a lifelong dieter and from as long as I can remember, she was always on a diet. She tried *The Stillman Diet, The Scarsdale Diet, The Grapefruit Diet, The Cabbage Soup Diet, Weight Watchers, Optifast*, and good old-fashioned calorie counting. One of the diets she attempted that I remember most vividly was *TOPS (Take Off Pounds Sensibly)*; there she was taught to substitute bean sprouts for pasta, which I thought was pretty weird. The other unforgettable weight loss program involved her receiving injections of urine from pregnant women. I'm not making that up. I thought it was pretty gross. Yet, with all her valiant attempts at weight loss, she kept gaining weight and remained obese her entire life. She suffered terribly, both physically and emotionally, from her weight, and died from complications of her morbid obesity, as did one of my brothers.

Although I was genetically predisposed to being obese, I do not blame my genes. Genetics only loaded the gun and made me more susceptible to developing addictions and putting on weight. It was my deplorable diet and sedentary lifestyle that pulled the trigger and caused me to become fat at the tender age of five years old.

I love what Dr. Baxter Montgomery, a Houston plant-based cardiologist, says: "It's not the diseases that are hereditary, it's the recipes!" And my family sure had their share of delicious, but very unhealthy ones. Some of my fondest childhood memories are the weekly Sabbath dinners at my beloved maternal grandparents' home. In their living room, there was a hexagonal shaped mirrored coffee table that spun around like a Lazy Susan, brimming with tempting treats. One large bowl contained unsalted, roasted mixed nuts, and I loved picking out all the cashews when no one was looking. None of my relatives ate salt while I was growing up because they had already developed high blood pressure and heart disease, even before I was born. The second irresistible offering was a beautiful candy dish made of china, which had a divider in the middle. I still recollect its pink floral print, but what I remember even more vividly was what it was filled with. Half of it contained *Peanut M & M's*, and the other half was an assortment of *See's Candy.* I loved sticking my fingers in the bottom of every piece, desperately searching for my favorite, the chocolate buttercream. If I accidentally bit into the maple one, I would immediately spit it out. After all, even as a young food addict, I had my standards! To this day, I can still tell you what filling is inside every single piece of *See's Candy* just by looking at it.

My grandmother was famous for her homemade chicken and matzo ball soup. After dinner, she would pour the leftovers into a glass jar, and as it cooled, the schmaltz (chicken fat) would congeal into a one-inch thick layer. The traditional high-fat, high cholesterol Jewish fare we ate growing up is among the unhealthiest on the planet. Maybe that's why so many Jewish mothers have encouraged their children to become doctors—to treat the myriad of illnesses caused by eating these disease-promoting traditional Jewish foods.

My grandmother was a Type 2 diabetic. I can still remember squeamishly watching her inject her very round belly with insulin every morning. She had to carry chocolate bars with her at all times and eat them if her blood sugar fell too low. As a young child with no understanding of diabetes, I actually thought having to eat a *Hershey Bar* was really pretty awesome and, as far as illnesses went, this was a pretty cool disease. Her mother, my great-grandmother, had died of complications of Type 2 Diabetes after having her leg amputated. I have very unpleasant memories of visiting my beloved grandfather in the ICU after he had open-heart surgery; how weak and anguished he looked after the operation really terrified me. I watched my own father languish, and suffer tremendously, after his own failed open-heart surgery, which ultimately killed him. He had a feeding tube surgically placed in his stomach and another tube in his neck that was attached to a respirator. His hands were tied down so that he would not pull out either of these tubes, which obviously caused him incredible pain and discomfort. He was not even able to communicate for the last three weeks of his life, but his eyes spoke volumes, as they were filled with terror. Growing up, I thought that all this was normal, that these diseases were just the natural result of aging, or as my parents put it, "the vagaries of old age."

It would be almost a half a century until I learned that all these diseases were completely preventable and largely reversible and that they were all caused by the foods my family ate. Starting at a very early age, I, too, ate all the wrong foods, and became addicted to them, while rarely engaging in any physical activity.

I had a very traumatic childhood. Early childhood trauma makes us more vulnerable to developing addictions. In her bestselling book, *The Hunger Fix*, Dr. Pam Peeke states that those who have endured a major trauma or abuse (as I did), have a family history of addiction (as I have) or have suffered from depression, anxiety or ADHD (as I have) demonstrate a higher predisposition to the disease of food addiction that causes us to self-medicate. She contends that women are even more susceptible to emotional eating and binge eating and that once you taste the food addiction waters, you can never reverse that memory.

Before I was born, my father was in an accident and suffered a traumatic brain injury that brought on recurrent violent outbursts. In addition to the highly processed junk food, emotional and verbal abuse was also on the menu every day. The physical abuse was at first reserved for my two older brothers and Snoopy, our beloved beagle. Finally, after twenty-five years of marriage, my father brutally attacked my mother right in front of me. At the urging of my grandparents, she finally left him. I would not see my father again for almost thirty years, until right before he died. My father was a part of my life only for the first eleven years, but the terror of my childhood still affects me to this day.

I do not tell you this story so that you will feel sorry for me. I'm sure that many of you have similar stories or even more horrific ones. I tell you this so that you will know that I truly understand how easy it is to use food to self-medicate and turn to it for comfort and love, especially if you didn't get that nurturing as a child and haven't found other ways to nurture yourself now. Yes, the things that were done to me were horrible, but the things that I ended up doing to myself were far worse.

I want you to know that whatever happened to you in the past, you can recover from it. It doesn't have to define you now. As long as there is breath, there is hope. But even with the best psychological or spiritual help you can receive—and if you experienced any trauma or abuse in your life, I strongly encourage you to seek that help—until you get the food right, you will never heal your food addictions and emotional eating or remain slim for very long. Even if we could channel Sigmund Freud to come back from the dead, I sincerely doubt that even he could help you if you continue to eat the highly addictive and nutritionally bereft foods that made you fat and sick in the first place: foods like cheese and other dairy products, fried foods, refined oils, animal flesh, and highly processed, refined carbohydrates like sugar, flour, and alcohol. The opposite side of the equation is important, too: while certain foods can destroy your health and your life, there are other foods that you will learn about here that can facilitate your recovery and help you heal.

My mom was an excellent cook, and we did have a salad and a vegetable with dinner. My meals at home were not the worst part of my diet. We rarely ate fast food, and soda was served only as a treat at a birthday party in a small *Dixie* cup. The problem wasn't so much the food that my mom served at mealtime; it was all the other crap that I ate, which was primarily highly refined carbohydrates (white sugar and white flour) like bread, cereal, pasta, and sweets.

We now know from brain imaging studies that sugar is highly addictive, yet I was starting every day of my young life with mega doses of this poison for as long as I can remember. For some reason, my mom allowed me to drink coffee from the age of five. I loved caffeine almost as much as I loved sugar, and together they just couldn't be beat. I would enjoy mass doses of this speedball combination of drugs, in one beverage or another, from childhood to my early forties. The only way I could drink coffee as a child was if I put a ton of cream and sugar in it. Being highly allergic to dairy, but not having that fact officially diagnosed until I was an adult, created all sorts of health problems for me in my youth.

Fortunately, I became vegan when I left home at the age of seventeen, and so dairy was no longer an issue for me. But the sugar and caffeine continued to be. In addition to my morning cup of Joe (which in college would become several cups of coffee and a cigarette), I would also ingest a highly processed sugary cereal like *Cocoa Puffs*. On the weekends, my mom would make pancakes or waffles. The pancakes would have chocolate chips mixed into the batter and the waffles would have a semi-sweet dark chocolate chip placed into each square. The melted chocolate would create a sweet, gooey, luscious contrast to the crisp hot waffle that was pure heaven. Yet even with all the decadence from the chocolate, they were still served with margarine and real maple syrup!

Because my father already suffered from heart disease and had his first heart attack before I was born, we never ate things like bacon and eggs for breakfast. Eggs were too high in cholesterol and bacon wasn't Kosher. The advantage to growing up in a Kosher home was that I was exposed to fewer varieties of animal flesh, like bacon, pork, sausage, crab, lobster, shrimp, or any of the shellfish. You can't crave something that you have never even consumed. I don't know a single person who has never smoked who has ever craved a cigarette. Have you ever met someone who has never consumed alcohol who has ever craved a drink? Because the Kosher laws did not allow us to mix meat with dairy, I also never developed a taste for things like cheeseburgers or pepperoni pizza. We develop taste preferences for whatever foods we habitually eat, and what I was habitually eating was processed sugar, refined grains, and other high-fat foods, while eating no fruits or vegetables whatsoever.

If you are a parent reading this, please understand that once you start feeding your kids unhealthy, disease-promoting foods like animal products, especially dairy, and processed food (particularly sugar and refined grains), you are planting the seeds for predisposing them to a refined food addiction by rewiring their delicate brain chemistry in an unfavorable way and adulterating their palate so that they are disinclined to enjoy the taste of healthy, whole, natural food. Processed foods like these are engineered to be addictive; they hijack our taste buds and our brain chemistry. Getting your family to eat healthy foods after they have been habitually eating these highly addictive foods will be an uphill battle, so please heal yourself from these addictions and stabilize your own brain chemistry first. The best strategy is not to feed your kids these poisons in the first place.

My mom was a chocoholic; I think she passed that gene on to me. I know that on some level she was giving me all these treats as a mis-guided way of showing love, but it was still very painful growing up the fat girl. While today one out of every five kids under the age of eighteen is obese[2], in the early sixties, that wasn't yet the case. In a classroom of forty kids, usually only one was fat—and that kid was me. I was mostly able to avoid ridicule over my weight by being the funniest kid in the class. What I did get teased about, though, was my gigantic lunch box. I was jealous of the other kids who had those cool (now vintage) lunch-boxes with *The Partridge Family* or *Flipper* on them. Mine was a huge, clunky, gray lunchbox, the kind that held a *Thermos* (in my case, filled with *Kool-Aid*). You know, the kind that construction workers use? In addition to the usual sandwich and chips that the other kids had, my trough also contained numerous treats, such as a full pack of *Hostess Suzy Q's* or *Hostess Cupcakes*. I can still recall the taste of that chemical, sickly sweet white filling as if it were yesterday.

Even though I didn't experience much teasing from my schoolmates, and thankfully never experienced bullying, I still have many painful childhood memories surrounding the issue of weight. Most of them have to do with the futile attempts that I made at exercise. If I did experience any shaming, it was from the nasty female phys-ed teachers. Because of my heavy weight and lack of coordination, I just couldn't run fast enough or do the crazy stunts they expected, like walking on a balance beam, climbing a rope wall, or swinging from the parallel bars. While I was a straight-A student and often the teacher's pet in my other subjects, I barely passed physical education and rejoiced the day it was no longer mandatory in the state of California. Having abrasions from your fat thighs rubbing together just doesn't make exercising very enjoyable. Nor is being made fun of for wearing an old lady, one-piece bathing suit because you are too fat to wear a bikini. Or being laughed at while trying to learn to ski because once you have fallen, you really can't get up. Is it any wonder that I grew up detesting all forms of exercise and wouldn't even attempt any type of physical fitness again until I was in my fifties?

My father, who grew up during the Great Depression, was a staff sergeant in World War II and a drill sergeant at home. "Take what you want but eat what you take," he would admonish us. And if we couldn't finish, he would yell at us and say, "Your eyes are bigger than your stomach." Even as an adult, I can still hear my father's voice from the grave and find that it's really difficult for me not to finish the food on my plate.

When I was eleven years old, my parents sent me to California to live with an aunt and uncle. I tell some of this story in my book *Unprocessed*, but what I didn't acknowledge there was that even though I ate the delicious, rich meals of gourmet French cuisine that were served at their home daily, I still continued to secretly indulge in those highly refined foods which I simply could not resist. My aunt was Swiss and one of her traditional snacks was bread and chocolate, so I remember coming home from junior high school and gorging on sandwiches made from *Wonder Bread* and *Nestle Crunch* bars. Every day, my aunt would give me a dollar to buy lunch at the school cafeteria, but instead, I would use the money to buy candy at the student store. Back in 1971, a candy bar was only a nickel, so a dollar could sure buy a heck of a lot of sweet treats.

I completely understood by the age of five that being fat was unacceptable. That I was not okay. But no solutions were offered and so every year I just kept getting fatter and fatter. I dreaded the month of September because that meant going back to school and buying new clothes, as last year's dresses no longer fit. Not because I had gotten any taller, but because I had gotten wider. I remember one rude sales clerk saying to my mother that if I got any fatter, the store would not be able to accommodate me and that I would have to shop at "Lane Giant's." She was referring to *Lane Bryant's*, a plus-size clothing store for adult women.

My uncle, a doctor who practiced internal medicine, must have noticed that I kept getting fatter, and he promised me that for every pound that I weighed under 160 pounds, he would donate a dollar to my favorite charity. So, being the altruistic person I am, I weighed myself, for the very first time in my life, and I was mortified to discover that at the mere age of eleven, I already weighed 160 pounds and was not yet even five feet tall! My weight was not only making me miserable, it was preventing funds from going to deserving causes.

While I'm sure that my uncle was well-meaning, he offered no real solutions for my weight problem. Although he was a doctor, and surely must have known a great deal about health, he had always struggled with his own weight, so he had little to offer me except generic advice, like, "Don't eat so much." I remember once, as we were serving ourselves at a buffet, we encountered a morbidly obese woman wearing a muumuu. Her plate was piled high with all sorts of fried foods. My uncle said to me, "You know, if you keep eating like her, that's going to be you someday, and you'll have to wear one of those fat lady dresses, too. I bet you could go an entire week without eating and it wouldn't hurt you one bit." And so, I did. Thus began my struggles with disordered eating. For the years that followed, I alternated between feasting and fasting, without ever understanding *what* to eat.

When I was nineteen years old and a junior at the University of Pennsylvania, my anorexia was so severe that I had to be hospitalized. They did not have very good treatment for this disease in 1979, so I was put in the locked ward of a mental institution along with some very interesting characters who were admitted for things like arson and appeared to be criminally insane. I was scared to death and didn't sleep a wink while I was there. My sister-in-law, Lauren, flew to Philadelphia to take me back to Los Angeles, where I was placed in another psychiatric hospital, which wasn't much better than the first. Nurse Ratchet was alive and well in these hellholes, and I feel lucky that I survived the ordeal.

Here is how they treated anorexia in the late seventies. You had a choice. You could either eat what they served you or two psychiatric aides who looked more like NFL linebackers would put you in five-point restraints and shove a tube down your throat and force-feed you like a goose cruelly being fattened for *fois gras*. Let me briefly describe five-point restraints: they take heavy leather straps and bind both of your wrists and ankles, and place an even larger leather strap over your abdomen, all so tightly that you cannot move even an inch. Telling them that I was an ethical vegan and didn't wear leather products did not seem to amuse them. After having been left in five-point restraints once for several hours, treated like a rabid dog, my will was broken. In order to avoid further trauma and humiliation, I ate. But once again, I ate all the wrong foods. Instead of eating wholesome, nourishing, and life-sustaining foods like fruits, vegetables, whole grains, and legumes, which is what my diet consists of today, all I chose to eat from what was offered at the hospital fell into my own four toxic food groups: flour, sugar, caffeine, and chocolate. I was already vegan at this time, so I still shunned all animal products, but ate instead only the least healthful vegan foods available, the highly processed and refined vegan junk food.

One of the nurses in the hospital told me that this disease had completely screwed up my hypothalamus and that my brain would never again be able to ascertain if I was hungry or full. (Where nutrition is concerned, you are best advised not to believe everything medical professionals tell you, since they are rarely trained in that field.) While this was true initially, I did recover, and so can you, but it took several years. The problem was that I was actually starving. The years of battling anorexia had wreaked havoc on my body. My hair started falling out and so did my fingernails. I stopped having menstrual periods and I developed an ulcer and an enlarged liver.

After years of alternating between severe dietary restriction and gluttony, once I started eating again, after my discharge from the hospital, I could not stop! I quickly gained over sixty pounds in the course of just a few months. The last time I actually remember weighing myself, I tipped the scales at 180 pounds! I was mortified and ashamed. While I had certainly been overweight at 160 pounds, I was always able to easily maintain that weight from the age of eleven, even while gorging on all the unhealthy crap that I desired. But now I was eating my way close to the 200 pound mark. My biggest fear in life, that I would end up morbidly obese like my mother, was now manifesting, but my appetite was insatiable. I felt completely out of control and became seriously depressed.

It was at this point that I attempted suicide. Needless to say, this was not a smart move for someone who hated being in a mental institution, and the aftermath was absolutely horrific. It was the darkest period of my life; I feel very ashamed about what I did and what I put my family through. The only reason I choose to share this personal information is this: since coming out publicly as a food addict, I have received numerous e-mails from people who have told me that they have attempted suicide or have contemplated taking their own lives, or that they have had friends and loved ones who have committed suicide because of this disease. I want people to understand that this is truly a biogenetic disease that you were born with. It is not your fault and you need not feel ashamed. It must be taken seriously because it can be fatal.

Food addiction, you see, is a chronic, progressive, and often life-threatening illness. Once you understand the gravity of the situation, it is your responsibility to seek the help that you need to recover, and that starts with getting the food right. It is essential that you abstain from eating the foods that will perpetuate the disease, and instead eat the foods that will restore you to health and stabilize your brain chemistry: fruits, vegetables, whole grains, and legumes. These are not only the healthiest foods on the planet but also the foods that will finally allow you to easily and permanently lose weight without going hungry.

After three months in the locked ward of an even worse psychiatric hospital, I was grateful to finally get home and be with my beloved, newly rescued mutt, Lucky. I had suffered with severe eating disorders, including anorexia, on-and-off for seven years, but because I was now no longer considered to be underweight, the doctors believed I was finally "cured." Even though I was not fasting or restricting my food intake, I was still starving on a cellular level for food that contained actual nutrients. But all I kept eating was essentially sugar and flour. And once I started consuming these foods, I simply could not stop eating them. Does this sound familiar to any of you? Having restricted my food intake for so long, my appetite was insatiable, and so I started bingeing.

Hitting 180 pounds officially put me in the obese category. While I never enjoyed weighing 160 pounds, at least I had been able to easily maintain that weight without gaining. But now my eating had spiraled out of control and I just didn't know what else to do to compensate for the binges that could easily be in excess of 10,000 calories. Having eaten very little for years leading up to my hospitalization, I was finally able to enjoy all my favorite treats that I had been depriving myself of for so long. It was not uncommon for me to ravenously consume dozens of freshly baked, gooey, warm semi-sweet chocolate chip and pecan cookies, followed by a dozen cupcakes with vanilla buttercream frosting and rainbow sprinkles. (All these junk foods were technically vegan.) If you are an addict, then you know that it is only the first bite that you can actually ever say no to and resist; after that, the disease takes over. Like Benjamin Franklin said, "It is much easier to suppress a first desire than to satisfy those that follow."

Feeling ashamed and guilty for eating these very unhealthful and addictive foods, especially in such massive quantities, I developed some very dangerous strategies for getting rid of the excess calories, including bulimia. And for the next six years, I battled with this other often life-threatening disease.

As I absolutely detested being obese, I discovered that by sticking my finger down my throat, I could induce vomiting and get rid of many of the calories. I purposely started smoking cigarettes, a behavior I had always deplored, thinking it would somehow decrease my appetite. I joined a gym and began exercising incessantly, blowing out my knee with multiple daily step aerobics classes. I also started abusing laxatives and diuretics so that I could get rid of the weight and the food even faster. But nothing could get rid of the shame, guilt, and humiliation that accompanies this disease.

Even with all these "strategies," the implementation of which felt like a twenty-four-hour-a-day job, I still could only get my weight down to 150 pounds. And the efforts that I had to go through to maintain that weight were gargantuan. I remember that during my anorexic years, while I felt weak, cold, and tired all the time, the only thing that I really had to do to maintain my weight was to barely eat. But having bulimia was absolutely exhausting. I started developing many medical problems from this insidious disease that wreaked havoc on my entire GI tract and even started affecting my teeth. I remember running from doctor to doctor, looking for symptomatic relief, never disclosing the real reason for any of my mysterious ailments. I still wonder if any of the "tummy troubles" I have today are a result of all the years during which I thoroughly abused my body.

Believe it or not, when I was twenty-two years old, I got thrown off a mechanical bull and fractured several of my vertebrae. I was rendered temporarily paralyzed, and once I could walk again, I spent three months in a body cast. That was followed by a year in a huge back brace, which was so tight that it made it impossible to binge. While in the hospital, I was given injections of a drug called *Demerol* every four hours, and as needed, for the pain. While I was never a person who drank alcohol or used recreational drugs, my addiction-prone brain absolutely loved this prescription medication. I requested it as frequently as possible during my stay, whether I was actually in pain or not. So, while I never became addicted to *Demerol*, I totally understand how people can easily get addicted to pain medication, alcohol, and other recreational drugs, and I was terrified at how much I truly enjoyed it. When you are an addict, it is very easy to develop cross-addictions, and so those whose consumption pattern of addictive foods like sugar, flour, and dairy raises a warning flag should be particularly guarded about their use of drugs or alcohol.

When I was twenty-five years old, I broke one of my ribs while coughing. Back in the eighties, they treated rib fractures differently than they do today, so I was wrapped very tightly in a rib belt. It was so painful that I could barely take the shallowest of breaths, so inhaling on a cigarette wasn't even an option. After six weeks of not being able to smoke, I was finally free from the physical addiction to nicotine. I had never tried to quit because I knew how powerful the nicotine addiction was; I held out little hope I could overcome it. So, I was actually grateful that I sustained this rib injury. I now think of it as a lucky break. Often, when we look back some of the most painful things that happen to us, it turns out that they actually were quite fortunate. Somehow, finally being liberated from one of the most powerful addictions, nicotine, gave me the confidence to begin to tackle the others.

Shortly after I quit smoking, I turned my attention to my eating disorders, with which I had suffered for more than half my life. I finally did what many addicts do when they've had enough. I turned it over to a higher power. I remember bingeing on an entire pan of triple fudge brownies and having my stomach distended to the size of a pregnant woman who is long overdue. The pain was so great that I couldn't even walk, so I crawled to the bathroom to induce vomiting to relieve it. I stared into that shiny porcelain toilet bowl with the fuzzy yellow toilet seat cover, as I had done so many hundreds of times before, and I finally had enough. I just couldn't do it anymore. While I have never participated in any twelve-step programs, I did literally hit my knees and prayed, asking God to take away this horrible disease, begging to be able to just eat like a normal person without fasting, bingeing, or purging, and in return I would accept any weight that I could easily maintain.

Note to self: Be more specific in the wording of your prayers. I should have asked for any *slim* weight that I could easily maintain.

Note to reader: Achieving and maintaining a healthy weight through healthy eating didn't seem to me at the time to be remotely possible. But the good news is that once you learn, understand, and implement *The Secrets to Ultimate Weight Loss*, losing weight and maintaining it will be effortless.

After finally discontinuing all my destructive eating behaviors, I gained about ten pounds, once again weighing 160 pounds, the weight I had been most easily able to maintain from the age of eleven without fasting, bingeing, purging, abusing laxatives, restricting food, or smoking. I was convinced that this must have been my "set point," my body's natural weight, what I was intended to weigh all along, and that there was really nothing I could safely do to change it. I also began doing some soul-searching and some of the deeper inner work that I believe is crucial to recovery: talk therapy, gentle yoga, and meditation. That work started with the reading of a wonderful metaphysical book by Louise Hay called *You Can Heal Your Life*, which I still recommend to all my clients today.

It would take another ten years before I even considered addressing my weight issue again. The year was 1995, and three wonderful things happened to me. I graduated college; I married my husband, Charles; and, most miraculously of all, a new pharmaceutical drug, *Phen-Fen*, was introduced! Touted as the magic bullet that would annihilate the obesity epidemic, a well-meaning doctor had given it to me because a knee injury from step aerobics prevented me from exercising. And miracle drug it was! Within just a few months, I lost over forty pounds, eating anything I wanted! You see, the drug tricked my brain into thinking I was full after only eating very tiny portions. (You will learn in the upcoming chapters that the fiber and water in certain foods will make you feel equally full without any need for drugs or restricting portion size.)

Needless to say, I had still never learned what foods to eat for optimum health. Thanks to *Phen-Fen*, I just ate smaller portions of vegan desserts, washed down with regular *Dr. Pepper*. For a while, I was truly on cloud nine, having finally found what I thought was the panacea. Until the day I walked to the mailbox and found a letter from the FDA. They don't usually write to me, so I immediately tore open the envelope.

The darned government had stepped in to ruin everything! I say that facetiously; actually, the FDA may have saved my life. Apparently, some people had suffered severe heart and lung problems from *Phen-Fen*; it was being withdrawn from the market. I was notified by my insurance company to stop taking it immediately and to see a cardiologist and have an echocardiogram to see if I had sustained any cardiac or pulmonary damage from the months I had spent taking this dangerous medication. Thankfully, I had not, but unfortunately, once the last traces of the drug were gone from my system, so was my newfound thinness. And the weight came back on even faster than it had come off. So, there I was, full circle, back to 160 pounds, the weight I had always easily returned to for the past twenty-five years. So, I began to accept the fact that pharmaceuticals were not the answer and that being thin was just not in the cards for me. I would always be fat, like my mother and my grandmother and my great-grandmother before me.

It would be yet another fifteen years before I would even seriously attempt to tackle my weight problems again. Twice in my life, I had been thin, once from anorexia and once from a dangerous drug, and both times it had been fleeting and required extraordinary measures to achieve and sustain. And then, in 2011, I learned *The Secrets to Ultimate Weight Loss*. And for the past six years, I have not only been joyfully and consistently slender, at 117 pounds, but free from the clutches of refined food addiction.

And believe it or not, my recent journey has been painless and relatively effortless. I do not have to weigh my food, or myself, to easily maintain my slim, ideal weight. While I do exercise regularly now to help manage my anxiety without medication, I engaged in absolutely no exercise whatsoever to lose the majority of these fifty pounds. I no longer have an insatiable appetite for unhealthy junk food or suffer uncontrollable hunger or cravings. I never feel deprived. I eat all the delicious, nutritious food that I want, as often as I want, until comfortably full, but of the *right foods*.

Like the hundreds of others who are practicing *The Ultimate Weight Loss Program*, you too can achieve your desired weight. And I would be honored to help you. No matter how long or how much you have suffered, or how much weight you have to lose, you finally can have both the health and the body that you so richly deserve. And you are about to learn how.

CHAPTER 2

The Secrets to Ultimate Weight Loss Revealed!

That sounds like a pretty sensational chapter heading, doesn't it? The truth is, it's really not a secret at all because this information has been around for a long time. I didn't invent it. As a matter of fact, there were two bestselling, yet unread, weight loss books that had been sitting on my bookshelf for years, that explained this concept some twenty years before. One was *The McDougall Program for Maximum Weight Loss* by John McDougall, M.D. The other one was *Eat More, Weigh Less* by Dean Ornish, M.D.

Both are wonderful books that I recommend to you. But it was actually a book that I happened to pick up at a *Dollar Book Store* that truly helped me to understand the lessons of Dr. McDougall and Dr. Ornish, once I finally read their books. The book was called *"The Volumetrics Weight-Control Plan; Feel Full on Fewer Calories,"* by Barbara Rolls, Ph.D. Dr. Rolls' book helped me grasp concepts embedded in the books of Dr. McDougall and Dr. Ornish because it was filled with many visual representations comparing the portion sizes of various foods. For example, for the amount of calories in a mere one-quarter cup of raisins, you could consume two cups of grapes. For the same amount of calories in two tablespoons of peanut butter, you could have over half a pound of crispy, delicious, oil-free, baked sweet potato fries. After reading this book, the works by Dr. McDougall and Dr. Ornish now made sense to me. The secret to weight loss was finally clear.

I can distill the fundamental secret to *Ultimate Weight Loss* down to two words; these words aren't *eat less*, they are not *exercise more,* and they certainly are not *gastric bypass*. The biggest secret to *Ultimate Weight Loss* is CALORIE DENSITY. Dr. Rolls calls this Energy Density, which she abbreviates E.D., but I tried using that once in a lecture and scared off a lot of men.

If you want to easily lose weight and keep it off, calorie density is so important to comprehend that I spend at least ninety minutes teaching it to every new client who comes to me for private coaching. I want to make sure that they truly understand it because it's the foundation upon which *The Ultimate Weight Loss Program* is built. Calorie density simply means the number of calories in a given weight of food, expressed in calories per pound. And foods vary in their caloric density from about 100 calories per pound to about 4,000 calories per pound. Most people erroneously believe that to lose weight, you need to "eat less and exercise more," but if that truly worked and was sustainable, then why do ninety-eight percent of people who lose weight on diets gain it all back within two years? Using calorie density as the basis for my own personal weight loss, I was actually able to easily and effortlessly lose fifty pounds, and keep it off, eating *more* and (initially) not exercising at all.

You see, feeling full is due to the weight and the volume of the food you eat, as opposed to merely the calories that the food contains. So, if you eat foods that are lower in caloric density, you can still feel full and take in fewer calories. In her research lab at Penn State University, where she studies human eating behavior, Dr. Rolls discovered that all people consistently eat pretty much the same weight of food every day. So, simply by changing the caloric density of the foods they ate, they could easily lose weight without the usual suffering associated with having to eat smaller portions of food. In other words, eating in accordance with the principles of caloric density allows you to feel full on fewer calories. You can literally eat twice as much food, yet take in half as many calories.

Most diets ask you to eat less, which makes about as much sense as asking you to breathe less. It's simply not sustainable. The problem with consuming smaller portions of food is that you get so hungry that you eventually go off your diet, and you simply cannot maintain an eating style that keeps you hungry all the time. Restricting our portions goes against our nature to eat to satiation. When we restrict calories, our body receives the message that it is starving. When your hunger signals have been distorted by chronic dieting, your body senses that you haven't consumed enough calories and drives you to eat even more food by sending you powerful hunger signals that even those who possess a great amount of willpower cannot ignore. And when your body thinks that it is starving, you will be drawn to the most calorically dense and fattening foods. Then you overeat and gain back all the weight that you lost through a great deal of suffering and deprivation, and then some.

Leptin is a hormone released by your fat cells to signal satiation when they sense that you have taken in enough food. When this happens, your hunger signals quiet down and you stop eating, as you are no longer hungry. (*Fen-Phen* worked by manipulating leptin levels.) When you eat less food by weight and volume, your body releases less leptin, so you are driven to overeat. Once you understand the principles of caloric density, you will find that you can actually eat even more food than you were eating before you started *The Ultimate Weight Loss Program,* without experiencing hunger or deprivation. And because you are taking in fewer calories, you will lose weight without the usual suffering associated with futile attempts at portion control or carbohydrate- or calorie-restricted diets. Using this approach, you could easily lower your daily caloric intake by about 500 calories a day and lose at least a pound a week. And this type of slow weight loss is the most sustainable because you are eating large, satisfying portions of food, so your brain never sends out those signals that you are starving, causing you to eat more, and of all the wrong foods. I lost fifty pounds, gradually and effortlessly, without restricting myself at all. As a general rule, the more weight you have to lose, the faster the pounds will come off at first.

So, here's how the program works: you fill up on the foods with the lowest calorie density *first*, minimizing or eliminating the foods with higher caloric density. And what exactly are these foods with the lowest calorie density? Well, as luck would have it, they are the healthiest foods on the planet: vegetables, fruits, whole grains, and legumes. The same four new food groups that you will find on the *Power Plate* created by Dr. Neal Barnard of *PCRM* (the Physician's Committee for Responsible Medicine) as a response to the USDA's absurd food pyramid. These four categories of unprocessed, whole plant foods have a caloric density ranging, on average, from 100-600 calories per pound. And a well-known study by the World Cancer Research Fund[3] established that by keeping the average caloric density of the food that you eat each day to 567 calories per pound or less, you will be able to reach and maintain a healthy body weight while eating satisfying portions of food, and without the usual pain associated with diets based on deprivation. If you use this scientifically proven method for weight control and management, there is no weighing, no measuring, and no counting anything. If you only eat from these four groups, most people can eat *ad libitum*—as much as they want, as often as they want, until they are *comfortably* full. That means that you feel satisfied and no longer hungry; it doesn't mean that you've stretched your stomach to the absolute limit, as you may be accustomed to doing every Thanksgiving.

I once saw a very accurate post on *Facebook* that read, "No one ever got fat from eating too much kale." With non-starchy vegetables (almost all vegetables except potatoes, sweet potatoes, winter squashes, and corn) having a caloric density of about 100 calories per pound when consumed raw and roughly 200 calories per pound when eaten cooked; it's virtually impossible to overeat them. Non-starchy vegetables are the first category of food on my calorie density chart (see back cover) and the food lowest in caloric density. In my *Ultimate Weight Loss Program*, participants are asked to eat a *minimum* of two pounds of non-starchy vegetables daily, in addition to any raw salads or vegetables that are included in recipes, starting their day with at least one pound of non-starchy vegetables as part of their first meal of the day.

That's right. I highly recommend, and try to insist upon, vegetables for breakfast (VFB). I know this may be a little bit of a shocking idea to you. I like to think that VFB is my personal contribution to the field of weight loss. I started to propose this idea before there were any scientific studies that I knew of on the subject, but since then the idea has been verified by studies that show that vegetables can turn off the hunger switch and help to fight food cravings.

Virtually all the people in *The Ultimate Weight Loss Program* have reported that just by implementing this one change, they are now losing weight effortlessly while feeling full and satisfied. People generally require at least ten calories per pound of body weight just to support their basal metabolic rate, so if you need to eat 2,000 calories a day just to maintain your weight, and you tried to do that by eating vegetables exclusively, you would have to eat ten to twenty pounds of vegetables in order to do so. That should give you an idea of how this style of eating keeps you feeling full as you achieve your optimal weight.

At first, many people have trouble just eating the two pounds that are recommended each day. Some non-starchy vegetables contain up to ninety-six percent water, and you could burn more calories in the chewing and digesting of them than you would ever absorb from eating them. Eating non-starchy vegetables is probably the only thing that virtually every diet style has in common, and their consumption is always encouraged and unlimited in almost all health or reducing programs. It would be exceedingly difficult to overeat them.

Whenever I have new clients, I have them fill out a forty-question intake form. One of the things I ask about is how many servings of vegetables they eat each day. It has gotten to the point where I can accurately guess their weight simply by how they answer that question. Invariably, the lower their daily intake of vegetables, the higher their weight. Research corroborates this. Those who ate the most vegetables consistently had the lowest body weight and BMI.[4]

So, another secret to *Ultimate Weight Loss* is to eat (not blend or juice) your vegetables. You don't necessarily have to like it; you just have to do it. And the more you do it, the more you will enjoy it. In this book, I will teach you how to enjoy your veggies by providing you with some delicious cooking techniques and delectable recipes. Once you see what regularly eating these nutritional powerhouses, especially for breakfast, does to annihilate your food cravings and give you the slender body you always dreamed of, you will absolutely learn to love them!

Moving along on my calorie density chart, right after non-starchy vegetables (with a caloric density of about 100-200 calories per pound), we have fruit, which has a caloric density of about 200-300 calories per pound. Zucchini, bell pepper, okra, eggplant, tomatoes, and cucumber, which are botanically fruits, average out at a mere seventy-three calories per pound! Most people enjoy fruit more than vegetables, as it's normal for people to prefer the taste of foods with higher caloric density. If you required 2,000 calories a day to maintain your current weight, and you did so with fruit alone, you would need to consume seven to ten pounds of fruit. As sweet and delicious as fruit is, if you've ever eaten a pound of it at one sitting, you'd know that eating that much fruit would be pretty difficult for most people. It is simply not possible to be overweight if all you eat is fruits and vegetables. Now I am not at all suggesting that you do this; however, I simply want to make you aware that the people who do follow this way of eating (fruitarians, low-fat raw vegans, and those following the 80/10/10 diet style, with its high intake of raw fruits and vegetables) are almost always extremely lean. It is impossible to be over-weight if the caloric densities of all the foods you eat are that low. But for *Ultimate Weight Loss*, it is important that you eat these foods in their whole natural state and not juice them, blend them, or dehydrate them. Allow me to explain.

I don't recommend liquid calories at all for weight loss, as they lack sufficient bulk to fill you up. Many clients often come to me consuming daily juices or smoothies because they think that these are healthy, yet they are still unable to lose weight.

This can easily be explained by the visual representation below.

Each glass container represents an empty stomach. In the first one, we place 500 calories of whole apples, which is about two and a half pounds of apples. Depending on the size and variety of the apples, that would be about six apples. The entire container is now completely full, as would be your stomach—that is, if you somehow managed to eat that many apples in one sitting, a dubious proposition. (I once tried and I couldn't even finish three apples.)

In the second glass container, we place 500 calories' worth of applesauce made from the six whole apples. Applesauce can be easily made by placing the whole apples in a high-powered blender without adding or removing anything. Now the same glass container is mostly empty, containing only about five cups of applesauce, but it still has the same number of calories. While the water and fiber are still present, processing the whole apples into applesauce makes it less bulky and greatly decreases the volume, so it takes up much less space in the glass container and therefore less space in your stomach. This is the same thing that happens when people drink "healthy" green smoothies; the fiber and water are left intact but the bulk has been significantly reduced, and bulk is what creates satiety, the experience of feeling full. When you blend your food, you greatly reduce the bulk so that you don't sufficiently activate the stretch receptors in your stomach, an important mechanism of satiety.

The third container we save for the liquid nourishment we are going to obtain from the very popular approach of juicing. As you can see, if we juice those same six apples, the apple juice takes up hardly any room at all in the glass container, because the most important components of the whole fruit have been removed: the pulp and the fiber. You are now left with a liquid that is also very high in sugar, which can raise your blood sugar more quickly than the whole apple, in turn raising your insulin levels more quickly. Insulin is the hormone that is responsible for driving fat into the cells. Water by itself does not directly contribute to satiety because it leaves the digestive tract too quickly. But when combined with the fiber in whole foods, it greatly increases the feeling of fullness and meal satisfaction.

Consuming calories that do not contain fiber significantly increases your risk of constipation, colon cancer, and other related diseases because the bowel requires fiber to function properly. Fiber is found only in plant foods. It passes through the intestinal tract to help eliminate cancer-causing substances as waste and binds with fat and cholesterol to remove them in the stool. This causes a decrease in calorie absorption, lowers blood cholesterol, and improves the elimination of waste and unused calories. Eating foods rich in fiber satisfies the hunger drive and helps to stabilize our blood sugar, and can help you to achieve *Ultimate Weight Loss*, as fiber binds with water and increases the volume of food in your stomach, bringing satisfaction sooner and with fewer calories. Foods rich in fiber, like fruits, vegetables, whole grains, and legumes, slow digestion to prolong the feeling of fullness and increase the sensitivity and efficiency of insulin. And chewing your food, not drinking it, also greatly increases satiety. It changes the level of satisfaction that you experience from your food. Fibrous foods require a lot of chewing, again helping to prevent overeating. Therefore, make sure that everything that you eat not only contains fiber and water but that you are eating it with both the fiber and water intact and in its whole food form.

In the fourth and final container, we place dried apple rings; I make these in my food dehydrator by thinly slicing those six apples on my mandolin. This process yields only 2 cups of dried fruit that would be very easy to eat when compared to six whole apples. Whole apples have only about 200 calories per pound, whereas dehydrated apples and other dried fruits have a caloric density of about 1,300 calories per pound. In making the applesauce, the bulk has been greatly reduced; in the juicing of the apples, the pulp and the fiber have been removed; and in the dehydrating of the apples, all the water has been removed. So, while each of the four containers still contains 500 calories from apples, which manifestation, the dried apples, the apple juice, the applesauce, or the whole apples, do you think is going to fill you up more? When you blend or juice your calories, or eat foods with the water removed, it's just too easy to over-consume them. Fiber plus water creates bulk. And bulk is what creates satiety, which literally means the end of hunger. Bulk is essential if you want to feel full. And bulk is what you get when you eat apples in whole form. Making sure that everything you eat has both the fiber and water intact is another essential secret to *Ultimate Weight Loss*.

Let's make the same comparison between apples in their whole and processed forms, this time keeping in mind the insulin factor. Fruit purées such as applesauce raise insulin levels much more quickly than the whole fruit, and fruit juice causes an even greater production of insulin, which is what drives fat into the cells. Remember that eating whole foods, which contribute the greatest degree of satiety, means eating foods with the fiber and water intact.

As we continue moving along to the right on my calorie density chart, immediately after fruit, with its caloric density of 200-300 calories per pound, we have the unrefined complex carbohydrates, a category that includes starchy vegetables, whole grains, and legumes, which contain 400, 500, and 600 calories per pound, respectively. Starchy vegetables, like all the numerous, amazing varieties of potatoes, sweet potatoes, and winter squashes like butternut, kabocha, or acorn, contain approximately 400 calories per pound. Whole grains like corn, rice, quinoa (technically a seed), millet, and oats, to name but a few, have about 500 calories per pound, while the legume family, including beans, split peas, and lentils, contain around 550-600 calories per pound. To get 2,000 calories from these foods, you would need to eat about three to five pounds of them. And because whole grains and legumes absorb water when you cook them, they make you feel even fuller.

You see, the foods with caloric densities of 100-600 calories per pound—the vegetables, fruits, whole grains, and legumes—are all whole plant foods found in nature. They are full of water, fiber, vitamins, minerals, phytochemicals, antioxidants, and micronutrients. When you eat foods that contain fiber and water, they create bulk, and bulk is what helps to create satiety, that feeling of fullness in our tummies that tells us to stop eating. This bulk takes up sufficient space in our stomachs so that our stretch receptors are activated and our hunger signals are shut off.

Animal products, on the other hand, contain absolutely no fiber, and processed foods contain little to no fiber, so they cannot create any bulk in our intestinal tract, and the only possible way for them to activate our stretch receptors and to feel full from eating them is to overeat them, thereby consuming more calories than we need. In addition, animal products and processed foods contain few or no micronutrients, so they cannot activate our nutrient receptors, another important mechanism of satiety. A diet composed of whole plant foods (vegetables, fruits, whole grains, and legumes) is truly the only way to feel full while consuming fewer calories, so of these eat freely, while you whittle away the pounds.

Initially, when I began giving *The Secrets to Ultimate Weight Loss* lecture to each new client, I used to write all this information out by hand on a big white dry erase board. (Thankfully, now I have *PowerPoint*!) I would write out the caloric densities of all the various categories of foods, but often the client would still be confused about what they could and could not eat for *Ultimate Weight Loss*. So, one day, to simplify matters, I drew a thick, vertical red line immediately following the legume category. I would explain that, for the next twenty-one days, they were to eat only whole plant foods to the left of the red line: vegetables, fruits, whole grains, and legumes. And there are literally thousands of healthy and delicious foods in each of these categories from which to choose! These four food groups have a caloric density ranging from 100-600 calories per pound, and, as noted before, the study done by The World Cancer Research Fund clearly shows that if you keep the average caloric density of your daily food intake to 567 calories per pound or less, you will be able to reach and maintain a healthy body weight while eating large and satisfying portions of food. You will also escape the usual suffering associated with diets based on deprivation.

So, what about the foods to the right of the red line? Well, believe it or not, these are the exact foods from which most Americans obtain the majority of their calories. That is why approximately three-quarters of our population is overweight, and more than half of those are obese. Americans eat over ninety-two percent of their calories from animal products and processed foods (which appear to the right of the red line) and less than ten percent of their calories from fruits and vegetables (which appear to the left of the red line). The foods to the right of the red line contain from 750 calories per pound to a whopping 4,000 calories per pound. When you eat foods with a higher caloric density, they take up much less space in your stomach, and you will have to consume significantly more of them in order to feel full. Foods with a higher caloric density cause us to overeat because they simply aren't as filling, and the more concentrated your food choices, the more likely that you will find yourself overweight. In order to feel full on these more calorically dense foods, you are going to have to consume a heck of a lot more calories from them. Not a great idea if you are trying to lose weight.

The first food to the right of the red line is avocado, containing about 750 calories per pound, primarily from fat. While avocado is a whole food fat and is not unhealthy, for many people, particularly those of us who have struggled with our weight, the reality is that it is simply too calorically dense to eat regularly if we are trying to lose weight or maintain our weight loss. In addition, avocado is so incredibly delicious—like nuts, seeds, nut and seed butters (such as tahini and peanut butter) and so many other high-fat foods—that the majority of people who come to me for weight loss, many of whom are food addicts, are simply unable to moderate their use of it. When we eat these high-fat foods, just as when we eat refined carbohydrates like sugar and flour, we crave more of the same and have a great deal of difficulty not overeating them. These high-fat, high-calorie, "pleasure trap" foods are ones that our ancestors did not have daily access to and consumed only seasonally. Nuts came in hard shells and each one had to be opened individually and by hand.

One day, when I was guest lecturer at *TrueNorth Health Center* in Santa Rosa, California, we were served a delicious guacamole as a topping for the baked potatoes. All of us took huge scoops of it, filling half of our oversized dinner plates with this luscious dip. Dr. Alan Goldhamer, the co-founder of the health center, asked us if we knew what constituted a single serving of this creamy, delicious topping. No one seemed to have a clue. He then said, "A serving of guacamole is two tablespoons." "Per chip?" I asked him. To which he replied, "No, per day."

When I got home, I looked at a container of commercial guaca-mole, and sure enough, it said that the serving size was a mere two tablespoons! I then found an avocado-promotion website, www.avo-cadocentral.com; it said that a serving of avocado was 1/5 of a medium avocado! I don't know about you, but I have never sliced a luscious, ripe avocado into five pieces and put four of the pieces back into the refrigerator, to consume the whole thing Monday-Friday. Have you? Avocado is just so darned tantalizing that eating even a little bit just makes me want more. So, personally, I avoid it now and make my *Sweet Pea Guacamole* (recipe in *Unprocessed*) out of defrosted frozen green peas instead of avocado.

I am not telling you never to eat avocado again or that it's unhealthy. I am saying that with a calorie density of 750 calories per pound, you need to be mindful of it if you're trying to lose weight. A single avo-cado can have over 300 calories and almost thirty grams of fat. For that same amount of calories, I can enjoy four pounds of my delicious *Oven Roasted Ratatouille* (recipe page 130), or two pounds of ripe strawber-ries, both of which contain virtually no fat. Which do you think you're going to find more satisfying and is going to fill you up more?

When the calories in the food that you eat come from fat, they are easily and effortlessly stored as fat, whereas the calories from carbohy-drates and protein, even if you overeat them, are either burned as heat or stored invisibly in the muscles or liver as glycogen. At nine calories per gram, all fat, regardless of its source, is more than twice as calori-cally dense as either carbohydrates or protein, each containing only four calories per gram. While dietary fat is easily and effortlessly converted to body fat (it takes less than three percent of the calories in the food to go from the lips to the hips), human beings cannot readily convert an excess of protein or carbohydrate to fat. This is called *de novo lipogen-esis*. For *Ultimate Weight Loss*, you need to fill up on the foods with the lowest caloric density, and ideally *eat them first*, so that you get full on fewer calories. If you are anything like me, you need to eat a lot more than two tablespoons of guacamole or 1/5 of an avocado to feel full.

Immediately following avocado with a caloric density of 750 calories per pound, we have the refined carbohydrates like bread, flour, and sugar, and the processed dairy products like cheese and ice cream. These are not whole foods and are especially deleterious to your health. These are calorie-dense manufactured foods, none of which are found in nature. It is within this category that most people's cravings and food addictions occur. At 1,200 calories per pound, we have ice cream; at 1,400-1,500 calories per pound, we have bread and flour; at 1,600 calories per pound, we have cheese; and at 1,800 calories per pound, sugar. The average American eats over 150 pounds of sugar per person, per year, which is almost a half a pound of sugar per person each day!

Even if sugars and flours were not addictive, at 1,400-1,800 calories per pound, they are simply too calorically dense for most people in general, and overweight people in particular, to eat if they wish to lose weight.

When you process a whole plant food, like beets into sugar or brown rice into brown rice flour, you exponentially increase its caloric density and thus your ability to overeat on it. It becomes calorie rich and nutrient poor. Whole beets are only about 195 calories per pound, but when processed into sugar they become 1,800 calories a pound and are completely devoid of their fiber, water, and nutrients. To yield a mere teaspoon of granulated sugar, you would need to start with about three feet of sugar cane. Do you think you could even chew through three feet of sugar cane? But how easy it is to down sixteen teaspoons of sugar, especially if they are hidden in a carbonated or caffeinated beverage or a rich dessert! If you take a pound of brown rice, which is about 500 calories per pound, and grind it into brown rice flour to make bread or bake a cake, you need roughly three pounds of the brown rice to make just one pound of brown rice flour. The brown rice flour has about 1,500 calories per pound, triple the caloric density of brown rice itself. If you ate 500 calories of brown rice, which I often do, your stomach would be completely full. But to completely fill it with bread, cake, or pasta made from the brown rice flour, you would wind up with about 1,500 calories. You see, the less a food is processed, the better it is for weight loss. The more a food is processed, the more it contributes to weight gain.

In addition to being more calorically dense, the foods to the right of the red line (with the exception of the few high-fat plant foods) have virtually no fiber or water, which have been removed in the processing, along with all the vitamins, minerals, phytochemicals, and antioxidants. These are the vital components of food that you need to prevent and reverse disease, and that most Americans are sorely deficient in. The more fiber you eat, the more weight you will lose because fiber fills you up with no calories. Fiber not only tricks the brain into thinking that it's full, it also helps remove toxins from the body and slows the passage of food through the digestive system so that satiety signals are stimulated for a longer period of time. When you refine a whole plant food to make sugar, flour, bread, or pasta, the plant's nutrients are destroyed and the fiber is either damaged or removed. This is also important because when you grind a whole grain to make flour, you now increase its surface area, which increases its absorption in your intestines, which increases your blood sugar more quickly, which in turn increases insulin. And insulin, again, is responsible for driving fat into the cells. This is another of the many reasons to eat your food whole in general, and your whole grains whole, in particular.

Always eating your food whole, rather than processed, is another secret to *Ultimate Weight Loss.*

With the exception of processed dairy products like cheese and ice cream, I intentionally did not include animal products in my calorie density chart. The majority of them average about 1,000 calories per pound or more, and so are found to the right of the red line. No animal products contain any fiber, and they are generally very high in fat and high in cholesterol. And when compared to all the miraculous foods to the left of the red line, they contribute very little to satiety. According to the satiety index developed by Dr. Susanna Holt, do you know what food tops the satiety charts? It's not bacon. If you guessed the potato, you would be correct!

There are a myriad of other reasons to not eat animal products besides weight loss. For a quick and easy way to fully understand why animal protein is so deleterious to your health as well as the environment, I strongly encourage you to watch the wonderful documentaries *Forks Over Knives* and *Cowspiracy*.

Even if dairy products were healthful, and they most certainly are not, their lack of fiber, water, and vital nutrients, married with their extremely high caloric density, make them completely unfavorable for weight loss. Having worked with thousands of clients now, I have discovered time and time again that when people abstain from all the foods in the refined carbohydrate and processed dairy products category, they not only lose weight, but their cravings disappear as their brain chemistry finally begins to stabilize.

As we continue to travel to the right on my calorie density chart, we encounter another luscious, high-fat food that is a favorite of just about every woman I have ever known. Chocolate has a calorie density of roughly 2,500 calories per pound. While chocolate may have some marginal antioxidant benefits, the company that it keeps, which is often full-fat dairy and almost always sugar, renders it unhealthful. It also contains some pretty highly addictive chemicals like caffeine and theobromine, plus its high caloric density and high percentage of calories from fat make it unfavorable for weight loss. Chocolate always tops the list of the most craved foods, and the only way to truly really get rid of cravings is to stop indulging them.

Most people whom you ask would agree that chocolate, and all the other foods to the right of the red line, taste way better than the foods to the left of the red line. We are genetically hardwired to prefer the taste of high-fat, high-calorie foods for survival; chocolate is both. The problem with frequent indulgence in these high-fat, high-calorie, highly stimulating foods is that the more you eat them, the more you desire them and the less satisfying whole natural food tastes by comparison. And when you eat processed foods that do not contain fiber and water, you fool the brain's satiety mechanisms, so you are compelled to overeat them.

A scientific experiment was conducted with people who were self-professed chocoholics.[5] They gave the subjects an injection of a drug called naloxone, an opiate blocker that is used in the emergency room to treat heroin overdoses. After the administration of this potent drug, the subjects had virtually no interest in eating the chocolate that they so adored. So, I ask you this: did the chocolate cease to become luscious, creamy, and delicious, or could it have been that the effect that the chocolate had on their brains was now obliterated?

You see, taste is very subjective and we actually develop taste preferences for what we habitually eat. What you eat today, you may crave tomorrow. The only food that we actually have an inherent taste for is breast milk; everything else is learned. You cannot possibly crave a particular food if you have never had it, and you will eventually stop craving all the high-fat, high-calorie foods once you stop indulging in them for a long enough period of time.

As we make our way to the right on my calorie density chart, immediately following chocolate, which has a caloric density of 2,500 calories per pound, we have nuts, seeds, and the luscious nut and seed butters, like peanut butter and tahini, which are made from them. These have an average calorie density of about 2,800 calories per pound. Seeds generally have a lower caloric density of about 2,600 calories per pound, while some nuts, like macadamias, can be as high as 3,200 calories per pound.

I have been accused of saying that nuts are not healthy and telling people not to eat them. This simply is not true. Nuts are a whole food fat and have some health benefits. But with a mere ounce of walnuts containing roughly 200 calories and twenty grams of fat, they are more likely to fill you out than fill you up. Learning not to indulge in them was crucial to my own weight loss. And when I finally stopped eating them entirely, for the first time in my life, I was able to get slim with little effort.

Even when I was eating a whole food plant-based diet free of sugar, oil, and salt, and carefully measuring out all my nuts and seeds and consuming only an ounce per day, I simply could not lose any weight until I stopped consuming all added dietary fat and reduced my dietary fat intake to fifteen percent or less of my total calories. There are individual genetic differences in how much fat certain people can consume without getting fat. There are some naturally thin people who can eat a lot of nuts and avocado and not gain weight. But if you are overweight, then it's probably not you!

Why not try an experiment in which you don't eat any fatty foods (no nuts, seeds, avocados, oil, coconut, olives, or animal foods) for just twenty-one days? I promise that you won't become fatty acid deficient in that time, especially if you still have fat on your body. There is fat in all whole natural foods. Greens have about three percent of their calories from fat, and even fruit has about one percent of its calories from fat. Some whole grains, like oats, for example, have almost twenty percent of their calories from fat. See if abstaining from fatty foods makes a difference in your ability to easily lose weight. If it doesn't work, then you can always go back to eating more fat on day twenty-two.

The truth is, I have never seen it not work.

The other problem with eating foods like nuts, seeds, avocado, and chocolate, is that they can also be trigger foods for many food addicts; including them in the diet, even in small amounts, can lead to cravings for more and more of these high-fat foods. If I could eat them without constantly craving them and overeating them, I would. If you are including these foods in your diet and are still overweight and wish to lose weight, then perhaps you are not able to moderate their use, either. I suggest you run an experiment for twenty-one days and avoid all the foods to the right of the red line and find out. If you truly could consume chocolate, nuts, seeds, sugars, flours, and alcohol and be slender and not constantly crave them, wouldn't you have done it already?

Many experts advise us to eat nuts every day. As far as I can tell, none of them have ever been overweight or struggled with food addiction or emotional eating. While I certainly don't think that nuts are addictive in the same way that sugar and flour are, many people, even slender ones, seem to have a problem moderating their use of them. If the person I know who has the most willpower and restraint, Dr. Alan Goldhamer, has to measure out his cashews in one-ounce bags and keep them in the freezer so he doesn't overeat them, good luck to the rest of us! If you are concerned that you'll become fatty acid deficient by following my advice to shun high-fat foods, then add one tablespoon of ground flax seeds, chia seeds, or hemp seeds to your daily salad. You can also boost your intake of dark green leafy greens, an excellent source of the essential fatty acids. (There is a blood test that can check the level of Omega-3 fatty acids in your blood if you are still concerned.)

We complete our calorie density chart with the final food (and I use the term "food" loosely), which at a whopping 4,000 calories per pound is the most calorically dense and nutritionally poor food on the planet, and that is oil. That means ALL OIL—yes, even some "health food" faves like olive oil and coconut oil, about which so many dubious health claims are made. Did you know that it takes almost sixteen ears of corn to make just one tablespoon of corn oil? Do you think anyone could honestly eat that much corn in one sitting? But it's very easy to down a salad with forty calories from lettuce and at least 400 calories from an oily dressing. It takes about forty olives to make a tablespoon of olive oil. When you process the olives into oil, everything that was beneficial in the whole natural food like the water, fiber, vitamins, minerals, phytochemicals, and antioxidants are destroyed in the processing. And you are left with a nonnutritive, disease-promoting toxin that will make you fat and sick. If there truly was anything health-promoting in the processed oils, don't you think that it would also be in the whole food that it was produced from? So, eat the olives, not the olive oil. Eat the whole flaxseeds, not the flaxseed oil. Eat the coconut, not the coconut oil. But remember, that even in their whole food form, they are still very calorically dense, high-fat foods.

It's amazing how effectively the calorie density approach works for weight loss, even for those not willing to go all the way in eliminating all foods to the right of the red line. Some of my clients are not willing to go plant-based right away, but I tell them to at least abstain from alcohol (a highly refined and addictive carbohydrate that has seven calories per gram, almost twice that of protein and carbohydrate, and no fiber or nutrients), oil, and all dairy products. By implementing those simple measures alone, many will lose up to ten pounds the first month. Giving up processed oils permanently is one of the best things you can do for your health, and your waistline. All oils bypass the normal mechanisms of satiation. Because oil has no nutrients, it never activates the nutrient receptors, and because it also has no fiber, it can never activate the stretch receptors. For any of the high-fat foods to truly activate your stretch receptors, you would have to eat an unthinkable amount of calories from them.

Oil is by far the most calorically dense, nutrient-poor food on the planet, as you will be able to see from this example. If I were to make a pasta primavera from brown rice noodles with my oil-free *Quick Sun-Dried Tomato MaRAWnara* (recipe page 133), topped with lots of veggies, I could eat a huge plate of this homemade version and consume about 500 calories, give or take. But here's what happens if you order what you think is a healthy dish in a restaurant. (Having worked as an Executive Pastry Chef in a restaurant for years, I promise you that they use more sugar, fat, and salt than you ever would at home). When they cook the pasta, they add oil (and of course salt) to the boiling water. When they drain the pasta, they pour on even more oil with a heavy hand. And of course, their marinara sauce recipe has probably an entire cup of oil in it as well. And they also add butter or oil to the vegetables. So, the same dish that I created at home for a mere 500 calories, at a restaurant contains a whopping 1,000 calories, and those additional 500 calories that come from oil simply won't register for you—they won't make you feel any fuller. Oil bypasses the normal mechanisms of satiation. Oil is insidious; it slips under the radar, undetected by your stretch and nutrient receptors. But those additional calories from oil and other high-fat foods never go unnoticed by your ever-expanding waistline.

Even if oil were truly health-promoting, wouldn't whatever is in the oil that's supposedly healthy also be in the whole food from which it came? If there were something truly magical about olive oil, flax-seed oil, or coconut oil, all of which contain 4,000 calories per pound, wouldn't it also be in the olives, the flaxseeds, and the coconut that it was produced from? Nothing remarkable and health-promoting happens in the transformation of a whole food into a processed food. It only serves to make the food more calorically rich and nutrient poor. Whatever you choose to eat, if you wish to experience *Ultimate Weight Loss*, please eat it only in its unprocessed, whole food form.

By now I hope you understand that for optimum health and weight loss, you're better off eating an ear of corn than the one-sixteenth of a tablespoon of corn oil that is made from it. But what about some relatively healthy foods that can be made from corn, like corn tortillas, oil-free baked corn chips (recipe in *Unprocessed*) or air popped popcorn? Well, let's first look at it from the perspective of calorie density. Whole corn, like any other whole grain, is a mere 500 calories per pound. But corn tortillas or even oil-free baked corn chips contain about 990 calories per pound, nearly double, because we have removed the water. And air popped popcorn contains a whopping 1,800 calories per pound, more than triple the damage! Keep reminding yourself that while these more processed versions of the whole foods are certainly not unhealthy, and you may be able to enjoy them occasionally once you become svelte, they are less favorable for weight loss because they have had their water removed. Remember, the more you process a food and move away from eating it in its whole, natural state, the less effective it's going to be for weight loss. In addition, foods like air popped popcorn and baked tortilla chips are generally eaten as snack foods, for reasons other than hunger, and are usually eaten by hand. Hand-to-mouth foods are never favorable for weight loss or for those suffering from food addictions. So, if you must eat these foods, I like the idea of my partner in the online *Ultimate Weight Loss Program*, John Pierre, who recommends that you eat them with chopsticks, which will slow you down considerably—and do so only occasionally after weight loss is achieved.

Sequencing your food intake by consuming lower calorie density foods prior to higher calorie density foods is another secret to *Ultimate Weight Loss*.

I've been very fortunate to be able to practice this technique during the last seven years as a visiting guest chef and lecturer at *TrueNorth Health Center* in Santa Rosa. Each of the three delicious meals we enjoyed each day, prepared by Chef Bravo, was an all-you-can-eat buffet, arranged in order of increasing caloric density. When you enter the dining room, there is a huge twenty-four-hour salad bar with a plethora of raw vegetables. Next is the fresh fruit, followed by the steamed non-starchy vegetables and then the cooked starches (such as potatoes, sweet potatoes, whole grains, and legumes). I was able to practice eating in accordance with the principles of calorie density at every meal, eating the more calorie dilute raw salads and steamed vegetables first, before enjoying the more satiating but more calorically dense cooked starches. By eating foods in order of increasing calorie density, you will actually enjoy them more, and feel full on fewer calories. What this will mean for you is eating a large raw salad, followed by steamed vegetables or a soup made from non-starchy vegetables, before moving on to a dish like my more satiating *Mexican Stuffed Potato* (a baked potato stuffed with corn, beans, and salsa—recipe page 174). I always save that dish for last, because if I eat it first, it would be very difficult for me to then go back and eat my salad and vegetables.

One of the principles I teach in *The Ultimate Weight Loss Program* is ***"If you are not hungry enough to eat vegetables, then you're not hungry!"*** That's why I always recommend taking advantage of their low caloric density and eating them first if you want to lose weight. After more than six years of practicing this important habit, it's permanently emblazoned on my brain and has become second nature. The natural extension of this approach of eating vegetables first is to eat them for the first meal of the day. Even my naturally thin husband has joined me in eating VFB (vegetables for breakfast) and on the rare days that we can't get them, we sorely miss them. As you begin to overcome your food addiction to refined carbohydrates, animal products, and high-fat foods, these health-promoting foods of a much lower calorie density will begin to taste good. And after eating this way for a while, you actually begin to prefer healthful foods and practically crave them. Eating any food can satisfy hunger, but cravings can only be satisfied with a particular food, or foods. When you are truly hungry, the unadorned basics like salad and steamed vegetables actually taste good.

After following an unprocessed, whole food, plant-based diet free of sugar, oil, and salt for three years, from 2008-2011, I still found myself about fifty pounds overweight. My diet was excellent by comparison with the Standard American Diet, but it wasn't excellent enough for me to achieve my optimal weight. I attribute my own success at weight loss to two improvements I made to my diet: 1) eliminating high-fat, calorie-dense foods such as nuts and nut butters, and replacing them with more satiating, less calorie-dense starches; and, 2) always eating vegetables for breakfast and continuing to eat the more calorie-dilute foods first throughout the day.

In *The Ultimate Weight Loss Program*, we encourage the participants to consume at least one pound of non-starchy vegetables for breakfast and a second pound later in the day, usually prior to dinner, before eating the other more calorically dense foods. It's not that you can only eat vegetables for breakfast; it's just that for *Ultimate Weight Loss* and maximum enjoyment of them, we highly recommend that you eat them first, before your starch. Consistently eating a raw salad or a calorie-dilute vegetable-based soup before meals will work just as well.

Keep in mind that if you are coming off the Standard American Diet or a highly processed junk food vegan diet, you may not be accustomed to eating large volumes of vegetables. In order to avoid the gas and bloating that some people experience when adopting this change, make sure you chew your food really well, to a cream. Most people cannot go from eating virtually no vegetables to eating two pounds a day, so your system may need some time to adjust. If this turns out to be the case for you, work up to that amount slowly, perhaps eating only ¼ to ½ a pound of vegetables at a time. While raw vegetables are even better for weight loss, it will be much easier for you to digest larger volumes of vegetables if you steam them or roast them, without oil of course. Also, remember that there are over thirty different varieties of non-starchy vegetables and that they vary in the degree to which they produce gas. Keep trying new vegetables until you find the one that works best for you. And if you are like I used to be, and dislike all vegetables, start out by eating the vegetable that you hate the least. At the beginning, the healthiest vegetable is the one you will actually eat!

You should be aware that, when eating in accordance with the principles of calorie density, you will need to eat way more food, in terms of volume, than you are accustomed to eating. This may be perplexing. Most people who have a long history of unsuccessful dieting have received only transient results from eating very small quantities of food while on diets, and have counterproductively restricted necessary food groups like the healthy unrefined complex carbohydrates, such as potatoes, rice, beans, or even fruit. You may be one of those unfortunate dieters. You are now being told to do the exact opposite and eat very large portions of the foods that you were told that you shouldn't eat at all. So, let me ask you this. If calorie counting, restricting carbs, or portion control truly worked, wouldn't you be thin by now?

Carbohydrates are our body's preferred source of fuel; it is the fuel that we process most efficiently. When your diet is deficient in complex carbohydrates, you will be hungry. As Dr. McDougall has said, "Carbohydrates are to hunger what oxygen is to the need to breathe and water is to thirst." I lost fifty pounds and kept if off for over five years now, by eating huge portions of potatoes, rice, and beans, along with lots of fruits and vegetables. And so did the hundreds of people who have participated in *The Ultimate Weight Loss Program*. And we did so joyfully without experiencing any hunger or deprivation. I actually eat more now as a slender person, in terms of quantity, than I ever ate as a fat person. People who see me sit down before enormous portions of rice or potatoes and are unfamiliar with the concept of calorie density often ask me, "Are you actually going to eat all that?" To which I gleefully say, "Yes, and then I am going back for more." When you truly understand that calorie density is the fundamental secret to *Ultimate Weight Loss* and implement it on a daily basis, you, too, can actually eat much more food and weigh much less.

Eating large quantities of food in public may be difficult for those who are still overweight because they may feel like others who do not understand calorie density are scrutinizing them. Even though a huge plate of rice, beans, and vegetables can have half as many calories as a single slice of pepperoni pizza, it is a much larger volume of food, and so to the nutritionally uneducated, it can look like you're overeating and you may feel like you are being judged. One of my clients was eating a huge plate of steamed vegetables and a plain baked potato at a business lunch, which maybe had a total of 300 calories, and a rude co-worker actually said to her, "See, this is why you're overweight. You just eat too much." This can be especially difficult for females, who were raised to believe that it's not ladylike to eat large portions. This is one of the many reasons that we insist upon no eating out during the first twenty-one days of the program. (Many food addiction treatment programs do not allow eating at restaurants or other people's homes for the first ninety days.) Unless you are not going to be bothered by these kind of snarky, ill-informed comments, or are able to fully explain the theory of calorie density to all your dinner companions, it might be better if you avoid these situations at first if they make you feel uncomfortable. If you must go to business lunches or eat with other people who don't understand this way of eating and you would feel uncomfortable eating large portions of healthy food in front of them, then I recommend that you eat before you go and have a cup of tea when you are in the restaurant. You never want to put yourself in a situation in which you will be hungry from not eating enough food.

If you've never eaten this way, I know that it must sound like I am making a bold promise, that you can truly eat and enjoy large quantities of food, even potatoes, and still lose weight. I didn't believe it was possible either until I went to *TrueNorth Health Center* and watched how all the doctors, patients, and other staff members ate. They were all trim. They would come to the dining room at every meal and take not one, but at least two, huge plates of food. And the food would be piled on high. One plate would usually have salad and fruit, the other lots of steamed vegetables and cooked starches. I was skeptical at first, but when I finally took the "when in Rome attitude" and "ran an experiment," as Dr. Doug Lisle, co-author of *The Pleasure Trap*, suggested, and ate all these foods with abandon, the weight melted off. The more potatoes I ate, the slimmer I got! I learned firsthand that the way to lose weight was with a full plate. Always remember that you will not gain weight if the calorie density of the foods you eat averages 567 calories per pound or less, which describes all the foods to the left of the red line.

Going to a residential treatment center like *TrueNorth Health Center* or the *The McDougall 10-Day Program,* both in Santa Rosa, California, can be enormously helpful for learning how to eat, with the buffets set up in order of increasing calorie density and everyone around you eating huge portions of the delicious food—and still losing weight! You'll feel embraced by a community of like-minded people who are all eating the same way. But even if you can't attend either of these wonderful programs, you still can do this at home.

It is imperative that you eat large enough portions of the right foods, including enough non-starchy vegetables to ward off food cravings, while still enjoying ample starch, and that you eat it all early enough in the day for satiation and meal satisfaction. You need to do this consistently and continue to eat this way even *after* you lose the weight. Regardless of the weight loss method you employ to lose weight, if you do not continue to eat in the same manner after becoming slender, you will most assuredly gain all your weight back, and possibly even more. This is exactly why dieting does not result in permanent weight loss. Using the calorie density approach with unprocessed, whole plant foods is not a diet, as you will be able to enjoy extremely large portions of delicious, satisfying foods like rice, beans, potatoes, fruits, and vegetables. And you will never feel hungry or deprived.

You won't be counting your calories or measuring your portions, but you should notice that the majority of the volume of your food will be coming from non-starchy vegetables, and the majority of the calories you ingest will come from sources of starch (potatoes, sweet potatoes, winter squashes, whole grains, and legumes).

Please don't worry about getting too thin. You won't keep losing weight forever. Your body will find its ideal weight and then you can still eat all the calorie dilute fruits and vegetables you want and reasonably larger portions of the unrefined complex carbohydrates like potatoes, rice, and beans. Just remember to eat your salad or cooked non-starchy vegetables first, at least during the active weight loss phase of the program. Then, feel free to eat your veggies and starch together, as long as you keep eating large enough portions of those veggies.

In the extremely rare case of someone who felt that he or she was getting too thin, an easy solution would lie in simply eating more starch or adding small portions of the whole food fats to the right of the red line such as an ounce of nuts or seeds or some avocado, assuming that these are not trigger foods for you. When you eat this way, it is very easy to maintain your weight, as long as you continue eating the same foods that you ate to lose weight.

Calorie density also takes all the emotional charge and judgment out of eating. Even though I have strong opinions about many things, including the list of health, ethical, and environmental reasons to shun animal foods, I no longer even bother arguing with people about which foods are "good" and which ones are "bad" when I teach *The Ultimate Weight Loss Program*. I often give my lecture on *The Secrets to Ultimate Weight Loss* on cruise ships, hospitals, and five-star resorts where none of the clientele is vegan. I never even have to use the "V" word (even though I am damn proud to be vegan for over forty years!), because guess what, folks? All the foods to the left of the red line on my calorie density chart are vegan! Now, I didn't skew the chart towards vegan foods; Mother Nature did. I explain to the people that they never really had a weight problem; they had a math problem. The calories in the food they eat, in the volume they need to eat them for satisfaction, add up to too high a number. The solution to the math problem is to simply eat from the *New Four Food Groups*: fruits, vegetables, whole grains, and legumes. These are the foods that are not only highest in nutrients, but also lowest in caloric density, and are also the healthiest foods on the planet. So, even though clients come to me primarily for weight loss and food addiction, they still end up eating a whole food, plant-exclusive diet to experience *Ultimate Weight Loss.*

The animals don't really care why we aren't eating them, now do they?

If you have been fooled by the purveyors of fatty foods and still don't believe that, in Dr. McDougall's words, "The fat you eat is the fat your wear," let me tell you about an experiment I conducted on an unwitting subject, my husband, Charles. In the summer of 2008, I saw a compelling DVD about preventing and reversing heart disease, featuring Dr. Caldwell B. Esselstyn, Jr. It convinced me that consuming all oil was very damaging to one's cardiovascular and overall health, so beginning on August 1, 2008, I immediately stopped consuming oil, as well as sugar and salt. I did not notify my husband of this dietary change because I figured he didn't need to be told since I was the one who prepared all the meals anyway. Since it's very easy to prepare food without oil, and it's even more delicious that way, he didn't know! Well, Charles doesn't normally wear a belt, but seven months into the experiment, he had to attend a formal event so he put one on. It no longer fit and he could not figure out how he could have lost so much weight! I told him to calm down, that I just stopped feeding him oil, the most calorically dense food on the planet. We didn't even own a scale back then, so we bought one and he realized that he had lost eight pounds, without his consent! And he was already slender to begin with. If someone who does not even need to lose weight can effortlessly lose eight pounds just by shunning processed oils, imagine what would happen to someone who actually needed to lose weight?

What's interesting to me is that Americans eat over ninety-two percent of their calories from animal products and processed foods (foods to the right of the red line), and less than ten percent of their calories from fruits and vegetables (foods to the left of the red line), and about seventy-five percent of Americans are overweight and more than half of those are obese. The Center for Disease Control (CDC) predicts that in a few short years, over forty percent of Americans will be obese.[6] All the foods to the left of the red line, the fruits, vegetables, and unrefined complex carbohydrates like potatoes, rice, and beans, from which I now eat one hundred percent of my calories, are the foods that most Americans actually eat very little of. Take a look at the foods to the right of the red line—most animal products, the refined carbohydrates, and high-fat plant foods—and you find the source of over ninety-two percent of the calories that Americans ingest. Do you see any correlation here between the caloric density of the foods that most people choose to eat and the inability of the majority of them to control their insatiable appetites and lose weight?

All the foods to the left of the red line are foods that are found in nature; we eat them largely the same way they were grown. With the exception of the whole plant foods that are comprised primarily of fat, like nuts, seeds, and avocado, all the foods to the right of the red line are foods that are not found in nature and we eat them as they were manufactured. To the left of the red line, we have whole foods. To the right of the red line (except for the high-fat plant foods) we have highly processed foods. As I said in my first book, *Unprocessed*, for optimal health, disease prevention, and even disease reversal, we are designed to eat our food whole, not processed. We need to eat foods that come from a plant, not foods that are manufactured in a plant. And as it turns out, these whole plant foods are lowest in calorie density, highest in nutrients, and unparalleled for weight loss too!

Sugar is put into almost every single processed food, from baby formula to geriatric formula, and because it's readily available, easily affordable, and socially acceptable, many people refuse to believe how highly addictive it is. Bread is "the staff of life," and we "break bread" with our loved ones, and so it's even harder for people to understand that flour is equally addictive. Just as there are some people who can drink alcohol and not become alcoholic, there are certainly people who can consume sugar and flour and not become addicted to them. But if you are overweight, or if you find that you can't stop eating these substances once you start, then it's time to consider whether you actually suffer from a food addiction.

Feeling full is important, especially for those with a long history of dieting based on deprivation and restriction, and for those who are food addicts and/or emotional eaters. While I am not a mental health professional, I did suffer from both of those afflictions as well as obesity. What's great about eating to the left of the red line is that while ideally you are dealing with your emotional issues, you could ostensibly overeat on these foods without it greatly impacting your weight or physical health. Let's face it, I never met anyone who was addicted to arugula and no one emotionally overeats on okra, but even if you did—well, go ahead, knock yourself out, you will not gain weight. It's all but impossible to put on extra pounds if you keep the average calorie density of the food you eat to 567 calories per pound or less—and if you need to lose weight, you will.

What I and all the participants in *The Ultimate Weight Loss Program* have discovered is that when you finally get the food right, by eating only whole plant food to the left of the red line and avoiding all animal products, refined foods, and the high-fat foods to the right of the red line, cravings permanently disappear and emotional eating is greatly diminished. Perhaps this is because for the first time in your life you are able to eat more than enough food to feel satisfied without restricting portions or shunning entire healthy food groups like complex carbohydrates. You will learn, from direct experience, that wholesome foods like potatoes and rice, that you were taught were bad, are the exact foods you can eat with abandon that will make you thin, and restore your health and vitality. And these health-promoting complex carbohydrates (a.k.a. "starch") are the only foods that will ever truly satisfy your hunger drive.

From now on, whenever you choose between foods to the left of the red line and the right of the red line, ask yourself, which will fill my tummy more? The only way the foods to the right of the red line can possibly ever fill your stomach is if you overeat them, taking in more calories than you need, which ultimately will make you fat, sick, or both. For most people in general, and overweight people and food addicts in particular, eating the foods to the right of the red line does not lead to satiety and merely perpetuates overeating because foods of a higher caloric density simply are not as filling. Eating the delicious bounty of whole natural foods to the left of the red line curbs overeating, eliminates cravings, and results in satiety, the end of hunger. And if you consistently eat to the left of the red line, you will reach satiety sooner, in a more healthful manner and on far fewer calories.

I believe that when you fully understand the concept of calorie density, you can create both the health and the body that you so richly deserve. When it comes to *Ultimate Weight Loss*, calorie dilution is the solution! And so, my friend, to achieve your desired weight and optimal health, and for disease prevention and reversal, here is the secret to *Ultimate Weight Loss*: eat to the left of the red line!

CHAPTER 3

Starting The Ultimate Weight Loss Program

*T*he *Ultimate Weight Loss Program* is a groundbreaking lifestyle intervention program in which individuals adopt a low-fat, whole food, plant-exclusive diet free of all processed food, including all sugars (including zero-calorie sweeteners), all flour and flour products, oil, salt, and alcohol, and eat only the foods to the left of the red line for a period of at least twenty-one days, and consume at least two pounds of non-starchy vegetables daily, starting with at least one pound of non-starchy vegetables as their first food of the day.

The results I have seen in the participants of this program over the past six years have been nothing short of miraculous. In as little as twenty-one days, I have witnessed people completely transform their health and their lives. It is not uncommon to see weight loss of ten to twenty pounds, depending on how much weight a person has to lose. (The most weight lost by a female during the twenty-one days was eighteen pounds; the most weight lost by a male was twenty-seven pounds). I have had participants whose doctors either reduced or eliminated their medications for high blood pressure, high cholesterol, high triglycerides, and diabetes. Perhaps more exciting than what people lost, like unwanted pounds and the need for expensive medications, was what they gained. Participants acquired peace of mind from experiencing freedom from their food addictions, perhaps for the first time in their lives. And they reported feeling better, calmer, and more balanced than they ever had before.

How do you do your own *Ultimate Weight Loss Program?* Well, if you lived in Los Angeles, there would be a few prerequisites for participating in my live, in-person *Ultimate Weight Loss Program*, such as having taken at least one of my introductory classes and having me come to your home for an inspection to see that all the unacceptable foods had been removed and that all the foods in your refrigerator and cupboards were compliant. Since it may not be possible for you to take a class with me or for me to come to your home, I will walk you through these steps and tell you exactly what to do.

Cleaning up your environment is going to be your first step. Your environment is the number one predictor of your success. If you are not willing to throw out noncompliant foods, then you must give them away, at least until you've completed *The Ultimate Weight Loss Program.* It would be better if you could get rid of these foods permanently, but if that is not possible, at least get them out of your sight. If you live with other people who are not embracing this way of eating, ask them if they can put their noncompliant foods into locked food safes, so at least they are out of your direct line of vision. If these foods were binge foods or trigger foods for you, it will be exceedingly more difficult if they are still visible in your home and tempting you. If it is absolutely necessary for you to continue to prepare these unhealthy foods for your family, this journey will be infinitely more difficult for you. Some of my clients have explained to their families that they are doing this because they love them and they want to be around for them for a very long time. They cooked only compliant meals for their families while asking them to eat all the other unhealthy foods outside of the home. Or, they would make one compliant meal for the entire family and if family members wanted noncompliant food added to these healthy meals, they were responsible for purchasing it and preparing it themselves.

Before you begin your Ultimate Weight Loss journey, please remove all the following items from your home:

1) All animal products
2) All processed food (with only these exceptions: salt-free canned or boxed beans; condiments like mustard or nondairy milks as long as they are all sugar-, oil-, and salt-free; and canned, jarred,

or boxed tomato products like tomato paste, tomato sauce, and diced tomatoes, again as long as they are all sugar-, oil-, and salt-free).

3) Sugar and all non-caloric sweeteners (in all their insidious forms)
4) Oil
5) Salt (including miso, tamari, Bragg's aminos, and coconut aminos)
6) Bread, Flour, and Flour Products (tortillas, boxed cereal, crackers, pasta)
7) Beverages containing alcohol or caffeine
8) Chocolate
9) Dried fruit.
10) High-fat plant foods, such as avocado, coconut, olives, nuts, seeds, and nut and seed butter (except for flax, chia, or hemp seeds)

Finally, whether it is on this list or not, any food that is a trigger food for *you*, causing you to indulge in what you now know to be unhealthy eating, should be permanently removed from your home.

Just as a recovering alcoholic should not keep bottles of beer and wine around for friends and family members, you must have the same approach to any of those addictive foods and especially to your personal trigger foods. Having a pristine environment will be critical to your success. When you come home from a stressful day at work, willpower alone may not prevent you from eating an entire sleeve of *Double Stuf Oreos*. It will be infinitely easier for you if this food is never in your home.

If you do decide to ever eat any noncompliant foods once the program is over, I recommend that you always eat them outside of your home and never have them in your home, because as every food addict knows, "If it's in your house, it's in your mouth." It's not a matter of *if* you will eventually succumb to temptation and eat it; it's only a matter of *when*. You can't eat it if it's not there. I have never met a single person who ever regretted not eating something off-plan. As Oscar Wilde used to say, "I can resist everything except temptation." Once you have cleared your home and work environments of all the contraband, go out and check your car. That emergency candy bar called an "energy bar" that you have in your glove compartment (for when you are suffering from a chocolate and peanut-butter deficiency!) has got to go. Now you need to replace all the unhealthy foods with health-promoting foods. Any temptation in your home or work environment must be removed or it will always be calling your name.

Now it's time to go food shopping. Here's what to buy:

1) Fresh fruit
2) Frozen fruit (with no sugar added)
3) Fresh non-starchy vegetables
4) Frozen vegetables (with no salt added)
5) Whole grains (corn, oats, quinoa, rice, etc.)
6) A good quality Vitamin B-12 supplement (1000 micrograms)
7) Legumes (beans, lentils, peas, and split peas, etc.)
8) Starchy vegetables (any kind of potato, sweet potato, or winter squash)
9) Flax seeds, chia seeds, or hemp seeds (unless they are a trigger for you)
10) Condiments (Herbs, Salt-Free Spices and Tomato Products, Vinegars)

While the idea of doing *The Ultimate Weight Loss Program* is to abstain from eating processed food (most anything from a can, box, bottle, or bag), as you can see from the lists above, I do allow a few exceptions such as canned or boxed beans, tomato products, and condiments, as long as these products obey the rules of being salt-, sugar-, and oil-free. If you don't like the idea of using beans and tomatoes in cans (and go for BPA-free, if you do), you can also purchase them in aseptic boxes or even jars. Processed foods, by design, are created to be addictive by containing large amounts of sugar, fat, salt, and other additives, which is why you will be hard-pressed to find more than a handful of processed food items that do not have one, or all, of these health-destroying ingredients.

Most Americans eat over ninety percent of their calories from animal products and processed foods; therefore, when people actually remove all of them from their homes, they become like Old Mother Hubbard: their cupboards are bare and they complain that they have nothing to eat. So, do your shopping as soon as you do your contraband-clearing. Please make sure that you always have plenty of delicious, compliant food on hand. We will give you many delicious recipes in the upcoming chapters, but think about this for a minute: the human race existed for millions of years without processed food, and our ancestors ate very little in the way of animal products. If you were born at another time in human history, or even in another part of the world today, the way that I suggest that you eat for weight loss, optimal health, and longevity, and to overcome your food addictions, would not represent a challenge. It would simply be the way people eat. While there are relatively few different types of animals people eat, there are literally thousands of varieties of fruits, vegetables, whole grains, and legumes from which you can choose, so you need never be bored.

You may have to shop a bit more often for your fresh produce, which is why I also suggest you also buy some frozen fruits and vegetables. Studies have shown that frozen produce is every bit as nutritious as fresh, sometimes even more so, because it's picked at its peak of ripeness and flash frozen retaining valuable nutrients. Even fresh organic produce often sits on a truck for days before you can purchase it, losing valuable nutrients.

If you can't afford to buy all your produce organic, please refer to a list put out by the Environmental Working Group (*www.ewg.org*) called "The Clean 15 and The Dirty Dozen." It will tell you which type of produce has the highest pesticide use. If it has a thick skin, which we never would eat, like a banana, it's generally safe to purchase conventional. You can buy large quantities of frozen fruits and vegetables at reasonable prices at warehouse stores like *Costco*, and they are often organic. Make sure you also have a variety of whole grains, legumes, and your favorite color of potato, sweet potato, or winter squashes on hand as well. These are very inexpensive when purchased in bulk. Whole grains like rice and quinoa that are often organic can be purchased already cooked in the freezer or aisle section of many stores. Believe it or not, you can now even buy organic produce at *Walmart* and other discount stores. While buying fresh produce will never be as cheap as eating at *McDonald's*, remember, you'll never get a million-dollar figure by eating off the *Dollar Menu.* You can either pay the grocer or pay the doctor.

I have facilitated several weight loss and lifestyle modification programs for almost ten years now, and my experience has taught me that the individuals who really stick to these protocols long-term and have lasting results in effecting permanent dietary and lifestyle change are the ones who truly understand the science behind the program. *Ultimate Weight Loss* is a knowledge-based program, just as much as it is a food-based program. When I gave quizzes to the participants, I found that those that had the highest scores generally did better with the program. It helps if you understand why I am asking you to abstain from meat, cheese, flour, sugar, oil, salt, alcohol, caffeine, and processed foods. It is not because I am a killjoy, trying to remove all the sources of pleasure from your life, but rather because once your palate and brain chemistry adjust to the flavors of whole, natural plant food, you will actually, in the long run, get more pleasure out of life. But this process can take at least thirty days to happen.

The process I am referring to is called neurological adaptation, sometimes shortened to *neuroadaptation.* To best explain it I will use an analogy. Think about a time that you went to a movie and arrived late. The theater was so dark that you couldn't find a seat. But if you just stood still for just a moment, your eyes would adjust to the new level of darkness and the light from the movie screen would be enough for you to safely find a seat. We develop taste preferences for what we habitually eat, and the only reason you may not love vegetables yet is that you don't eat them often enough. We have to first eat properly, and then give our palate and brain chemistry some time to adjust. But in time, this process of neuroadaptation occurs, as long as we don't keep assaulting our taste buds and brain chemistry with highly processed and addictive foods, like dairy and other animal products, refined carbohydrates, and addictive substances like sugar, oil, and salt, that fool the brain's satiety mechanisms.

How long it takes to adjust depends on the individual, how compliant he or she is, and how long he or she has been eating these toxic, addictive foods. I have seen many people neuroadapt in a few weeks and for others, it has taken a few months. The secret is to eat lots of non-starchy vegetables, especially greens, as these help reset the taste buds and stop the cravings for processed foods, especially the sugars and flours. Nutritional scientists are discovering that we have taste receptors in the gut that release hormones that trigger satiety, and that bitter compounds, such as those found in vegetables like broccoli, can turn off the hunger switch.[7]

If you have been eating a lot of salt, either in the form of processed foods or by your own use of the salt shaker, it can take at least thirty days for you to really enjoy the taste of foods prepared without salt. Then when you eat a piece of celery or some chard, it actually may taste too naturally salty to you. It can take a bit longer get over your cravings for high-fat foods and adjust to a lower fat diet. And while we never completely lose our sweet tooth, if you permanently abstain from sugar you can learn to satisfy it with fruit, the whole fruit, and nothing but the whole fruit.

When people refrain from the more calorically dense foods and eat only the calorically dilute foods, they often experience unpleasant symptoms of detoxification and withdrawal, such as headache, fatigue, and irritability. Even though they are eating enough calories and feel physically full, at first, they often report having cravings for the more calorically dense foods. Cravings are almost always emotional and a sign of food addiction and they can also be brought on by stress. For most people, if they truly commit to abstaining from these higher calorie "pleasure trap" foods, these cravings will eventually go away in a few weeks to a few months. That's why it's so helpful to be part of a program and have group support while undergoing this process of neuroadaptation, especially if you are unable to abstain from your drug of choice for even twenty-four hours. When you stop consuming highly addictive foods like alcohol, caffeinated beverages, dairy, sugars, and flours, you may feel really bad for a few days, or even longer, as you physically detoxify from these substances. The emotional cravings, grief, and sadness that often can accompany giving them up may go on even longer, especially if you are unwilling to go deeper and look at the reasons you have been using foods to medicate and numb yourself.

If these feelings persist, you may want to consider speaking with a qualified therapist or counselor about the underlying emotional issues.

Now, you have removed all the noncompliant foods from all your environments and replaced them with superior low-fat, unprocessed, whole food plant-exclusive choices. Maybe you've also done some of the recommended reading so that you better understand the science behind your new approach to health. These are big changes, I know, but hang tough, you can do this. Remember, you're just running a three-week experiment. You can do anything for twenty-one days. There's a holiday called Lent based on this premise; those observing it throughout history have abstained from the things they loved for forty days, so a mere twenty-one days should be a piece of kale!

Next, you will need to get a journal. It needs to be one that you write in with pen and paper, not one of those computer apps. Your brain gets more involved in the process when you actually write and not type. That's because when you commit ink to paper you activate a part of the brain called the reticulating activating system that gives greater importance to what you are focusing on. And, when you use your favorite piece of technology to log your food, it's just too easy to lose focus and get sucked into a time-wasting addiction like checking *Facebook* or watching the latest *YouTube* video of *Dining with Dogs* (my personal favorite).

If you were taking the program with me in person, we would meet for dinner, yoga and meditation classes, culinary instruction, education, and support over the course of four consecutive weekend evenings. Doing it on your own, feel free to start on whatever day works best for you. (This year, though, please, and as soon as possible—no excuses! Have you ever noticed how most people wait until January second to start a diet and have already broken all their New Year's resolutions by Martin Luther King Day?)

Please write on your calendar what your start date and end date will be for your initial commitment to the program for twenty-one days. It is my hope that you will want to continue past day twenty-one, but there is a reason we run the program for that length of time. The rationale is that it can often take only three weeks for people to begin to form a new habit, and we know that this length of time is doable for most people, and we want you to be successful. Keep in mind, though, that it can take two months, or more, for a new behavior to become an automatic habit. Often if you tell people, especially at the onset of a lifestyle program, that they can never have something ever again, they will want it all the more. That is why I emphasize that this is just an experiment that I want you to try for only twenty-one days. If there's a non-compliant food that you think you will struggle to live without for twenty-one days, then mark down on your calendar that on day twenty-one, your long nightmare will be over and on day twenty-two you will again get to eat or drink that particular item.

What happens to most of my clients is that after they have lost so much weight, started to feel their brain chemistry stabilize and feel free from the clutches of food addiction, have gone off their medications and begun to feel better than they ever have in their lives, very few actually indulge in the treat they had promised themselves for day twenty-two. And guess what happens to those who do? They report that the food which they thought they couldn't live without not only doesn't taste as good as they remember, but it now makes them physically ill.

You can always choose to go back to your old way of eating. But why not give this your best effort for just three weeks and see how you feel? You can expect amazing results!

If you were taking *The Ultimate Weight Loss Program* with me in person, we would be interacting several times a day through our private online group, where you would be supported by hundreds of amazing people who are at various stages of recovery but all on the same journey. People who have this kind of strong social support do better with weight loss and weight management. Here you would be able to ask questions and share your triumphs and challenges. If you aren't able to be part of our growing community of "Lefties" (people who eat exclusively to the left of the red line), I strongly encourage you to find a like-minded, supportive community to take this journey with, as it will greatly increase your chances of success. It does not have to be a live group of people, although that is wonderful if you can find one or create it; a virtual community can work just as well. And if you can't find a group of people, having even one person who will join you in this twenty-one-day journey will help you immensely.

It is crucial that you fill out your Daily Food Journal every single day. I cannot tell you how many people have seen weight loss achieved, often for the very first time, once they started writing down what they actually ate. By reporting what you eat, you become accountable. The most overweight people tend to underreport what they eat. When making a peanut butter sandwich for your child, do you lick the spoon clean before putting it in the dishwasher? Well, there are probably 100 calories still stuck to that spoon, and almost all of them are from fat! When you cook, do you taste each recipe over and over again until it's just right? Well, those calories still count, even if you eat them standing up. Research shows that people who log their food lose almost fifty percent more weight than those who don't.

The people who have been most successful on this program still log their food, even though many of them have reached their goal weight. Let me give you an anecdote to help explain why it's so important to keep a food journal, especially at the beginning or if you reach a plateau. The summer between my sophomore and junior year at the University of Pennsylvania, I stayed on campus and I was constantly broke, even though I had a job. I asked my oldest brother for a loan; he said he would help me but he needed to see my budget. I was nineteen years old; I didn't even have a bank account, let alone a budget! So, he told me to write down every penny I spent for the next thirty days and send it to him and then he would send me some money. Desperate people do desperate things, so for thirty days I complied, and what I learned from doing this has helped me to this day.

It turned out that I had been engaging in mindless spending. And writing down every nickel that I was spending for a cup of coffee or package of gum made me very aware of this. For one thing, I was eating my meals out quite a bit, which is much more expensive than cooking them yourself. For another, I had acquired a bit of an addiction to a pinball game called *Jungle Queen*. While playing a single pinball game may have only cost a mere quarter, when you play it every day for an hour, it can really add up. So, I was able to quickly and easily figure out where all my money was going. And because I had to write it down and I knew that someone else would be reading it, I really didn't want the number one expense on my monthly budget to be an arcade game! Writing it down made me accountable. Similarly, if you know that someone else is going to be reading your food journal, you may think twice about having that hot fudge sundae or *Big Mac*.

My private clients send me their food logs every single day while we are working together, and the participants of *The Ultimate Weight Loss Program* are encouraged to log their daily food on our private online group page. Many of them do this simply by taking pictures of their meals, but I urge people, especially at the beginning, to write it down by hand. One of the things I have noticed is that when people relapse on this program, the first habits they abandon are logging their food and eating vegetables for breakfast.

In addition to writing down what you eat, it can also be very helpful if you write down how you feel before and after eating, and turning your food journal into a food/mood journal. This is especially important if you are not yet willing to do the deeper work and address the *why* of your emotional eating. I had a client who would do a stellar job at breakfast and lunch and eat perfectly, but every day around five in the afternoon, she would eat something non-compliant, like an entire bag of chips. This happened every Monday through Friday. She got in touch with how she truly felt emotionally, which was stressed and pissed off. (Remember, if hunger isn't the problem, then food isn't the solution.) She was stuck in horrendous Los Angeles rush hour traffic for over an hour each weekday. She tried to rationalize that the *Nacho Cheese-flavored Doritos* were her "reward" for eating on plan for her first two meals, but in reality, they were her coping mechanism for braving the maddening freeways of L.A. In our online *Ultimate Weight Loss Program*, we help you to find nonfood rewards and appropriate ways to handle uncomfortable and unpleasant feelings without using food. By adding her mood to her food journal, we could analyze what was really going on emotionally with her at that time, and we were able to create and implement a strategy. Now she uses her commute time to eat her second pound of non-starchy vegetables, like sugar snap peas or jicama, which give her the crunch she wants without derailing her health and weight loss goals and destabilizing her brain chemistry. She follows it with a small, therapeutic dose of a sweet potato so that she is not starving when she gets home from work and has to prepare dinner for her family.

I am not interested in how much you eat or even how often you eat. What matters most is *what* you eat. If you eat only whole natural foods like fruits, vegetables, whole grains, and legumes without the addition of animal products, processed foods like sugars, flours, oil, or high-fat plant foods like nuts, seeds, avocado and coconut, you can eat to satiation and not worry about weighing, measuring, or portion control. It is only when you choose to include the higher-fat plant foods that you have to worry. While nuts and seeds and avocado are certainly healthful foods, they are too calorically dense for most overweight people to include if they are trying to lose weight. And for those who have already lost weight, re-introducing nuts, seeds, and other high-fat foods, even in measured amounts, can result in weight-gain. (This has been the experience of many successful participants in *The Ultimate Weight Loss Program*.) For many people, these are also trigger foods that cause them to overeat. Some people cannot keep nuts, seeds, or avocado in their home without gorging on them. If you are one of these people, I recommend not keeping them in your home to tempt you. Any food that is a personal trigger food for you, a food that you cannot moderate your use of or that causes you to overeat or crave other foods, should also not be kept in the home. And what may be a benign food for you at one part of your journey could quite possibly become a trigger food for you at another. When I was fat, I was actually able to moderate my consumption of chocolate, nuts, seeds, and dried fruits; they caused me to remain fat but I didn't binge on them. But now that I have been eating so cleanly for over six years, with only one relapse, I know that I can no longer include them safely in my diet anymore, in any amount. I have tried a few times to eat them "under medical supervision" while working at *TrueNorth Health Center*, and have found that when I do occasionally indulge, I just can't stop thinking about those "pleasure trap" foods and when I can eat them again. I also find that even a few of the so-called healthy foods that I used to enjoy that are to the right of the red line, like unsalted air-popped popcorn, corn tortillas, or baked tortilla chips, all of which lack water and are easy to overeat, have become problematic for me and I now have to avoid them.

When embarking on your journey to *Ultimate Weight Loss,* we ask you to go at least the first twenty-one days without any high-fat foods, to give your taste buds and brain chemistry a chance to adjust to a lower-fat diet. (For some, an even longer period of adjustment may prove necessary.) Then, after weight loss is achieved if you decide to include the higher fat plant foods in your diet, and you're confident that they're not trigger foods for you, then I suggest you eat no more than one ounce of raw, unsalted nuts or seeds per day. Dr. Caldwell B. Esselstyn, Jr., author of *Prevent and Reverse Heart Disease*, often makes the point that as we rapidly down-regulate the fat receptor in our brains (by not eating fats), we begin to lose the craving for fatty foods. Dr. Esselstyn argues that it's therefore much easier for his patients to go "cold turkey" and make drastic dietary changes at once than to attempt to make gradual adjustments to a profoundly unhealthy and fatty diet. If you try to make these changes gradually, you will find yourself in a situation of misery and denial because you have not down-regulated the fat receptor.

If you are truly worried about getting enough of your essential Omega-3 fatty acids, simply sprinkle a tablespoon of ground flax seeds, chia seeds, or hemp seeds on your food.

Personally, I eat purslane almost daily either raw in my salads or steamed. It is the absolute highest plant source of Omega-3 fatty acids and it tastes delicious. If you purchase it at ethnic markets it is called *verdolaga* and you can get three to four large bunches for a dollar. It would be practically impossible to become fatty acid deficient during the twenty-one days of this program, especially if you still have fat on your body. According to Dr. Alona Pulde and Dr. Matt Lederman, authors of the *New York Times'* bestselling *The Forks Over Knives Plan*, it is "significantly more important to worry about not consuming excess fat than it is to worry about consuming sufficient Omega-3."[8] As Drs. Pulde and Lederman point out, only one-to-three percent of our calories need to come from the essential fatty acids. That said, if someone is truly worried about Omega-3 fatty acids and cannot or does not wish to consume nuts and seeds, an algae-derived DHA supplement is available.

The one supplement that is absolutely required on a plant-exclusive diet is Vitamin B-12. 1000 micrograms daily should be more than adequate.

The goal is to consume as many non-starchy vegetables as you possibly can. Believe it or not, after consuming vegetables infrequently for the first forty-three years of my life, I now eat about four pounds of non-starchy veggies daily. But keep in mind that this is not a vegetable-based diet, as most of your calories have to come from starch (unrefined complex carbohydrates). Strive to eat a minimum of three pounds of produce a day, divided this way: at least two pounds of non-starchy vegetables and one pound of fruit. A mere two pieces of fruit can weigh a pound. Be mindful that you don't just eat frozen fruit sorbet all day while ignoring your veggies and starch. You are welcome to consume all your vegetables raw, as in a big salad, but most people find it easier if they eat at least some of the non-starchy vegetables, especially the greens, cooked.

If you have trouble eating salads and vegetables, adding some fruit can make them delicious and may even reduce your need for dressing. I love putting some pomegranate seeds, a grated or chopped apple or pear, or even some cut-up grapes or strawberries in my salads. Some fresh pineapple, or even canned, unsweetened pineapple, on your cooked greens tastes absolutely delicious. But don't just transfer your sugar addiction to bananas and tropical fruits, which I see many of the participants do; instead, focus on some of the lower glycemic fruits like apples, berries, citrus fruits, and pears, and try to include those every day. You can even add cooked starches (rice and/or beans, for example) to your salads to make them more interesting, satiating, and delicious.

Remember that that what sets *The Ultimate Weight Loss Program* apart from all the other wonderful plant-based programs is that we strongly suggest that your breakfast includes at least one pound (of your daily two pounds) of non-starchy vegetables. Many people initially freak out about having to eat a pound of vegetables for breakfast (VFB), but once you have been doing the program for awhile and realize what eating non-starchy veggies first thing in the morning does for you, not only in terms of weight loss but in annihilating your cravings for sugar and flour and turning off your hunger switch, you will absolutely fall in love with them and realize that (unless all you are eating is raw greens) a pound of steamed or roasted non-starchy vegetables is really not that much food. For example, when you take a pound of Brussels sprouts and make the delicious *Balsamic Dijon Glazed Roasted Brussels Sprouts* (recipe page 123), the yield is a mere two cups of food.

The number one reason people are afraid to try *The Ultimate Weight Loss Program* is that they resist the idea of eating vegetables in the morning. And the number one reason participants in the program succeed is VFB, which generally becomes their favorite part of the program. They learn to love vegetables in the morning!

The reason we are eating VFB is because *The Ultimate Weight Loss Program* is much more than a weight loss program. It is a program that has been carefully designed to permanently extinguish your food cravings, overcome your food addictions, and stabilize your brain chemistry. Starting every day with at least one pound of non-starchy vegetables will be essential to your success. I cannot stress how important VFB is. When we asked every single person who has been successful on *The Ultimate Weight Loss Program* what they feel that they could most attribute their success to, they unanimously said VFB! The private online support group came in second. Conversely, we have discovered that when people have relapsed on the program, VFB was one of the first habits to go. Once their VFB was reinstated, they were back on track.

If you think I am crazy for suggesting that you eat vegetables for breakfast, consider this. In every country that I have ever visited, other than the United States, I was served vegetables as part of my breakfast. And this was not because I was a vegan chef or on a weight loss program, but because that's what they ate in these countries. When I was teaching in Mexico, breakfast was oil-free black beans and corn tortillas with steamed vegetables. In Japan, it was miso soup, rice, and steamed vegetables. Whether it is the kimchi in Korea, the pickled vegetables in China, or the onions, tomatoes, and cucumbers that accompany the herring in Denmark, the rest of the world that has not yet been poisoned by our Standard American Diet eats a savory breakfast. Only in the Good Ole U.S.A. would a caffeinated, high-fat, high-sugar *Cinnabon*, *Frappucino*, *Egg McMuffin* or *Captain Crunch with Crunchberries* be considered an acceptable breakfast. So, while oatmeal and fruit may certainly be a healthy breakfast for some people, if you struggle with sugar and flour addiction, or need to lose weight, the best thing that you can do is to start your day in a savory way, with vegetables.

You see, almost all the people who participate in *The Ultimate Weight Loss Program* suffer from varying degrees of food addiction, especially to sugar, so the last thing we want to do is have their first taste of the day be something sweet, as it will just perpetuate their cravings for sweets all day. The earlier in the day that you activate that sweet taste, even with something healthy like fruit, the more you will crave sweets all day. Vegetables, especially the dark green leafies, stop these cravings in their tracks. Remember, when the taste receptors in your gut are activated by the compounds in bitter foods, they release hormones that trigger satiety. Let greens by thy medicine!

Other programs simply encourage you to eat less of any problematic foods that contain sugar and flour, or change the type of them you are eating and use the non-caloric sweeteners like stevia, xylitol, erythritol, or artificial sweeteners (which virtually all food addiction experts say are far worse than even real sugar). Advising a person addicted to refined carbohydrates to merely change the type of sugars and flours he or she consumes is like telling an alcoholic to get sober by drinking lite beer instead of vodka. If you had lung cancer, would you ask the doctor what is the optimal number, or the best brand, of cigarettes to smoke? Are you beginning to see how ludicrous this is?

Now back to VFB. I had help developing the idea of urging the consumption of vegetables for breakfast, which is the foundation of *The Ultimate Weight Loss Program*. It was something that I discovered by observing which of the participants were the most successful. In my initial program, called *The 30-Day Unprocessed Challenge,* I also rec-ommended that the participants eat at least two pounds of non-starchy vegetables daily—one pound raw and one pound cooked—but when they would send me their food journals every night, most of them were barely consuming even half of a pound. And yet, I noticed that a few participants were just on fire! They were losing weight faster than all the other participants and they were also the ones who reported that their cravings for unhealthy food, especially sugar and flour, had completely disappeared. These were the only ones who were consistently eating their two pounds of non-starchy vegetables every day, and by the end of the challenge, they were also the ones who had lost the most weight and had the greatest improvement in their blood tests.

So why were these folks able to attain such spectacular results and eat their two pounds of non-starchy vegetables daily, while the rest of the group struggled to eat even one pound? Because they all ate at least one pound of vegetables for breakfast. It set the tone for their day and encouraged them to eat even more vegetables as the day progressed.

The truth is that I asked them why they were eating their greens for breakfast because I, too, thought this was odd, at first. And they unanimously said that if they didn't eat them first thing in the morning, they just couldn't find the time to do this. After witnessing the spectacular results of the breakfast vegetable eaters in comparison to the rest of the group, I permanently changed the program to require at least one pound of non-starchy vegetables as the first food of the day. And of course, everyone resisted. Especially the folks who were used to starting their day with just sweet fruit, very sweet green smoothies, or oatmeal with a lot of fresh and dried fruit with walnuts sprinkled on top. (The oatmeal became their "flour," the fruit became their "sugar," and the nuts were their fat.) Once they finally got on board with VFB, they observed their cravings disappear and finally achieved the weight loss they desired; they were sold on its efficacy because they were finally able to achieve permanent weight loss, annihilate their food cravings, and be forever free of their food addictions.

I am not asking you to do anything that I do not do myself. Since I started my own *Ultimate Weight Loss* journey in January of 2012, with very rare exceptions such as international travel, I have started every single day with at least two pounds of non-starchy vegetables and eaten at least another pound of them with lunch and another pound while hungrily waiting for my husband to come home for dinner. As a slender person, I now consistently eat a minimum of four pounds of non-starchy vegetables daily, so I am completely confident that you can eat two pounds of them. I have come to believe that this requirement is such an integral part of one's success on the program that I even travel with my *Instant Pot* electric pressure cooker so that I can cook and eat vegetables in my hotel room, and I have been traveling extensively for over seven years now.

When I am traveling internationally and absolutely cannot get VFB, I travel with a green powder such as *Vitamineral Green* and drink it in water. This idea came to me from John Pierre, who used to teach these programs with me when he lived in Los Angeles and runs the online version of *The Ultimate Weight Loss Program* and *The Ultimate Weight*

Loss Mastery Program with me. While I do not recommend green powders as a substitute for eating vegetables, they can help in a pinch when you are having sugar cravings and can't get vegetables. Many of our participants, especially in the early stages of their recovery, like to put the powder in their water bottles and sip it throughout the day or whenever a craving strikes in a vegetable-free setting. In our online *Ultimate Weight Loss (UWL)* program, John Pierre also offers many other strategies for combating cravings, such as the judicious use of essential oils like peppermint or clove.

Eating these 200-400 daily calories of non-starchy vegetables will be paramount to your success. This quantity of vegetables, when compared to animal products, processed foods, and high-fat plant foods, represents a much larger volume of food. It will fill you up so that you can eat fewer calories while still feeling satiated.

You may not like eating VFB at first, but you are an adult and you don't have to like something to do it. Hey, I don't like going to the dentist, but I still do it. Why? Because I dislike the consequences of not doing it even more. But let me tell you this. As you do it, you will begin to like it, once you see what eating these miraculous vegetables does for your waistline and brain chemistry. It's almost magical! Once you make eating veggies for breakfast a habit, you will learn to love it. People actually develop taste preferences for what they habitually eat. When you can't get your VFB, you will miss them. And one day you will wonder why you didn't think of doing this sooner.

I have a friend from Thailand who says that Pad Thai is the best food in the world. My friend from Mexico completely disagrees and says that enchiladas are the best food in the world. Is Pad Thai really better than enchiladas, or are enchiladas, in fact, better than Pad Thai? While you may prefer one of these foods over the other, many people would consider both of them delicious. I recognize that both of my friends grew up eating their particular favorite, which is why they love them so much. There are people in certain parts of the world who consider eating crickets a delicacy. If you grew up eating vegetables for breakfast, as you would in many other cultures, you would love them too. Americans eat less than ten percent of their calories from vegetables, and most of them come from French fries!

Instead of eating over ninety percent of your calories from animal products and processed foods, I am suggesting you eat one hundred percent of your calories from unrefined whole plant food. Your taste buds will adjust and so will your brain chemistry. You can actually learn to prefer the taste of whole natural food. According to a study published online in *Nutrition & Diabetes*, MRI images showed that as people ate more fruits and vegetables, they exhibited more brain pleasure from them.[9] At a mere 100-200 calories per pound, finding ways to add more non-starchy vegetables to all your meals and recipes is the best way to reduce the overall calorie density of your meals. And the regular consumption of raw vegetables will cause you to lose weight even faster.

But what if you hate vegetables? Then do what I did when I finally started exercising after being sedentary for over fifty years; I did the exercises that I hated the least. So, eat the vegetables that you hate the least. People always think because I sign my e-mails with "Love & Kale" that they can only eat greens! Not true. While greens are certainly very nutritious, if you aren't yet able to, as my *newer* clients lovingly say, "choke them down," eat any non-starchy veggie. Just *Google* the words "non-starchy vegetable" and you'll be amazed at the list that comes up. If you abhor kale, try artichokes, asparagus, broccoli, carrots, cauliflower, sugar snap peas, or zucchini, to name just a few. Almost everyone who has tried sugar snap peas loves them. They are delicious and crunchy when eaten raw and become really sweet when you cook them. If you really hate all of those, then try the recipe for *Balsamic Dijon Roasted Brussels Sprouts* (recipe page 123). Even people who never liked Brussels sprouts before, myself included, absolutely love this recipe. You can also roast any vegetable in your oven or an air fryer with nothing on it and it will taste amazing because roasting brings out the natural sweetness of the vegetables. Always roast more vegetables than you can eat because the aroma of roasted vegetables is irresistible and others in your home will want to eat them, and you won't get your full dose. You can even eat the leftover roasted vegetables cold in salads and puréed with beans for a delicious no-added-fat hummus dip for your raw veggies. Always look for ways to sneak more veggies into your life. Remember, the people who eat the most veggies consistently are leaner and have the lowest BMI.

If you eat all your vegetables raw, be prepared to do a lot of chewing because you are going to be eating a huge volume of food. That is why I recommend cooking at least half of your daily two-pound vegetable allotment, especially the ones you eat in the morning. How you cook them and flavor them is up to you. Greens work well in an electric pressure cooker like the *Instant Pot.* Some veggies, like zucchini, get too mushy when pressure-cooked, so I prefer to steam them on the stove. Another way I like to cook my vegetables is in a sauté pan. You want to make sure you get a good stainless-steel pan. What I love to do is sauté some chopped onion, garlic, and mushrooms in *No-Sodium Veggie Broth* (recipe page 194) and then add some kale or rainbow chard and cook them until they are bright green. Then I drizzle a bit of my favorite balsamic vinegar on them, like *Garlic-Cilantro* or *Smoke-Infused*, and I have what I call *Lip-Smacking Mouthwatering Kale* (recipe page 128). When I started this practice of eating vegetables for breakfast over six years ago, I wasn't exactly bounding out of bed to eat kale. So, I made it delicious by using many of the flavored vinegars widely available today both online and at specialty stores. Using flavors like *Ripe Peach, Wild Blueberry, Cucumber Melon, and Jalapeño Lime*, I actually started to look forward to eating vegetables and learned to really enjoy them. Almost all the flavored balsamic vinegars are free of oil, sugar, and salt, and come in myriad flavors for every palate. They truly make eating vegetables a joy. Hey, they even come in chocolate and espresso, but I don't recommend indulging in those flavors while you're on *The Ultimate Weight Loss Program.*

It is unlikely, especially at first, that you'll get as much pleasure from those mandatory 200-400 calories of veggies that I recommend that you consume twice a day as you will from the rest of your daily fare. You see, all eating stimulates the production of dopamine in the brain, a neurotransmitter that causes you to experience pleasure. But the more calorically concentrated the source of calories, the more dopamine that is released into the brain. Once you eat foods of a higher caloric density such as fruit (300 calories per pound), starchy vegetables (400 calories per pound), whole grains (500 calories per pound) or legumes (600 calories per pound), it will be infinitely more difficult to try and choke down those veggies that contain a lowly 100-200 calories per pound. That is why it is critical that you always eat them first!

Hunger is the sensation you feel when your body requires food. Cravings are your desire to have a particular food. True hunger can be alleviated by eating any type of food. Emotional hunger can be alleviated only by eating the specific food that you're craving. That is why it's so important to wait until you are truly hungry to eat. And you will know that you are eating for emotional reasons, or engaging in what is known as "hedonic eating," if you continue eating in the absence of hunger.

Traditionally, I was never a breakfast eater and have never even woken up hungry. But I make sure that my veggies are ready when hunger does strike. I either cook them as soon as I wake up or roast several days' worth in advance. Even if I am not really hungry in the morning, I would always be able to eat a pastry or even some delicious ripe sweet fruit or oatmeal. Those foods will always appeal to me. But it's not until the aroma of those four pounds of *Oven Roasted Ratatouille* (recipe page 130) becomes enticing and irresistible to me that I know that it's time for me to eat.

If you really hate even the mere thought of eating vegetables for breakfast, that's simply another reason to start your day with them. Do you think you will be more or less likely to consume them as the day progresses, once you've eaten a bunch of other delicious foods at a greater caloric density like fruit, potatoes, rice, and beans? The only way I am able to maintain a fitness routine after fifty years of inactivity is if I do it first thing in the morning. If I don't, the day just slips away from me. Trust me, it's the same thing with eating your vegetables! Just do it and get it over with. It will become just like brushing your teeth. You don't think about brushing your teeth. You just do it because the consequences of not doing it (like cavities, root canals, or losing your teeth) are worse than any "pain" you have to go through in order to make the effort to brush your teeth. It has become an automatic habit. The same thing can happen with VFB.

For me, it really became a self-esteem issue. Starting every day with at least a pound of non-starchy veggies said to the universe that I meant business. If you could only implement one permanent dietary change for the rest of your life, after giving up all dairy, animal products, and processed foods like sugar, flour, oil, and alcohol, this would be the one I recommend the most. But that almost understates its value because making this change will help you give up those unhealthy products. I can honestly tell you that while I have lost a substantial amount of weight several times in my life, I have never been able to easily maintain a slender physique before implementing this program, and neither have the hundreds of other participants of *The Ultimate Weight Loss Program* who continue to faithfully eat their VFB. It really sets the tone for the day and makes it so much easier for us to make healthy choices throughout the day. And best of all, those of us who have been doing this for several years are finally free of the intense food cravings for unhealthy foods that have plagued us our entire lives. And the freedom from food addiction feels so much better than those foods themselves ever made us feel.

Please keep in mind that you will not be able to get enough calories, or achieve satiation if you eat only fruits and vegetables, so you will need to add lots of the "good stuff," the unrefined complex carbohydrates (also known as starch), after you eat your VFB. A pound of cooked non-starchy vegetables, roughly 100-200 calories, will not keep you full for very long, so once your hunger returns, and it will, feel free to move onto your favorite starch. This can be whatever you like, such as beans, lentils, starchy vegetables, or whole grains. For me, that usually means eating *Potato Waffles* (recipe page 179) or roasted sweet potatoes with broccoli. Some of *The Ultimate Weight Loss* participants enjoy eating whole grains and/or legumes after their vegetable meal as their "second breakfast," and that's fine. (Think rice, beans, and salsa—*muy sabrosa!*). Legumes are great for balancing your blood sugar for hours, so try to have some every day, especially at breakfast or lunch. Think about having a potato or sweet potato after eating your vegetables, as soon as your hunger returns. Potatoes are delicious baked, roasted, cooked in an air fryer, or even a non-stick waffle iron with your favorite toppings, such as corn, beans, and salsa. Make soups or stews out of lentils or split peas, or eat starchy foods that you already love like corn and peas. I enjoy cutting up a cold, leftover baked sweet potato or leftover roasted butternut squash and mixing it in my huge salads. I also enjoy adding garbanzo beans, wild rice, and sliced grapes in them as well.

This is a very important concept in *The Ultimate Weight Loss Program*: you have to make sure you are eating *enough food*. If you have been eating mostly animal products and processed foods, you may have gotten used to eating relatively skimpy portions of high-fat, high-calorie foods. Vegetables, fruits, whole grains, and legumes are comparatively much lower in calorie density, so you are going to have to eat more of them. You must never let yourself get too hungry because that is when are more vulnerable to making poor food choices and to overeating.

I would recommend that as you start this program, you visit your doctor and have your blood pressure, blood cholesterol, blood sugar, and triglycerides measured. (Some pharmacies also will measure your blood pressure, blood sugar, and total cholesterol.) Do it again on Day Twenty-One to see the amazing changes that have occurred. If you are able to get your doctor to order these lab tests, it would be helpful as it would provide you with measurable results. If not, many pharmacies now offer machines where you can test your blood pressure for free, and offer very low-cost cholesterol testing.

We don't believe in using scales on an ongoing basis in this program, whether it's to weigh yourself or your food. However, to show how effective and powerful dietary changes can be, we *do* weigh the participants on Day One and again on Day Twenty-one. We also take their waist measurements. Even people who don't lose much weight in the first twenty-one days of the program still may lose an inch or two off their waists. If you would like to weigh yourself after the first twenty-one days, we recommend that you do so no more than once a month. As you truly commit to this lifestyle, your body will find its ideal weight. Don't let the number on the scale determine your success on this program or your self-worth. Instead of chasing skinny, we want you to pursue optimum health. We don't want you to get thrown by what may be a weight gain caused by temporary water retention, often the result of salt sneaking into your food. Lasting weight loss is the result of following a health-promoting diet. And once you deal with your food addictions and permanently abstain from any highly addictive foods and any personal food triggers, your brain chemistry will stabilize and your body weight will normalize.

While it is not mandatory for you to exercise to lose weight, there are myriad other reasons that moving your body on a regular basis is vitally important. When it comes to your bones, muscles, joints, and brains, "use it or lose it" is really true. You can never out-exercise a bad diet, but you can supercharge a good one. Regular exercise also boosts your mood, decreases anxiety, increases self-esteem and will-power, improves brain and bone health, enhances cognitive function, and helps you sleep better. It also makes it easier to stick to a healthy diet and makes you more resilient to stress. (If you have heart disease or any reason why you believe you should consult with your doctor before beginning an exercise regimen, then you are advised to do so.)

Probably the best way to start moving is by simply walking. If the weather does not cooperate, you may live near a shopping mall that opens early in the morning and can serve as a place to walk. Get yourself an inexpensive pedometer and wear it every day. Begin to notice how many steps you are accruing at the end of the day, and the next day, see if you can just get in a couple more, with the ultimate goal of working your way up to 10,000 steps a day. You can get more steps in while doing things you are already doing, such as talking to your buddy on the phone, by simply by standing up and moving as you do it. If you are unable to walk, see if you can join your local *YMCA* and do gentle water exercises or walk back in forth in the shallow end of the pool.

So, now what? This is your Day One, the first day of a healthy new you. Let your *Ultimate Weight Program* begin!

CHAPTER 4

The Seven C's To Success

Your environment is the key that will determine your success on *The Ultimate Weight Loss Program,* or any dietary or lifestyle change program. It is the number one predictor of your outcome on this program. If you did not clean up your environment as I suggested you must do in the previous chapter, you may be able to get through the first twenty-one days, but you are not likely to succeed long term.

When alcoholics get out of rehab, how easy do you think it would be for them to abstain from alcohol if they return to their former jobs as bartenders or keep hanging around the old gang who is still drinking? I had a client, an admitted alcoholic, who still kept booze in her home "for company." Not exactly a foolproof relapse-prevention plan, is it? You won't be surprised to learn that she has not been very successful at maintaining her sobriety. Even with the very best inpatient treatment, regular attendance at AA meetings, and family support, the recidivism rate for alcoholism is still very high. The statistics are far grimmer for weight loss and food addiction. As I mentioned earlier, ninety-eight percent of people who lose weight will gain it all back, and usually more, within two years. Clearly, diets do not work. But what makes this a more difficult problem to treat is that while nobody ever needs to engage in destructive, health-compromising behaviors like drinking, smoking, or taking recreational drugs, we must all eat food to survive. And while it's possible to go places and avoid alcohol and heroin, junk food can be found everywhere. I recently saw a vending machine full of *Cheetos,*

Snickers, and *Red Bull* in the parking lot of a major hospital. How's that for ensuring repeat business?

While it's certainly possible, and recommended, to permanently abstain from alcohol, tobacco, and recreational drugs, you can't do that with food. Even if you clean up your home environment, you really can't go to very many places without constantly being bombarded with disease-promoting, unnatural, food-like substances. Whether it's the obligatory candy dish that they now have at almost every business establishment, the "free" samples at *Costco*, or the aroma of buttered popcorn at the movie theater, it's difficult to go anywhere where unhealthy fare isn't practically being forced upon you. If you watch TV, there are constant images of the worst food imaginable (much of it specifically targeted to children on Saturday mornings) and the most popular blogs, magazines, and cooking shows today are nothing but a constant array of food porn. In fact, there are entire networks now whose sole purpose is to get you to watch their shows and entice you with these nutritionally bereft treats that are guaranteed to make you fat, sick, and addicted. Trying to resist the temptation in the modern world is going to be difficult enough, but if you haven't cleaned up your act at home, you haven't got a prayer, and it's not a matter of *if* you will relapse, only *when*.

So, at the start of this twenty-one-day journey, if you haven't completely sanitized your environment, I implore you to do so. It is imperative that you remove all the unhealthy and addictive foods, and any personal trigger foods, from your home *now and forever*. No excuses. You must get rid of all the animal products and processed foods. Just because you are motivated and feel strong right now, all it takes is one bad day at work and you will be licking the bottom of that peanut butter jar or eating frosting right out of the can again. If you were truly an alcoholic, wouldn't your spouse insist that you get alcohol out of the house? Well, your food addiction is every bit as serious. In fact, it can become life threatening, and I ask you to take this as seriously as you would any other addictions. You need to explain to those living with you that you are suffering from the disease of refined food addiction and that these measures must be taken to ensure your recovery. Tell your family that you must do this because you love them and want to be around for them as long as possible. Make everyone in your household understand that if you don't do this now, the day may come when you will not be around. How will they feel then? Ask them to please remove all their noncompliant food from your home. They can eat whatever they want outside of the home, but you cannot have any amount of noncompliant food in your environment. Not a drop, not a morsel, not a crumb. If they absolutely refuse to cooperate, then your only option is to keep all your food separate and get a food safe for the noncompliant food. Food safes that can be locked are not hard to find in stores or online; they can be kept in or out of the fridge.

I could tell you literally hundreds of stories from my clients who fail at co-habiting with addictive foods. They thought they could handle keeping things like sugar, flour, bread, pasta, chocolate, peanut butter, tahini, ice cream, cheese, or alcohol in their homes for their families or "for company." Some even made it several months before they experienced a relapse. And then something happens. The boss yells at them, their spouse says something unkind, their dog dies. And guess what? They are instantly sucked into the "pleasure trap" and right back into the throes of their addiction. But now it's even worse because, after a period of abstinence, it takes less of the drug to get an even more pronounced effect. The sleeping dragon of addiction never wakes up in a good mood. As they say in *Alcoholics Anonymous*, while you are getting sober, your addiction is out in the parking lot doing push-ups. When it has even the slightest opportunity to make a comeback, and I promise you that it will, it is going to return with a vengeance and be even more powerful than it was before your attempt at recovery. That "one bite" that everyone promised wouldn't hurt becomes a binge that can last for days, weeks, or even months. And I am sorry to say, I have seen some people never fully recover from a relapse and get back on track.

This process—learning a new way of eating, and overcoming food addictions—is already difficult enough. Why would you make it any harder by having these foods in your home to tempt you? Keeping noncompliant or personal trigger foods in your home is dangerous. It doesn't matter if the ice cream isn't your favorite flavor. It will remind you of your favorite flavor. You already know how the story will end, and it's not happily ever after. You swear that you are strong enough, that you aren't going to touch their food, that this time it's going to be different. But it's never going to be different until your environment is different. That is why psychologist Dr. Doug Lisle says that you have to work even harder on your environment than on yourself.

Willpower is a limited resource. You won't have to rely on it to not eat something that isn't there.

Mae West is credited with saying, "I generally avoid temptation, unless I can't resist it." As a food addict, you know that this is true. So why on earth would you think you could have the temptation in your home? I wish I could say that you will never have a stressful day, have your feelings hurt, or grieve the loss of a loved one. But that's not very likely, is it? You can't control what happens to you, only how you respond to it. And if you keep using food as a drug to fix your mood, you will never be able to permanently lose weight or overcome your food addictions. There are some whose food addictions are so severe that a craving will actually drive them to leave their homes at midnight for a run to the nearest *7-Eleven*. And it's never to buy broccoli slaw, is it? But for most of us, thankfully, these cravings will pass, or hopefully, we have learned some techniques to distract ourselves long enough and not indulge them. (Taking a warm bubble bath, going for a walk, using essential oils like peppermint or clove, doing some deep diaphragmatic breathing, or calling a friend are all good strategies.) Willpower is only necessary when you have to make a decision. It does not take any resolve to decide to not eat something that isn't there. And I have never met anyone who regretted *not* eating something off-plan. Remember, your cravings are merely a symptom of your food addictions and a sign that the disease is active; giving in to them only intensifies them. It is simply your disease talking to you. But you don't have to listen. And the only way that cravings will ever go away permanently is to eat to the left of the red line and to stop indulging them. That is how you silence them forever.

If you have been eating a nutrient-poor diet, deficient in fruits and vegetables for a prolonged period, you may still be experiencing cravings as you go through withdrawal and a period of detoxification. How long this takes varies from person to person and will depend upon how poorly you have been eating, for how long, and how clean you are eating now. That is why it can be so helpful to go to a place like *TrueNorth*

Health Center or the *McDougall 10-Day Program* so you get a chance to reset your taste buds in an environment of complete rest. But your cravings will go away, I promise you, if you stop indulging them. Just continue to eat to the left of the red line, and keep temptations out of your environment.

I've spent a lot of time on this, I know. But it is imperative that you understand that if you don't completely sanitize your environment (home, office, car, or anywhere you spend time) it will be far more difficult for you to be successful long term because you will have to rely on willpower. And please remember that while a certain food may seem innocuous and perfectly healthy for some people, if it's a trigger food for you, you simply cannot have it in your home. Avocados, pistachios, and baked tortilla chips can be part of a healthy diet for some people, but for me, they are like crack! How do you know whether a food is a trigger food for you? It's easy. If you continue eating it in the absence of hunger and you are unable to moderate your use of it without a great deal of difficulty, that's how. If you can't stop thinking about it, or if you feel bad after you eat it, then that's another clue.

After witnessing hundreds of people having success on *The Ultimate Weight Loss Program*, I noticed that they had certain behaviors and characteristics in common, which I have termed *"The Seven C's to Success."* Those who lacked these attributes struggled significantly more to achieve their goals.

The first "C" in the *"The Seven C's to Success"* is the one that without which, none of the other 'C's' are possible, and that "C" is COMMITMENT. *Merriam-Webster's* dictionary defines "commitment" as "the promise to do something; the attitude of someone who works very hard to do something." What is your attitude when it comes to commitment, in general, and specifically when attempting a permanent lifestyle change? John Assaraf, the behavioral expert, says, "If you are interested, you'll do what's convenient. If you're committed, you'll do whatever it takes." My mom used to always say, "It's easy to do what's easy." If eating healthfully, losing weight, and keeping it off was easy, more than three-fourths of Americans wouldn't be overweight or obese. If it were easy, then everyone would do it. But just because something isn't easy doesn't mean that you won't be able to do it. I know hundreds of people who have had success doing *The Ultimate Weight Loss Program*, and it wasn't necessarily easy, at least initially, for most of them. Very little that anyone has ever accomplished in life was easy at first. But avoiding the problem or giving up when things get difficult doesn't help. And with this particular disease, the longer you wait, the harder it gets to treat, because food addiction is a chronic, progressive, and debilitating disease. But it's only too late if you don't start now.

You have likely accomplished in your life some things of which you are justifiably proud. Maybe you have a successful marriage, raised wonderful children, earned a degree, or have a flourishing business. I bet that your greatest successes have involved an extremely high level of commitment. For those of you who are married, did you commit to be faithful to your spouse fully, or only unless someone more appealing didn't come along? For all the parents out there, did you commit to loving your children only if they were perfect little angels who never misbehaved? If you earned a degree, did you commit to finishing the program only if all the courses were easy? And for those of you who have had great financial success, did you immediately throw in the towel if you hadn't earned a million dollars in the first quarter? Anything you've done in your life that is worthwhile, that you are proud of and that has been meaningful, has been difficult at times. For me, commitment doesn't imply that something is going to be easy; it simply means that I refuse to give up. Once you truly commit, it's infinitely more difficult to quit.

If you want to know what you are truly committed to, just look at your life. You may say that you are committed to your job, but you show up late for work every morning. You may say that you are committed to exercising, but you use your treadmill to hang your clothes on. You can always tell what you are truly committed to by the results you have in your life in that area. If you want to increase your level of commitment, then write down what you wish to accomplish. If you want to up your level of commitment even more, then make your commitment public. One of the reasons that so many of the participants of *The Ultimate Weight Loss Program* have been so successful, at least during the duration of the program, is that they made a verbal commitment to the group and to their buddy, and they didn't want to let them down.

The second "C" in the *"The Seven C's to Success"* is COMPLIANCE. In medicine, the word compliance simply means "following a prescribed course of action." I love the word compliance for the same reason I love calorie density. People have no emotional attachment to those words whatsoever. Clients will call me up berating themselves because they were "bad" because they ate a brownie. I try to teach them that they are not bad if they eat something off-plan, nor are they good if they eat steamed kale. They simply were either compliant or non-compliant. If they want to achieve their weight loss goals and overcome their food addictions, then it's going to take a high degree of compliance. The greater the degree of compliance, the easier the program becomes. Compliance does not imply perfection. There is a difference. Your success on this program will be determined by how quickly you get back on track, in the event that you relapse. And the more compliant meals you can string together for longer and longer periods, the greater your chance of success. Many participants have concluded that 100% compliance is actually easier than 99% compliance.

Remember, *The Ultimate Weight Loss Program* is a revolutionary, life-changing, lifestyle intervention program in which individuals agree to adopt a low-fat, whole food, plant-exclusive diet free of all processed food, including all sugars (including zero calorie sweeteners), all flours, oil, salt, and alcohol, and eat only the foods to the left of the red line for a period of at least twenty-one days, and consume at least two pounds of non-starchy vegetables daily, starting with at least one pound of non-starchy vegetables for breakfast.

Should you indulge in any noncompliant food, immediately make sure that the very next bite of food that you put into your mouth is a non-starchy vegetable, and *voila*, you have once again become compliant. Then go back to the first "C," COMMITMENT, and recommit. When you truly commit, it's infinitely harder to quit. If taking it "a day at a time" seems too daunting, then take it a meal at a time or even a bite at a time. The more compliant meals eaten in a row, the stronger your compliance muscle gets, until one day, this is just how you eat. You don't even have to think about it. Thankfully, I have endured only one relapse in the past six years, and after experiencing all the shame and humiliation that went with it, I realized that for me, it was far easier to stay compliant than to have to try to re-establish compliance again after a relapse, experiencing the symptoms of detoxification and withdrawal all over again.

Eating with a reduced degree of variation may be difficult for some of you who thrive on variety. But variety can be the kiss of death for the food addict because it encourages overeating, and can threaten your compliance. I am not saying that you have to eat the same exact thing every day, but the more you learn to simplify your meals, the more success you will have. Still, it's not like you have to eat like a monk. Have as much variety as you please within the confines of your *New Four Food Groups*: fruits, vegetables, whole grains, and legumes. Vary the grain, the bean, the vegetable, and the sauce within every meal to keep it interesting and flavorful. The possible combinations are endless. In the recipe section, you will find over one hundred delectable recipes.

The third "C" in the "The "Seven C's to Success" is CONSISTENCY. By this I mean steadfast adherence. Those who were successful on *The Ultimate Weight Loss Program* were unwavering.

Think about all the people in life in various fields who you admire. Itzhak Perlman may have played the violin since he was three years old and been a virtuoso by the age of ten, but you can be certain that he also practiced consistently, and that he still does. Think about all the great athletes you admire and some of the amazing feats they've accomplished. Do you think there has ever been an Olympic champion who only worked out every other Tuesday? When you do something consistently, it means that you are doing it in the same manner with little variation. And when you do something consistently, it becomes a habit. Even small changes, when done consistently over time, can have enormous benefits. You are being asked to make some pretty big changes, and I promise you that if you do them consistently, the payoff will be profound.

The fourth "C" is COOKING. Everyone who was successful at losing weight and maintaining their weight loss in *The Ultimate Weight Loss Program* was willing to learn how to cook. They didn't go to culinary school, but they did develop some basic kitchen skills and figure out how to prepare at least a few simple, healthy and delicious meals. And with time and money-saving tools like the *Instant Pot* electric pressure cooker, this process has never been easier. I once had a client, a woman in her 40's, who literally did not know how to bake a potato; and while it's not necessary to become a Julia Child, if you want long-term success it's a good idea, at a minimum, to know how to prepare whole grains, legumes, and a few entrees and sauces. Most people don't eat thirty different breakfasts, lunches, and dinners every month. They find their favorites and repeat them. You will need to do the same with the new foods that you are eating.

Instead of always searching for new recipes, they learned to assemble wholesome meals from simple ingredients. Batch cooking allows you to always have healthy food ready. When you cook grains and beans, you can eat some and freeze some for later. Then you can always assemble delicious one-bowl meals such as rice and beans with *One-Minute Salsa* (recipe page 228) with steamed vegetables or over greens. When healthy food is always available, you will eat it when you are hungry. (Unless, of course, you still have unhealthy choices in your environment).

Cooking your food may never be as cheap and quick as going through the drive-thru, but living with a foodborne illness like heart disease or diabetes is expensive and will slow you down. The time you spend cooking pales in comparison to the time it takes for frequent visits to the doctor's office. While you are cooking, you can use that time to listen to your favorite music or podcast. I use the time to listen to audiobooks or Dr. Lisle's podcast called *Beat Your Genes*. The more you cook, the easier it gets and the less time it will take you, especially if you eat simply.

The fifth "C" is CHANGE. If you truly want your life to change, then you have to be willing to change your lifestyle. First and foremost, you are being asked to change the foods that you eat, many of which you may have eaten your entire life, and you may have a physical addiction or emotional attachment to. To do this, you will have to change the way you shop, change the foods you keep in your home, and change the way that you cook. You will not only be changing the foods you eat but the preparation methods and the seasonings you use. You may have to change the restaurants you go to or even decide whether or not you will continue to eat out. If you choose to still eat at restaurants, you will certainly have to change what you eat and how you order. You may even have to change your friends, at least temporarily, if they don't support your healthy new lifestyle or try to sabotage you. And you may need to change whether you accept many social engagements or family events if you are not yet strong enough to withstand those environments.

That's a lot of change, I know. Most people spend their entire lives resisting change. Many people will not even consider making a dietary or lifestyle change until the pain associated with change becomes less than the pain of staying the same. Change *is* hard. But if you are carrying around excess weight, in physical pain, and living with the shame and guilt that accompanies food addiction, not changing may prove even more difficult. While I do believe that any change you make in the direction of optimum health is better than doing nothing, the more changes you are willing to make and the faster you are willing to make them, the sooner you will see results. Once you make the commitment to change, the universe will open up its arms to support you.

The sixth "C" is COMMUNITY. Believe it or not, for many of my clients, this is by far the most important of the "C's." In the words of the poet John Donne, "No man is an island entire of itself." For most people, eating differently than their family or friends makes them feel like an island, isolated and all alone. It is important for them to fit in and be accepted by their community, even if their community is as fat and sick as they are.

You will see how hard it is for you to change. It is going to be infinitely more difficult, if not impossible, to get your friends and family to change. Whether they are overweight or not, it's very likely that they are just as addicted to sugars and flours, fat, salt and dairy and other animal products as you were at one time, and perhaps still are. You will be about as successful in attempting to get others to adopt this lifestyle as King Sisyphus was in pushing that boulder up a mountain. So, as enthusiastic as you are about discovering the solution, I would suggest that you don't even discuss it with them, at least while you are still losing weight. I understand your enthusiasm. Once you start losing weight, feeling great, and reversing your diseases, you want your loved ones to experience the same healing. But don't be surprised if they never hop on board. I have lost most of my family to preventable lifestyle-related diseases, including severe food addiction, and I have been shouting this from the rooftops for many years. For now, let's just concentrate on you and your recovery. You can't force your loved ones to embrace your newfound healthy lifestyle. Many of you have spent your entire lives being highly agreeable people-pleasers or even martyrs, and it can be very difficult finally putting yourself and your needs first.

Having a community of supportive people, like the participants of *The Ultimate Weight Loss Program,* who are experiencing the same challenges and difficulties as you are, can be helpful in providing the support you may not be getting from your friends and family. I promise you that once you lose the weight and reverse any lifestyle-related diseases, some of your friends and relatives will come running to you, asking you how you did it.

So, how do you create a new community that supports your recovery and newfound health and well-being? On August 1, 2008, I adopted a whole food, plant-based diet free of sugar, oil, and salt. I had already been vegan for thirty-one years, since the age of seventeen, so all my current friends and family were used to that. But when I started eating unprocessed food without sugar, oil, and salt, no one had a clue as to what to feed me. Heck, I couldn't even figure out how to feed myself at first. So, I turned to the internet and for just twelve dollars a month, I became an organizer of my own *Meetup* group called *UNPROCESSED/ Whole Food Plant-Based People.* I was very specific in the description, stating that I wanted to have a potluck with like-minded people who did not eat processed food in general, and sugar, oil, and salt in particular. I figured I might get one or two kooky people, like me, attending. The first potluck was in January of 2009. I was shocked that twenty-five people showed up, and how fun and (relatively) normal they were. I had no idea that anyone else in the world ate this way. The second month, fifty people showed up and by the third month, we had seventy-seven people in my modest apartment. There are now over five hundred people in the group, so we are no longer meeting in my home. But some of the people from the very first potlucks are still my close friends today.

Even if you don't want to become an organizer, you can still join *Meetup* for free, and look for a nutritionally kindred group. Once you adopt a healthier lifestyle, you will begin to meet people who share an interest in healthy eating. They will come out of the woodwork. And you will find plenty of camaraderie if you attend any of the various plant-based health conferences.

If you don't live in a city that offers such events, or if you can't afford to attend, you can still be part of a virtual community. There are many free programs and resources available for little or no cost online where you can connect with people of like mind. There are numerous groups and forums for both food addiction and emotional eating. And your community doesn't have to be an entire army; sometimes having even one person who supports your healthy lifestyle can be enough.

The seventh "C" in the *"The Seven C's to Success"* is COMPASSION. Even if you are not yet a vegan or someone who has an animal companion, I would ask you to consider including all living creatures in your circle of compassion. Albert Schweitzer said, "Until he extends his circle of compassion to include all living things, man will not himself find peace."

While I have spent my entire life extending my circle of compassion to those with fur, feathers, and fins, I needed to learn to be compassionate with myself, instead of beating myself up because of my weight. For you, too, maybe it's time to direct some of your compassion inward. The road you are about to travel may not always be easy, but I promise you that it will be a worthwhile journey to take. It will be a lot easier if you are loving and compassionate towards yourself, especially if you stumble along the way.

I will give you an example from my life in which I applied *"The Seven C's to Success"* even before I knew what they were.

For the first fifty years of my life, the only exercise I ever got was jumping to conclusions, but after meeting John Pierre right before turning fifty, that all changed. He started teaching *The Ultimate Weight Loss Program* with me and said that I was not being a good example by not engaging in any movement. I told him that I didn't enjoy exercise; he countered that I was being just like my clients who exasperated me. He pointed out that I would get upset when people in the program wouldn't eat their vegetables. I would tell them, "Well, you're an adult, you don't have to like it, you just have to do it." And so, he threw this right back in my face with fitness. When I met him, I really did have a broken knee and it took me another year and a half until I could really do any significant type of movement, so here's how I started. Since I didn't like exercise, I figured I would do the form of exercise that I hated the least.

In August 2011, I went to the closest yoga studio and signed up for their new student special, fifteen days of unlimited yoga for twenty bucks. I made a COMMITMENT to take as many of the classes and try as many different teachers as was humanly possible during those fifteen days. At the end of those fifteen days, I loved it so much, I bought thirty more classes and committed again.

I showed up to class on time, followed the rules, and did all the poses to the best of my ability, hence I was COMPLIANT and CONSISTENT. All the people taking the classes were my COMMUNITY, many of who are now dear friends. I also enrolled my current friends at the time to join me in these classes, creating even more community.

I had to be willing to CHANGE my schedule, stop wasting so much time on *Facebook*, and get to bed earlier so that I could get up in time for a class. I also had to change my belief that exercise was no fun. Although I had tried the hot yoga before and detested it, there were many other forms of yoga that I had never even heard of, and two of them, Yin and Restorative, I ended up absolutely loving.

My COOKING itself didn't change much but I learned to commit to weekly batch cooking which freed up time for me to devote to yoga. And I had to learn to have even more COMPASSION for myself than ever before with the out-of-shape, overweight body that I brought to class. When I started yoga, I could barely spread my legs apart without intense pain; it felt like they were being ripped from my body. The teacher would have to prop up several blocks just so that I wouldn't cry. Now I can put my legs behind my neck and am almost able to do the splits.

Thank you for listening to my story. And *Namaste.*

CHAPTER 5

How to Eat Healthfully Anywhere

Since my book *Unprocessed* was released in 2011, I have had one suitcase that I have not even bothered to put away. I have been on the road, speaking about the miracles associated with eating a whole food, plant-based diet. I get emails almost daily asking me how one can still eat healthfully when eating outside of one's home. I have cruised the Caribbean, journeyed from Alaska to the North and Mexico to the South, and stayed everywhere from five-star resorts to *Motel 6's*. I have traveled several times to a number of cities in Texas, the heart of cattle country, and frequented many towns and cities in the Midwest and Deep South. I have flown coast-to-coast, and just about everywhere in between, multiple times, and visited towns so small they didn't even have a real supermarket. And I even survived a couple of trips to Las Vegas! Yet even with all this traveling, I have consistently managed to find not only vegan food, but also whole plant food that was free of sugar, oil, salt, gluten, nuts, seeds, and soy, to accommodate my unique dietary restrictions, food allergies, and preferences. From California to the New York Islands, I promise eating healthfully while you travel can work for you and me!

Eating away from home is never going to be as easy, or in my opinion, as delicious, as eating at home. It does require planning and preparation. But it can be done. Before I tell you how I do it, I'd like to explain why I think it's so difficult for so many people to eat healthfully when they are away from home, and why I think it's even more important to stay compliant in these situations. One of the main reasons that people have such difficulty when attempting to eat healthfully outside of the home is because they never have really fully committed to eating healthfully *inside* their homes. When you have followed this way of eating for a prolonged period of time and have successfully met your health and weight loss goals, it will truly become your preferred way of eating; you will not want to deviate from the program and jeopardize all that you have achieved.

Often the foods they once loved taste so sickly sweet, oily, or salty to them now that they simply don't enjoy them anymore and they don't feel well when they consume them.

Occasionally, they may even get physically ill from eating what most of the rest of our society considers normal. Or they immediately notice several unpleasant and uncomfortable symptoms, such as bloating, flatulence, or weight gain, and they can't wait to return home and get back to eating their health-promoting diet.

The longer you eat healthfully, the better healthful food tastes. And the more you eat simply, the better simple foods taste. You will begin to favor the taste of the unadulterated, unprocessed whole natural plant food. And once you have finally escaped the dietary "pleasure trap," you will actually begin to prefer eating whole natural foods. Many people simply do not give *The Ultimate Weight Loss Program* enough time for their taste buds to fully adjust to this new way of eating so that they can begin to appreciate how amazing simple, healthy, left-of-the-red-line food can taste. If you have only eaten healthfully for a mere twenty-one days, it is unrealistic to think that you will suddenly enjoy organic lightly steamed purple carrots with fresh chives as much as a piece of *Sara Lee* carrot cake. But once you have neuroadapted, you will become just as satisfied with a simple supper of rice, beans, and fire roasted salsa over salad greens as you previously were with a *Taco Bell* bean and cheese burrito. But because you haven't fully neuroadapted to these simpler, less stimulating, less concentrated foods, you are always going to be looking for that next hit of dopamine from these more "exciting" foods. (Remember that the more concentrated the source of calories, the more dopamine is released.)

While you can make the foods we eat in *The Ultimate Weight Loss Program* taste as gourmet as you desire, the reality is that most of the rest of the world just isn't able to do so yet. The only foods that are routinely available when you attempt to eat healthfully outside of your home are the very simplest of foods. Things like a plain baked potato or dry salad. This makes steamed vegetables and brown rice seem exciting by comparison when you can actually get them. Some people feel that this is unfair, especially since it seems like everyone else gets to eat all the "good stuff," meaning all the disease-promoting crap. They feel that they, too, should be able to enjoy their vacation and splurge or celebrate at restaurants. They see these restrictions as a punishment. But I promise you this: when you eat healthfully long enough, you start feeling like eating out is the real punishment. Once you start eating for hunger instead of emotional reasons such as boredom, loneliness, or stress, you will be satisfied with the choices you can find anywhere in the world. Of course, this will never occur if you are still using food as a drug, whether it's to celebrate or to medicate.

While you may feel that it's extreme to avoid treats entirely, consider that having a slender, healthy body is the real treat. If you have read this far in the book, you understand that I am still a food addict, albeit in recovery, and it's not possible for me to have a treat without relapsing. If you are the kind of person who can, as the author Michael Pollan says, "treat treats as treats" without it affecting your mental or physical health or jeopardizing your program and hard-earned recovery, then, by all means feel free to do so. But if you could have been moderate in this area without experiencing negative consequences, wouldn't you have done so already? You see, I believe that many of you are waiting for a socially acceptable excuse to go off your program. You are still a food addict and haven't been in recovery long enough, so you use these outside eating opportunities as a chance to "legitimately" go off plan. I mean, how can you be expected not to eat the BBQ beef sandwich and fries when that's all you could find at the Memphis airport?

I have had clients tell me that they couldn't possibly go to San Francisco without eating the sourdough bread or enjoy a *Dodger* game without eating a *Dodger dog*. I have heard them say that they shouldn't be expected to not eat the cheese in France or the pasta in Italy. And I have seen them, in a moment of weakness, succumb to one of these temptations and undo all the hard work that they have accomplished.

Beginning with a single bite of a pecan praline on a trip to New Orleans, or an innocent "fun-size" *Snickers* bar at Halloween, some have gone so far deep back into the "pleasure trap" that they have gained all their weight back, and then some, and even had to go back on their medication or watch their health deteriorate drastically. It breaks my heart when I see this happen. Because it all happened with "just one bite" that they were erroneously told, and they believed, wouldn't hurt them. I believe it is far easier to stay out of the "pleasure trap" and stay compliant than having to neuroadapt all over again and continually become compliant.

As Saint Augustine once said, "Complete abstinence is easier than perfect moderation."

The other problem with straying off your plan is this: once you have abstained from the hyper-palatable foods that have become your drug of choice for a prolonged period of time, it takes a smaller dose to get an even more pronounced effect. So, you actually now get a bigger blast of dopamine from a much smaller amount of the substance. The feeling is much more intense than you remember and now you really can't get enough. In her insightful book, *The Hunger Fix*, Dr. Pamela Peeke says, "We now know that when you awaken the sleeping dragon of addiction, it becomes stronger, more powerful, and twice as deadly as before."[10]

A plain baked potato doesn't sound so bad, after all, now does it?

The truth is, it's important for you to become more vigilant, not less when eating outside your home. Most of your friends and family members have probably been your "pushers" for years. They will constantly try to entice you with their tempting treats, saying things like, "Aw, c'mon, one bite won't hurt," or, "All things in moderation." One bite can kill and moderation has never, ever worked for an addict. I have known several people who have died from diseases caused by the consequences of food addiction, and others who have contemplated suicide from not being able to deal with this disease, so I do not believe in "moderation" as a solution. The only thing that has ever worked is abstinence. Before eating something that may send you on a downward spiral, ask yourself, will it be worth it? Will you be able to recover quickly and easily and get right back on the program with the very next meal? If the answer is no, then consider all your other options, including skipping a meal. I have seen slender people at *TrueNorth Health Center* fast on water only for over forty days. Unless you are on medication that does not allow this, you probably could skip a meal if there was nothing compliant to eat. People actually have survived flying from Los Angeles to New York without eating the stale peanuts.

One of the things I constantly ask my clients when they are faced with these often-challenging outside eating situations is to remind themselves what their goals are and ask themselves if eating or drinking this particular item will move them closer to their goals or further away from them. Truly committing to healthful eating does make it easier to manage these often-complex social situations. And remember, you will never regret *not* eating or drinking something non-compliant. Every meal is a choice: you're either eating for your recovery or for your addiction. You can't do both.

All outside eating events always fall into one of three categories: situations where you have complete control over your food; situations where you have partial control over your food; or situations where you have little to no control over your food. The solution is to set yourself up for success by creating as many outside eating situations as possible where you can have complete control over your food intake. Other than in your own home, an example of a situation where you can often have complete control over your food is travel. Whether by automobile, bicycle, bus, foot, plane, or train, you are allowed to bring food with you. When arriving at your destination, be it at a hotel or someone's home, if you have a refrigerator and are allowed to prepare your own meals, then you have complete control. The same would be true of a potluck. Any place that you are allowed to bring food, such as a park, school, or your workplace, you can choose to bring the absolute healthiest food possible. And if there are other people who will be eating with you, make sure you bring plenty to share because they will often end up liking your food better.

An example of a situation where you have some control would be a restaurant. You can often navigate the menu to find suitable choices and I will give you some tips on how to do this. Eating at someone else's home is another example, if at least some of the food offered to you is compliant and you are willing to politely turn down the foods that are not.

The most difficult situations are those in which you have no control over the food served. Examples would be a large event like a wedding or Bar Mitzvah or a host who refuses to make accommodations for your special dietary needs. I try to avoid these situations and people like the plague, and if I can't, I make sure that I pre-eat something extremely healthy and very filling like a sweet potato before I go, and have compliant food with me in my cooler in the car.

One of the things that all outside eating scenarios have in common is that they all require some degree of planning. And with the exception of not being able to bring liquids onto an airplane (unless you purchased them after going through TSA), you really can bring almost any other food you want on board. You can even bring an ice chip to keep your food cold, so long as it's frozen solid and you take it out of your bag so that TSA can see it when it goes through the x-ray machine. You can also use frozen foods, like bags of frozen fruits and vegetables, or entrees you froze ahead of time, to keep your food cold and you can actually eat them when you arrive at your destination. I always bring at least twenty-four hours' worth of food with me whenever I travel. Having been on the road relentlessly since 2011, I can't tell you how many times I have met delays where it has taken me twenty-four hours to get to my destination or return home. In my cooler bag, I always take several cooked potatoes or sweet potatoes and raw vegetables like sugar snap peas or baby carrots and some *Blueberry Mill-Oat Muffins* (recipe page 140). I also carry non-perishable food with me in my backpack such as fruit like apples, bananas, and oranges. I may also take some nonperishable snacks like freeze dried apple chips or dried bananas. They are made from just fruit. (Hummus seems to be a gray area. If it is spread on a wrap, TSA may let it go through, whereas in a container they often confiscate it. You may not believe this, but my colleague, John Pierre, dehydrates his hummus and reconstitutes it with water when he arrives at his location.) In my suitcase, I also take organic salt-free beans that come in aseptic cartons to add to my salads. You can tear the box right open and don't even need a pair of scissors. I also bring shelf-stable precooked brown rice or quinoa in individual servings. The food that they sell on airplanes and most airports is just overpriced junk food, so I always make sure that I am never hungry or tempted.

Occasionally, I will buy food at airports. You can get plain steel cut oatmeal made with water at *Starbucks* (there is one in just about every airport); add a banana as your sweetener. Keep in mind that the oatmeal from *Jamba Juice* is precooked in soymilk, which contains sugar, so it's always good to ask first how the oatmeal is prepared. I am allergic to soy anyway, but even a small amount of sugar in a recipe is enough to set me off. *Jamba Juice* will, however, make a custom smoothie with just greens, water, and fruit, and they are located in many airports now. It is in these travel situations that I allow myself the occasional smoothie. Apples, bananas, and oranges are pretty easy to find at every airport. Many airports have a *Wendy's* where you can get a plain, hot baked potato or two, or a *Pei Wei* or similar Asian restaurant where you can get plain brown rice and steamed vegetables. If you don't see it on the menu, ask. I have even had chain restaurants like *Panda Express* make me plain steamed vegetables, even though they weren't on the menu (they normally cook their vegetables with chicken broth and oil, so it's important that you always inquire about what the exact preparation method is). I always offer to pay more money for my special order; the worst that can happen is they will say no. I like to find out what the food choices are at every airport I will be traveling to before I fly. You can look this up online by *Googling* the airport to see what the different food options are. Or check out the airport travel guide at *www.pcrm. org.*

As fewer and fewer nonstop flights become available, I actually choose my connecting airport based on how healthy their food options are. For example, when I have a choice of flying into either Midway or O'Hare airports in Chicago, I always choose Midway because they have a build-your-own salad bar restaurant with an oil-free dressing. I was once stranded there for eight hours, so this really paid off. When I have the option, I always choose San Francisco Airport for a connection because they have a fresh juice bar (which means that they also have fresh fruits and vegetables) and a yoga room. So, do your homework before you make your reservations.

Once you arrive at your destination, you are most likely going to be staying with someone you know, or at a hotel or a place you have rented.

I will cover eating at other's people's homes in a bit, but here are some tips for staying at a hotel. Always try to get a room that has a refrigerator. And if your room doesn't have one, ask. Even when I have been told no at first, I was able to get a mini fridge. I told a "little white lie" that I was on medication that needed refrigeration and asked them to please store it for me and said that I would come down a few times a day to get it. Next thing you know, a mini fridge was sent up to my room! I find it's best to call the hotel in advance to make this request. (And if you absolutely can't get a fridge, you can always get ice to keep your food cold.)

Many hotels now routinely have coffee pots and microwaves. This makes it easy to make oatmeal in your room every morning. I always bring with me *Ziploc* bags of my *Anytime Oats* (recipe page 138) and single-serving cartons of unsweetened, non-dairy milk when I travel, one for every day that I'm away. I add the liquid and the fruit when I get there. *Umpqua Oats* makes a sugar-free oatmeal called *Not Guilty* that's great for travel. It's sold in many stores, on *Amazon,* and I've even seen it sold at several airports, including the one in Burbank, which is where I usually depart from. Believe it or not, I always travel with my *Instant Pot* electric pressure cooker so that I can steam vegetables and potatoes for breakfast in my hotel room. I can even make rice in it. I always go to the grocery store when I arrive in a new city, even before checking into my hotel, so that I will have what I need during my trip. Now with *Uber* and *Lyft,* it's very easy and affordable.

One of the most frequent questions I get asked is how to eat healthfully in restaurants, so here are some tips that I've used over the years. It can be difficult enough eating out when you are vegan, but even more challenging when you don't consume oil, and nearly impossible when you don't eat salt. So, here is my number one tip for eating out, whether at a restaurant or someone else's home: *Eat before you go.* If you aren't starving when you get to the restaurant, you are less likely to make poor choices. Then if all you can get is a dry salad, you won't feel as deprived. Restaurants use more sugar, fat, and salt than you ever would at home, so don't be surprised if it is very difficult to get a healthful meal out. There are websites like *www.HappyCow.net, Yelp,* and *Trip Advisor* where you can look up these restaurants in advance, but keep in mind that just because a restaurant is vegan does not mean that it's healthy.

In fact, I'm sorry to say that I have frequently eaten more healthful and more satisfying meals at non-vegan establishments. At *Morton's Steakhouse*, I was able to get a huge baked potato and salsa with a variety of fresh vegetables. And they were willing to cook them for me to order without any salt or oil, any way that I desired. But before setting foot in any restaurant, I will always pre-eat.

If you know in advance where you will be dining, you can often look up the menu on their website. Many restaurants now also list their nutritional information online, so if you notice that a "healthy kale salad" has fifty-three grams of fat, you know to steer clear. If a restaurant has multiple locations, they are required to list their nutritional information online. If a chain has more than twenty locations, they must now post that information on their menu as well. Gone are the days where chefs actually cook from recipes and prepare the food. Most restaurants' cooks merely assemble the prepackaged food. Almost every restaurant preps all their food in advance, so it's not always possible to request substitutions, but if you can, there are ways to navigate the menu. For example, if you don't see spinach offered on the menu but you notice they have a spinach omelet for breakfast, you can ask them if they will steam some spinach for you. If you don't see rice or beans listed on the menu a la carte but notice they offer them as part of a burrito, you can always ask if you can get a side order of rice and beans. Just make sure they don't put oil in them. Many restaurants, like *Chipotle*, put soybean oil in both their rice and beans. Remember: soy, corn, and wheat are the three most heavily genetically modified crops.

I was recently in a small town with a population of 1,500 and the only eateries were fast food joints and taverns that served everything fried. At the tavern at which I was dining, I noticed that they had both French fries and sweet potato fries on the menu, so ostensibly they had to have potatoes. I asked if they would cook me a potato in whatever manner they were willing, other than fried, such as baked, steamed, or even cooked in the microwave. They gladly made me both a microwaved potato and sweet potato and served it to me with some salsa. Was it the best meal I ever had? No. But does every meal you eat have to be like dining in a five-star restaurant? If it does, I'm not sure how much success you are going to have long-term on this program. In another town, at a *Marriott Hotel*, I saw "French fries made from Yukon gold potatoes" listed on the menu. When I asked if they could make me a baked potato, they said no. They bought their fries premade and already frozen. Unfortunately, that is what more and more restaurants are doing now: assembling their food instead of actually cooking it. Whenever any eatery goes out of their way to accommodate my special dietary needs, I tell them how grateful I am and tip very generously. I also will write a glowing review on *Yelp* and mention how they went out of their way for me.

When I have to dine in an unfamiliar restaurant, I will call them in advance during non-peak hours (after the lunch rush and before the dinner rush) and ask if they are able to accommodate my special dietary needs. I apologize in advance for appearing difficult and I explain that it is "doctor's orders" and that I am vegan and on a special diet for medical reasons and unable to eat any oil. If the food is served with any oil on it, I send it back and say I'm very sorry but I'm *deathly allergic*, which is what Dr. Esselstyn advises his heart patients to do. Sometimes restaurants say they can accommodate me, sometimes they can't. The worst that they can say is no. But when they say yes, I am very grateful and I tell everyone. If you are unsure if your needs will be accommodated, it is always best to pre-eat. And remember, you always have the option to not eat in any situation.

I know people who carry a small business card with them that says what they can eat and what they are unable to eat and ask the server to hand it to the chef. I have had success doing something similar. I wrote on a piece of paper that I could eat any fruit, vegetable, whole grain or legume and could not eat any sugar, oil, or salt and I thanked the chef for their ingenuity. If the chef is available, I will ask to speak to them in person to explain my dietary needs. I've had some rather creative and delicious meals this way. A very successful *UWL* member who wanted to remain compliant on a cruise ship gave the chef a list of what she could and could not eat, and reported that all her meals met her exact specifications and were delicious! Since it's difficult to get oil-free dressings in a restaurant other than lemon or vinegar, I discreetly bring my own dressing with me in a small sealed container called *Dressing 2 Go* that you can purchase at *Amazon* or *Bed, Bath & Beyond*. It's always best if you are the one who gets to choose the restaurant. I will choose a restaurant that I know has a salad bar or a baked potato. At *Souplantation* or *Sweet Tomatoes*, I can get both but I still bring my own compliant salad dressing and salt-free salsa in my cooler purse.

At many vegan restaurants, I have been told that I could not get anything without oil and that there were no substitutions. Not a fan of fake meats and faux cheeses, I find it easier to arrive completely full and just order a cup of tea. If my dining companions ask why I'm not eating, I will just say that I had a late breakfast or late lunch. If they are food bullies and just won't relent in their efforts to try and get me to eat noncompliant food, I just tell them I am having a colonoscopy the next day. That usually shuts them up. I have offered to consult with restaurants for free so that they will offer healthier choices and some of them have actually been amenable to my suggestions. Keep in mind that in most restaurants, the majority of the food is cooked and prepped in advance, so it's going to be difficult to guarantee that it doesn't have oil or salt. If the restaurant sees that a healthy option will sell and that people will order it, they will keep it on the menu. That's how I got *Sharky's Woodfired Mexican Grill* to carry the *AJ Burrito*, which expanded to the *AJ Bowl* and the *AJ Plate*. I often have to fib and say that I'm allergic to oil to be absolutely sure that I don't get any in my food. At many Asian restaurants, when I've said no oil, they interpreted that to mean less oil. In general, at ethnic restaurants, it's usually fairly easy to get steamed vegetables and brown rice. I find it's often less challenging eating at restaurants than other people's homes because the server doesn't take it personally if you can't eat something, don't want something, don't like something, or even send it back. Try doing that at your Mother-in law's house!

If you are just starting out on *The Ultimate Weight Loss Program*, we recommend that you steer clear of eating at restaurants or other people's homes for as long as possible and at least for the first twenty-one days of the program. While some may feel that this is extreme, if they truly understood what a slippery slope dining out can be for a food addict, especially one who hasn't been abstinent for very long, they would see that this is a very sane and reasonable request. Taking care of your needs like this isn't selfish; it shows a great deal of self-love and self-respect, which is something that many of my clients need to cultivate more of. Self-care is health care. Many are chronic lifelong people-pleasers and it's difficult for them to put their own needs first, so turning down a social invitation, pre-eating, or bringing their own food to a social gathering proves to be very empowering for them.

Eating at other people's homes, especially if they don't eat in the same healthful manner as you do, can be extremely challenging, to say the least. Navigating social situations when you don't want to offend other people yet want to remain true to your own healthy eating plan can be difficult indeed, so here are some strategies that I have used in the past. The first thing I do when invited to someone else's home for a meal, whether I know them well or not, is to ask if I can bring a dish to share, and I make it sound as specific and enticing as possible ("Can I bring my *Bodacious Beet Salad with Barefoot Dressing*?" (recipes on pages 206 and 205), so that I rarely get refused. If the host says yes, I'm home free. (I have now just created an outside eating situation in which I can have complete control over my food). I can't tell you how many times that my dish was met with appreciation and had everyone asking for the recipe. If the host says no, then I will say that either I have severe food allergies or I am on a very special diet, "doctor's orders," and would they mind my bringing my own food just for me? In the rare case that they say no even to that, then I either won't go or I will pre-eat and push the food around on my plate, eating any compliant food when I get there. If the host is willing to make something special for me, then I will ask for something really simple like a plain baked potato so they don't have to go to too much trouble.

If it's a potluck, well then, you're in luck! You can bring anything you want and as much as you want. And you can use this as an opportunity to show others how delicious healthy, compliant food can be. I've never had anyone turn their nose up at my *Red Lentil Chili* (recipe page 180), *Chipotle Bean Burgers* (recipe page 161), *Herbed Quinoa Tabbouleh* (recipe page 242) or *OMG Watermelon Salad* (recipe page 226). At some very exclusive resorts where I've worked, I served these dishes to people who eat the Standard American Diet and they loved them and even asked me for the recipe! I've been eating differently for so long now that I'm just in the habit of bringing my cooler filled with healthy compliant food everywhere.

Growing up in a Kosher household, I just accepted the fact that the world was not going to cater to my special dietary requests. I learned that if I wanted to eat, it was up to me to bring my food. The same thing happened when I first became vegan in 1977. If I wanted to eat, I had to bring my own food. So, it really isn't difficult for me to now make sure I have *UWL* food with me wherever I go. When I have been to places where there is nothing I could eat, I have actually excused myself and gone out to my car to nourish myself. I will intentionally leave my cell phone or wallet in the car and if I get hungry, politely excuse myself to go get it. Then I eat my food. I can't tell you how important it is to always carry food with you everywhere, once you embrace any type of a healthy lifestyle. The world is not set up for us to eat healthfully; forewarned is forearmed. Like a Boy Scout, you must always be prepared because everywhere you go there will be unhealthy food to suck you right back into the "pleasure trap." And when you are hungry, it's infinitely harder to resist. Heck, I can't even go to the pet store now to buy my dog a leash, or the hardware store to buy nails, without having to look at all the candy they sell at the cash registers of these non-food stores! Always remember how critical your environment is to your success.

There are many places other than actual restaurants and other people's homes where people go that it is very difficult or impossible to find healthy food. Places like amusement parks, business conferences, courthouses, fairs, hospitals, malls, movie theaters, museums, and sporting events, to name just a few. The difficulty one encounters in trying to obtain healthy food outside of the home is the primary reason why it's so important to not only pre-eat in most situations but to also carry a cooler with healthy options with you at all times. At a wedding or Bar Mitzvah, or similar event, if you know the host well and are comfortable asking for special foods, you may be able to have your needs accommodated. You can also find out who the caterer is and talk to them yourself; however, I have found that the larger the event the more difficult it is to ask for special food, so I just pre-eat and have my purse cooler full of delicious, compliant food waiting for me in my hotel room or the car.

Thankfully, I don't have to go to very many of these types of events where I have no control over my food, as I have learned that it's almost impossible to get my dietary needs met at these types of functions. Keep in mind that when you attend these special events, you really aren't going there for the food anyway. You are going to share in the special day of a friend or family member. The food should be inconsequential.

Even at special family gatherings, like birthdays and holidays, it doesn't have to be just about the food. In the Jewish household in which I was raised, whatever the problem, food was the answer. We ate when we were happy because a baby was born and we ate when we were grieving because a loved one had died. So, if you are lucky enough to still have a grandma or other special relative who shows their love gastronomically, explain to them how much you appreciate all the special foods they make for you, but that if they really love you, to please help you take this program seriously. Tell them that you have finally decided to do something about your health challenges and you would like to enlist their help. Ask them to show their love by serving food that is on your plan. Explain the program to them. If they remind you that your previous diets have failed, you can point out how different this program is, and how nutritional science is now finally on your side. Ask them to please not bring tempting treats into your home and to not be offended when you are no longer able to enjoy them. If they don't listen, take the love they have to offer, not the food. Never, ever eat anything you don't want to eat because you think if you don't you will hurt someone else's feelings. You need to learn to love yourself enough to just say no.

While some people offering these irresistible hyper-palatable foods may truly be well meaning and doing it out of love, there is another group of individuals out there doing it to intentionally sabotage you. They're called *Food Bullies*. I know it's hard to believe that anyone would intentionally thwart your weight loss efforts and health goals, but trust me, they are out there. And you may even be living with one of them. All bullies are motivated by fear, and if our friends and loved ones are not joining us in getting healthy, they may, consciously or unconsciously, try to derail us because they fear if we get healthy we may leave them behind. It's sad to say, but some of them are acting out of jealousy, especially if you start losing weight and they remain overweight. Or they may feel that because you are finally losing weight and getting healthy that you are somehow superior to them. How you deal with people who are unsupportive or actively try to sabotage you, is going to depend on what their relationship is to you and how important it is, so you may need to seek the help of a qualified therapist to help you deal with this situation should it arise.

The late, great Reverend Dr. O. C. Smith often gave a memorable analogy in his marvelous Sunday sermons. He talked about how when crabs were caught in a bucket, every now and then one of them would figure a way to crawl out to save its life, by climbing over the other crabs. And sure enough, all the other crabs would pull him back down to his certain death. Just understand that for many of us, those other crabs are our friends and family. But you're probably better off not sharing this analogy with them.

So many of our traditions, relationships, and even our emotions are intimately tied with food. You have developed so many of these over your lifetime; they aren't going to just magically disappear when you read this book. You can, however, be aware of them and seek to make changes in this area. Overweight people tend to have overweight friends, and if your entire relationship has been based solely on eating crap together, unless your friend wants to join you in healthy eating, you may have to find other activities that don't involve eating to do together or you may have to make some new friends. But I promise you that those potential new friends who share your commitment to health are out there; in the last chapter, under "COMMUNITY," you learned some of the ways to find them.

If you are the only one in your family eating this way and you still have to prepare unhealthy food for them, this can be excruciatingly difficult, if not impossible, to accomplish without relapsing. Remember the golden rule of *UWL*: "If it's in your house, it's in your mouth." I recommend preparing healthy food and offering your loved ones two choices: Take It or Leave It. Now that you know what the healthiest way is to eat, how could you possibly feed the most cherished ones in your life food that will promote disease? If they want to eat crap outside the home, you may not be able to stop them, but why do you have to be their executioner?

In *The Ultimate Weight Loss Program*, we recommend that you don't eat out at all for at least the first month of the program. If a person absolutely must dine out due to a previous commitment or work situation, here is what one of my brilliant students did when she was on the program. She called the restaurant in advance and explained the situation and asked if she could please bring her food to the restaurant and have them heat it up and plate it and she would gladly pay for the cost of a meal. They said it would be absolutely no problem and that they do this all the time. She got there a bit early to deliver the food and when her dinner came, her colleagues didn't bat an eye or even know she hadn't ordered it from the menu. They charged her for the cost of the least expensive entrée on the menu.

Everyone is always willing to do what's easy. But the ones who truly succeed are those who are willing to do not just what is easy, but whatever it takes. And if you want to be one of the only two percent of people who permanently keep your weight off, it will take an extraordinarily strong level of commitment to *The Ultimate Weight Loss Program*.

In the live *UWL Program*, we spend almost four hours discussing the subject of eating outside of the home because it can be so difficult for people, especially the women in the group, who tend to be the more agreeable "people pleasers." If you are going to succeed in eating differently than almost everyone else in America, you are going to have to learn to be a bit less agreeable and uncompromising in this area. The stress of eating differently than their friends and family causes some of the new participants terrible angst. If they are completely new to healthy plant-based eating, it can take some time for them to get comfortable in social situations. When they were overweight and eating at *McDonald's*, no one said a word to them. But now that they are losing weight and eating a plant-based diet, everyone is suddenly concerned about their health. That is why I try to impress upon them the importance of eating plant-perfectly at home one hundred percent of the time and never having any noncompliant foods in their homes. That way, if they absolutely feel that they must eat something off-plan, at least it will not be in their own environment.

The healthier you eat, the healthier you want to eat. I have been eating this way for so long now that when I absolutely have to dine at a restaurant or at the home of someone who doesn't eat like me, I truly experience it as a punishment. In my opinion, the food is so much better-tasting, and infinitely healthier, at home. And it's certainly more bountiful and less expensive. Because I am a volume eater who eats in accordance with the principles of calorie density, and because I eat much more now as a slender person than I ever did as an obese one, I simply cannot get enough food at a restaurant or someone else's home. Even though I am a gregarious person, I still suffer a bit from social anxiety, which can cause the levels of ghrelin (the hunger hormone) to increase so that one actually feels hungrier. When I am in these social situations, even if I have pre-eaten, I just wish I could click my heels together and be back in Kansas, which for me is at *TrueNorth Health Center* where I don't have to feel different for eating huge volumes of delicious, nutritious, calorie-dilute foods. You know you have truly succeeded on *The Ultimate Weight Loss Program* when home is your very favorite place to eat because when it comes to delicious, healthy, and compliant meals, Dorothy was right: there truly is no place like home.

CHAPTER 6

Overcoming your Weight Loss Obstacles

Here is an added bonus for continuing to eat to the left of the red line, even after you have met your health and weight loss goals: as someone who has been a severe food addict and emotional eater for over fifty years, and lost several loved ones to this disease, I can honestly tell you that it's the sanest and safest treatment I know of for both of these disorders. If you are using food as a drug to medicate yourself, then you will always be seeking the foods to the right of the red line to get your hit of dopamine or to numb yourself out. If you simply commit to eating to the left of the red line, you can greatly decrease or even eliminate your struggles with food addiction and emotional eating. While I also recommend that you do some of the deeper emotional work, eating to the left of the red line will do the trick physiologically.

Americans on average consume nearly 1,000 calories every single day from a nutritionally bereft, disease-promoting substance—sugar—that shouldn't even rightly be considered food! Sugar rivals cocaine and heroin as an addictive substance, and while many people, whether they are sugar addicts or not, would agree with this, it is much more difficult to get folks to understand that dairy and flour products can also be addictive.

For recovering food addicts like me, eating refined flour products like bread and pasta, even when made from healthy whole grains, is not favorable to our brain chemistry. The scientific mechanisms involved are described in detail in Dr. Joan Ifland's *Sugars and Flours: How They*

Make Us Crazy, Sick, and Fat. As Dr. Ifland explains, sugar and refined flours go through the same type of processing and refining as drugs and alcohol.

While some people don't believe that food addictions exist, I would contend that you certainly can be addicted to particular foods, and if you think about it, all the foods that people have a problem with are to the right of the red line. I have known plenty of people who were addicted to alcohol, but never met a single one who was actually addicted to the barley or rye or other whole grain from which it's made. I have worked with hundreds of people who were addicted to refined sugar, yet I have never met a single person who was addicted to beets. I meet many people unable or unwilling to give up bread, but none of them had a problem resisting wheat berries. When it comes to potato chips, "Betcha can't eat just one," is a natural fact, but with a delicious baked potato, you probably can. And as far as I know, no one has ever become addicted to poppy seeds from the poppy seed plant, only to the opium that's made from it. You see, it is not these complex carbohydrate foods in their natural unrefined state that are the problem; it's the *refining* of these complex carbohydrates that creates the problem. The addiction is always to one form or another of the *refined* carbohydrates. And all flours and sugars, even the zero calorie sweeteners like stevia, xylitol, and erythritol, go through a refining process similar to that used in the production of drugs and alcohol.

Caloric density is but one reason I don't drink any alcohol or recommend it to my clients. All proteins and carbohydrates contain four calories per gram. All fats contain nine calories per gram. And alcohol falls in between at seven calories per gram. So, fat is more than twice as calorically dense as either protein or carbohydrates, and alcohol is almost twice as calorically dense. Like oil, it contains no fiber or nutrients and it simply does not fill you up. Alcohol is a drug, not a food, and has recently been linked to many cancers. In fact, the World Health Organization recently stated that they can no longer recommend any amount of alcohol as safe, as even light drinking can increase your risk of most cancers. It's also the case that when people consume alcohol, it fuels their hunger and, unsurprisingly, their risk of making less-than-stellar food choices. It decreases your self-control so that instead of having a baked potato, you may go for the potato chips, and then one or two potato chips becomes the entire bag. I can't tell you how many clients I have who, upon stopping the consumption of alcohol, lost their cravings for the other refined carbohydrates, like sugar and flour. For the first time in their lives, they were easily able to achieve and maintain their slim ideal weight.

One of the most important things to be learned from Dr. Doug Lisle and Dr. Alan Goldhamer's groundbreaking book, *The Pleasure Trap*, as it pertains to calorie density, is how the caloric density of different foods affects the release of a neurotransmitter called dopamine, a chemical that is released in the brain whenever we have a pleasurable experience. While all eating stimulates the production of dopamine in the brain, the more calorically concentrated the calories, the more dopamine is released. So, it makes perfect sense that most people would rather eat chocolate than chard and bread instead of broccoli. We are genetically hardwired to prefer the most concentrated source of calories for survival, but our ancestors did not have to deal with the constant lure of these highly processed and refined foods, while the high-fat plant foods of a higher caloric density and animal products were seasonal or infrequent indulgences. Our ancestors were nomadic and none of the processed foods to the right of the red line (sugar, flour, alcohol, dairy products, and oil) even existed until comparatively recently in the timeline of human history. If our ancestors saw a ripe avocado, which was seasonal, of course, they undoubtedly ate it, as humans are genetically hardwired to prefer the taste of high-fat/high-calorie foods for survival. Our ancestors struggled with getting enough calories, a problem that few of us will ever experience. Nuts were also seasonal and certainly not eaten every day. Nuts come in very hard shells and as far as I know, our ancestors did not have nutcrackers and had to open each nut individually. They certainly weren't downing three-pound bags of roasted and salted nuts from *Costco* while lounging on their recliners.

It is normal to want to feel good. If you had a difficult childhood, using food to numb your pain may have been the only way you were able to soothe yourself and feel better. Eating highly concentrated, hyper-caloric, and hyper-palatable foods to the right of the red line stimulates much more dopamine in our brains than eating nature's bounty; but we can easily become addicted to this artificial stimulation of dopamine in our brains so that whole natural foods (to the left of the red line) aren't as satisfying to us, especially at first. In addition, many of us are chronically stressed, sleep deprived, or were born with a lower receptivity of dopamine in our brains and do not regularly engage in any of the more healthful behaviors that can increase dopamine naturally, such as exercise or sex.

I included both cheese and ice cream on my calorie density chart because foods made from dairy are, for many people, highly addictive. To truly understand why milk and other dairy products do no body any good, I urge you to read *The China Study*, by Dr. T. Colin Campbell. As a matter of fact, most of the food addiction treatment programs that I have investigated completely shun dairy, as well as sugar, flour, alcohol, caffeine, chocolate, and nuts. When I interviewed Howard Lyman, aka "The Mad Cowboy," for my weekly teleclass, he told me that giving up cheese was infinitely more difficult for him than even quitting cigarettes.

Dr. Neal Barnard, who has written excellent books on the subject, one called *The Cheese Trap*, and another called *Breaking the Food Seduction*, also has a popular *YouTube* video called *How to Magnetize a Baby*, in which he explains the science behind dairy addiction. It has to do with casomorphins, protein fragments in dairy. The first part of the word comes from casein, the protein found in dairy that, as Dr. Campbell discovered, is a potent carcinogen. You will recognize the rest of the word from the word morphine because when you ingest these highly concentrated compounds from the milk of another mammal, they have an opiate-like effect on the brain. As sugar and flour do. That is why it is so hard to stop eating them once you start.

Eating to the left of the red line is your solution, as all the foods with an addictive effect on your brain exist to the right of it. It truly is that simple.

So why do some people have trouble transitioning to this new way of eating? What are the obstacles that hold some people back?

In November of 2016, I started using *Facebook Live* so that I could interact with the participants of my *Ultimate Weight Loss Program*.

Not being very tech savvy, I accidentally did my very first broadcast to everyone on *Facebook* instead of to just my private group. Much to my surprise, there were over 200 people watching live and thousands more watched the replays, so I decided to do a weekly broadcast, which I call *Weight Loss Wednesday*. I have now done over sixty episodes that you can watch on *YouTube*. Viewers are able to ask me questions live, and at the end of one of the broadcasts, someone asked me if there were any characteristics that the people who are not successful in losing weight had in common. After thinking for a minute, I said yes and gave my answer. But when the broadcast was over, and after giving the question more thought, I realized there was more than one characteristic; in fact, there were several.

I thought this topic might make a good lecture, so when I was at *TrueNorth Health Center,* I decided to test it out in front of a live audience. It was a Sunday morning and there was a patient in the audience who was a Baptist preacher, so I decided to call the talk *Chef AJ's 10 Commandments for Overcoming Your Weight Loss Obstacles.* I delivered it like a sermon, complete with fire and brimstone.

My Ten Commandments are a set of rules to help you achieve and sustain permanent weight loss. I will present them to you starting with the tenth one first so that I can save the first, and most important Commandment, for last.

My tenth commandment is THOU SHALT EAT SIMPLY.

While at first this may sound boring and restrictive, the truth is that the more simply you eat, the more that simple foods will taste good to you. Variety may be the spice of life, but as Heather Goodwin, who has lost over 300 pounds on *The Ultimate Weight Loss Program,* likes to say, "Variety is the spice of obesity." That is because variety is the kiss of death for the food addict. The more choices you allow yourself at every meal, the more you're likely to find yourself overeating.

There is a phenomenon that Dr. Barbara Rolls talks about called sensory specific satiety. To give you an example of this, you could be stuffed to the gills at Thanksgiving dinner but still find room for that piece of pumpkin pie. I learned this firsthand at *TrueNorth,* where I am a guest presenter at their annual *Holiday Cooking Extravaganza.* One of the cooking instructors had made a delicious entrée of a potato stuffed with corn and beans and topped it with salsa and guacamole. It was very filling and satisfying. She then asked everyone in the class if we would like another and we said, "No, we're too full." She then went into the kitchen and brought back a beautiful carrot cake and said, "Would anyone like a piece?" All the hands in the class shot up like a rocket. This merely illustrates that the more courses you allow yourself in a meal, the more you will eat. Think about how much more you eat at a smorgasbord or buffet-style restaurant than you would at home or even at a restaurant where you have fewer items on your plate. This is why people pack on the pounds on cruise ships. When I eat a meal, I usually limit it to no more than two or three items such as sweet potatoes and broccoli for lunch and a hearty soup, stew, or chili with rice for dinner, and sometimes fresh fruit for dessert. So if you're following the principles outlined in *The Ultimate Weight Loss Program* and are still struggling with losing your last few pounds, consider simplifying your meals. You will save money and time, and ultimately learn to enjoy your food even more.

The ninth commandment is THOU SHALT NOT EMBELLISH THY FOOD WITH CHEMICALS.

The chemicals that I'm specifically referring to are sugar, oil, and salt, none of which exist in nature in any concentrated forms. They fool your brain's satiety mechanisms and cause you to exponentially overeat. They are really more drug-like than food-like and will stimulate your appetite, causing you to have food cravings and to overeat.

Similarly, I also don't recommend using flour and alcohol in your recipes, just as I also don't advise eating bread and pasta or consuming alcoholic beverages. I use the acronym SOFAS (sugar, oil, flour, alcohol, and salt) to help people remember what to avoid, and I tell people that if they want to lose weight and get healthy, stay off the SOFAS.

The more you season your food, in general, the more you will eat, and this is not just true for salt. Anytime you use spices to season your food, you make it more hyper-palatable and increase your propensity to overeat it. For foods that you're having trouble eating at first, like vegetables, this may be a good thing. But for foods that you are already overeating, this may not work in your favor.

Now I'm not telling you to just eat everything plain, with absolutely no seasoning. I'm simply telling you to be aware that the more you embellish your food, the more food you will eat. When I started my *Ultimate Weight Loss* journey in January of 2012, I initially used lots of spices and seasoning to make it easier to choke down my morning pound of kale. I now find that I truly enjoy and appreciate the taste of even plain steamed zucchini and prefer to eat simpler foods, even unadorned vegetables. I can really taste the flavors now in whole natural food and I enjoy them immensely. This did not happen overnight. It took time for me to fully neuroadapt to the more subtle flavors of less stimulating foods. I really believe that the less you rely on your food to entertain you, the more excitement you may look for and find in other areas of your life. That will help the intense food cravings go away. I love how Andrew "Spud Fit" Taylor, the man who ate nothing but potatoes for an entire year and lost 120 pounds, says, "Keep your food boring and make your life interesting."

The eighth commandment is THOU SHALT NOT EAT AT NIGHT.

Unless you have plans to run a midnight marathon, there is no reason whatsoever that you need to eat after dinner. Calories eaten at night will be stored as fat because there's no way you'll be able to burn them. There's an old saying, "Eat breakfast like a king, lunch like a prince, and dinner like a pauper," and this is a great parable to live by for both health and weight loss. I have interviewed several medical doctors, including gastroenterologists, for my *YouTube* show *Healthy Living*, and they all concur that we need a minimum of three hours between our last swallow of food and lying down. Five hours, in fact, is even better, especially if you have any digestive issues such as gastroesophageal reflux disease. Some participants in the *UWL Program* who suffered from GERD and gave up eating at night have completely eliminated this disease and were able to stop taking their medication for it. Your digestive system needs this much time to rest. When you eat before bedtime, it's like trying to put gas into a car that already has a full tank.

When you stop eating into the night, you will find that you will also sleep more deeply and wake up feeling more refreshed. And, as a welcome surprise, you may find yourself actually hungry in the morning. Many people who struggle to lose the last few pounds utilize a technique called intermittent fasting, in which they narrow their eating window to about six to eight hours of the day. For example, one might eat one's first meal of the day at 11:00 a.m. or noon and eat dinner at 5:00 or 6:00 p.m., so that sixteen to eighteen hours of the day is spent fasting. You can find more information about intermittent fasting and how and why it works on the *TrueNorth* website: *www.healthpromoting.com.*

While many believe that weight loss is just a result of calories in versus calories out, the research now being done on this subject shows that calories consumed at night, even if within your caloric budget, are more likely to cause you to gain weight. Often people eat at night because they are seeking stimulation to stay awake to keep working. They confuse being tired with being hungry and what they really need is to go to sleep because what their body needs is rest. Any eating you do at night is not for hunger.

So why do so many people engage in nighttime eating? Well, this brings us to my next commandment.

The seventh commandment is THOU SHALT NOT EAT EMO-TIONALLY.

If hunger is not the problem, then food is not the solution. People eat for so many reasons other than hunger that many people have completely lost touch with the ability to even ascertain if they are hungry or not. And if you can't even tell when you're hungry, how will you ever know when you're full? People often eat because they are angry, anxious, bored, depressed, lonely, or stressed. One way to identify whether you're eating because of true hunger or for emotional reasons is to look at what type of food you choose to eat. If you're opting for a plain baked potato, then perhaps you really are hungry, but if you're reaching for the potato chips, probably not. If what you are hungry for is a hot fudge sundae, you can bet your last *Dorito* that you are eating for emotional reasons. True hunger can be quelled by eating any real food with nutrient value. Emotional hunger can only be alleviated by eating *particular* foods, usually with little or no nutritional value. That is why you will often hear me say to my clients, "If you're not hungry enough to eat vegetables, you're not hungry." Once you learn to deal with what is really eating you, it'll be far simpler to change what you're eating so that you can finally experience *Ultimate Weight Loss*.

The sixth Commandment is THOU SHALT EXERCISE.

Some people believe that they should not exercise while they are losing weight because it will deplete their willpower. Nothing could be further from the truth. Dr. Doug Lisle points out that exercising actually increases your willpower and thus your ability to stick with a healthy eating plan. Another benefit of exercise is that it actually raises your self-esteem. Dr. Lisle notes that the number one predictor of self-esteem in a female is her weight.

I don't recommend exercise as a primary means of weight loss because you can never outrun a poor diet. But regular exercise makes you feel better about yourself, which in turn makes you more likely to stick to *The Ultimate Weight Loss Program* and less likely to overeat. There are myriad other health benefits to exercise such as improved bone, brain, and cardiovascular health. It is also been shown to decrease anxiety and depression and greatly improve your mood. People who exercise sleep better at night and have less need for the stimulants, such as caffeine and sugar, that can thwart your weight loss efforts. And building muscle will make you appear even more fit and trim and allow you to burn more calories, even at rest. Research now shows that regular exercise can not only help prevent you from developing an addiction but actually can rewire the brain and help you overcome an addiction.

The fifth commandment is THOU SHALT NOT MAKE EXCUSES OR BUILD EXCEPTIONS.

I once heard someone say that you're either committed to the results you want or you're committed to your excuses and that you can't be committed to both. Excuses are just a justification or rationalization as to why you can't do something that you really don't want to do in the first place. Making excuses allows you to save face. There are really no alcoholics who want to stop drinking or smokers who want to stop smoking—more precisely, they don't want it enough to endure the agony of detoxification and withdrawal—and you often hear them say that they're going to quit *"tomorrow"* or someday in the future, when things are less stressful for them.

People who want to lose weight make the same excuses, especially when they relapse. Sure, it's difficult to make these positive dietary changes, but it is doable. It will only happen, though, if you stop making excuses about how hard it is, why you can't do it, and why this isn't the right time. There will never be a better time than right now. The road to someday always leads to never. As difficult as it is to make dietary changes, you will find that they become so much easier once you stop making excuses and, as the old saying goes, *"Just do it."* Whether it's eating vegetables for breakfast or beginning an exercise program, you don't have to like it, you just have to do it. But, guess what? Once you start seeing results and having that calm stable brain and the slender body you've always dreamed of, you actually learn to love both.

Exceptions are different than excuses but they can still impede your weight loss efforts and many people build exceptions into their weight loss program before they have achieved their goals. Then they wonder why they are having such difficulty in reaching them. Many people do a decent job eating at home but make exceptions when going to restaurants. Unfortunately, the amount of oil and salt in a single restaurant meal can derail your weight loss efforts. Making exceptions to go off-plan for special occasions like birthdays, anniversaries, vacations, and holidays is a near-guarantee of failure.

On *The Ultimate Weight Loss Program,* we recommend that you abstain from all drugs like alcohol and caffeine and any food-like substances like flour and sugar in all their insidious forms that have an addictive effect on many people. Many people cherry-pick the program—making exceptions for one food-like substance or another—and do only the parts they like and then wonder why they don't lose weight. For example, many people attempt to do the program while still indulging in a nightly glass of wine or their daily *Diet Coke* habit and then they wonder why they still have cravings and are overeating and not losing weight. Then they say that the program didn't work for them. But they never did the program as designed; they did their own loose interpretation of the program. So, my advice is that you do *The Ultimate Weight Loss Program* as designed for at least twenty-one days before you consider making any exceptions. Once you resolve to permanently make addictive substances like alcohol, caffeine, diet soda, flours, and sugars non-negotiables, it's much harder to make them exceptions.

The fourth commandment is THOU SHALT NOT ENGAGE WITH ENABLERS.

An enabler is a person who makes it easier for an addict to continue his or her self-destructive behavior. If you've ever watched the television show *My 600-lb Life*, you would understand that it would be very difficult for these people, many of whom have been bed-ridden for years, to continue with their self-destructive eating unless someone was continually providing them with the unhealthy food. Some of these enablers are actually out-and-out food bullies. They will say things like, "But I made it just for you," or, "C'mon, one bite won't hurt." (If you are a food addict, one bite, in fact, *will* hurt because the first bite is the only one that you have the power to resist).

While these food enablers may appear innocuous, and may even be your beloved, bespectacled grey-haired granny, they can actually do great harm, especially if you never call them on their behavior and explain to them how their "concern" and "well-meaning" ways are in fact hurting you. They can hurt you with the food they insist you eat, and they can also do a great deal of damage simply by the words they speak. They will often say things like "you're too thin," or will ridicule your dietary choices or repeatedly make you aware of your past dietary failures.

It would be extremely unlikely for someone to offer liquor to a person who they know to be a recovering alcoholic or to insist that they taste "just one sip." When this type of behavior is directed at someone suffering from a food addiction, it is every bit as detrimental. It is unlikely that you will be able to change these people, so you need to either disengage from them or find ways to co-exist without allowing them to drive you into a relapse. This can be very difficult because sadly, these people often are your friends, co-workers, or loved ones. Sometimes they are living in your home, which can make it very difficult for you to recover. When you lose weight and get healthy, it can be very threatening for them, especially if they are still overweight or have a lifestyle-related disease. It can be a simple case of misery loves company, or they may be afraid that if you recover and lose weight, you might leave them.

Sometimes working with a qualified therapist is the only way to resolve this problem. Most importantly, carefully choose the people you spend time with, and select people who are caring enough to be supportive.

The third commandment is THOU SHALT NOT ELIMINATE STARCH.

My obese brother, who was a medical doctor, probably weighed close to 300 pounds when he died, far too young, from the complications of his obesity. In the mid-80's, when I first encountered the work of Dr. McDougall, I sent my brother a copy of his book. He sent it back to me, unread, with a note attached that said, "I can't eat carbs, they make me fat." What I, of course, wanted to say to him but didn't because it would've been socially inappropriate, was, "But you're not eating carbs and you're still fat." My brother was a highly intelligent and conscientious person. In fact, he had a genius IQ and was valedictorian of his Princeton University graduating class. Unfortunately, intelligence alone is unlikely to be enough to help you to crawl out of the "pleasure trap" and stay out. And while most doctors are highly educated, they do not have the training to help you understand how to lose weight healthfully. Nutrition is not taught at most medical schools, so expecting your doctor to know anything about nutrition is like expecting your plumber to know something about quantum physics.

While the majority of your food volume can come from produce, at least three-quarters of your calories need to come from the satisfying starches, such as potatoes, sweet potatoes, winter squashes, whole grains (such as corn, oats and rice) and legumes (beans, peas and lentils). If you limit yourself to fruits and non-starchy vegetables you will be hungry and you'll stray to foods to the right of the red line, which will sabotage your weight loss efforts. This is not only one of *The Secrets to Ultimate Weight Loss* but the secret to satiety. Healthy unprocessed starches will keep you safely to the left of the red line while keeping your belly full and a smile on your face.

The second commandment is THOU SHALT EAT VEGETABLES FOR BREAKFAST.

As I've often heard Dr. Alan Goldhamer say, "Show me an overweight person, and I'll show you someone unwilling to eat enough raw salads and steamed vegetables." Many people completely eschew vegetables, but what I would like you to do instead is to *chew* vegetables. Vegetables are the food most correlated with losing weight and gaining health. So, if your weight loss has stalled, examine the amount of calorie dilute food you are eating relative to the amount of calorie dense food. If you keep the average calorie density of the food you eat per day to 567 calories per pound or less and are not overeating, you should be able to lose weight quite effortlessly. Think of it as nature's gastric bypass.

By eating vegetables for breakfast, you get your day off to a calorie-dilute start and help your taste buds get in the groove for a day of healthy eating.

The first and perhaps most important commandment is THOU SHALT COMPLETELY SANITIZE THY ENVIRONMENT.

By now, you are probably sick of hearing me say that your environment is the number one predictor of your success on *The Ultimate Weight Loss Program* and that if it's in your house it's in your mouth, and that it's not a question of if you will eat it, only when.

Now, I'm not saying that you won't have some success if you don't remove all the non-compliant foods from your home. But I've yet to have someone achieve their goal weight and easily maintain it when their environment did not support them. In order to succeed at all when your environment does not support you, you will have to work all the other aspects of the program a thousand times harder. I can honestly say, of *The Ultimate Weight Loss Program* participants who have lost 100 to 300 pounds and are keeping it off, all have pristine environments. They do not allow anyone to ever bring non-complaint food into their homes for any reason. Remember, your environment is anywhere that you are, and we can't always control all the environments that we spend time in. That is why it's crucial that at least your home is free of temptations. If you have non-compliant food in your house for any reason, then either on some level you want it there so that you can make your relapses easier and more justifiable, or you do not love and respect yourself enough to create an environment that is conducive to your recovery. Your environment either supports your recovery or it supports your addiction. It simply cannot do both.

I hope this book is a welcome addition to your environment. May it be the solution that you've been waiting for. I truly believe that you can have the health and the body that you so richly deserve, and I hope that the ideas expressed in the previous pages, and the recipes presented in the coming pages, help you achieve both.

Love and Kale,
Chef AJ

Recipes For Ultimate Weight Loss

E very recipe in this section is compatible with *The Ultimate Weight Loss Program* and free of sugar, oil, salt, flour, gluten, and nuts. The recipes that I created were tested on "regular people," in other words, those who were not following the *UWL Program* or even eating a health-promoting diet, and received two thumbs up. Where applicable, I have provided options to those who are making these recipes for others who are not following the *UWL Program*. You may notice that there are no pretty photos of food here. Being constantly bombarded with visual images of enticing food is not a good idea if you are trying to lose weight or recover from food addiction. For many food addicts, intense visual cues like these can trigger them to want to eat these foods, or at least make them unable to stop thinking about them. That is why I opted not to put photographs in this book.

NOTE: Eighteen of the over one hundred delicious recipes that follow use beans as an ingredient. Beans are one of the healthiest, most fiber- and protein-rich foods in the plant kingdom. They are eaten in all of the "Blue Zone" communities around the world associated with longevity. If you find that they give you gas, make sure to soak them overnight before cooking them, and then cook them with a one inch piece of kombu (a sea vegetable) to help increase their digestibility. If you are not used to eating fiber-rich foods in general, start with a small amount and work your way up. If you like to cook your beans from scratch, then, after soaking, either simmer them on the stove until tender (this can take two hours or more), or cook them in an *Instant Pot* electric pressure cooker (this takes ten to twenty minutes). If, for convenience, you prefer canned beans, try to buy BPA-free cans. Salt-free canned beans are widely available and preferred, but if you cannot find them, please make sure that you thoroughly rinse the beans before cooking to remove as much of the residual salt as possible.

You will do best on this program if you simply find a few meals that you enjoy and repeat them often. Do you really prepare thirty different breakfasts, thirty different lunches, and thirty different dinners each month? Or do you have a few favorites that you eat over and over? Variety is the kiss of death for the food addict and it encourages overeating. The less time you spend in the kitchen, the more time you have to meditate, work out, and create a vision board. Healthy and trim people who are not food addicted, like Dr. John McDougall and his wife Mary, tend to eat the same meals over and over. I have often heard him say how they eat the same breakfast every day (oatmeal and fruit), leftovers from the previous night's dinner for lunch, and a starch-based bean, grain, or potato dish for dinner. If you don't yet enjoy the taste of these foods, it is not because they are not delicious. It is because you have been eating so much sugar, fat, salt, processed foods or animal products that you are not yet able to enjoy their taste. The longer you have been eating these unhealthy foods, the longer it will take for health-promoting foods to taste good. But if you give it enough time, it will happen.

If you want variety, then vary the grain, the bean, and the type of vegetables. Did you know that there are over 18,000 different types of legumes? When preparing the *Mexican Stuffed Potato* (recipe page 174), switch it up by changing the type of legume you are using and the variety of potato. Change the grain, the bean, and the green. Use a different flavor vinegar or *Yummy Sauce* (recipe page 235). Instead of making recipes, cook food. Batch-cook grains and beans and freeze them in individual portions. Steam some vegetables and then eat your food in your favorite dish. I love the one-bowl method of eating. At each meal, fill your bowl with non-starchy vegetables so that it is at least one-half to two-thirds full. Then add a starch, or variety of starches like corn, beans, potatoes, rice, or sweet potatoes (or a soup or chili recipe made from these ingredients) and a sauce if you like. Have a piece of fruit or some fruit-only sorbet for dessert, brush your teeth, and call it a day.

My advice to you, especially if you are early in your recovery, is to make only *UWL* meals for your family, whether they need to lose weight or not. Put a salt shaker on the table and let them add salt if they must. If they want to add some higher fat foods like avocado, guacamole, or nuts to their salads or entrée, have them feel free to do so. And if they absolutely insist on adding animal products or other non-compliant food, then they are responsible for procuring and preparing them, and keeping them locked up and out of sight when not in use. Do not make separate meals. Serve everything buffet style and let them choose the foods they want. If you want them to eat healthy foods, then give them two choices: Take it or leave it. ☺

VFB Vegetables for Breakfast (or anytime)

These are my favorite non-starchy vegetable dishes. Not everyone can eat a pound of plain steamed vegetables in the morning, but don't be surprised if, after practicing *UWL* for a while, you may actually learn to enjoy them and eventually prefer them. After a grueling hour on the spin bike, my two pounds of steamed summer squash that I eat as my VFB taste like manna from heaven. But you never have to eat your veggies plain, or even steamed, if you don't want to. These recipes are delicious any time of day—yes, even for breakfast. They can be eaten alone as your VFB (Vegetables for Breakfast) or VBD (Vegetables Before Dinner), as snacks, side dishes to meals, incorporated into recipes like salads, and even cold as leftovers. Even if you now hate vegetables, once you see what they do for your figure and to diminish your sweet cravings, you will absolutely fall in love with them. The more you eat them, the more you will like them, and you will eventually crave them, and wonder how you managed to live without them for so long. Remember, we develop taste preferences for what we habitually eat, so the more you eat vegetables, the more you will prefer them.

In addition to weight loss and recovery from food addiction, another side effect of eating lots of non-starchy vegetables is beautiful glowing skin. I have the privilege of lecturing at five-star resorts like *Rancho La Puerta*. Guests often tell me that I have beautiful skin. I am almost sixty years old and have no discernible skin care routine. The only way I can account for this improvement in my complexion so late in life is my high intake of antioxidants from all the vegetables in my diet. I eat a minimum of four pounds a day, so I think it's reasonable to ask you to eat at least half of that, or two pounds per day. Do that and watch yourself literally become more beautiful from the inside out.

If you are still a card-carrying member of Veggie Haters Anonymous, then start out by eating salads or eat the vegetable that you hate the least. The non-starchy vegetables that are classified botanically as fruits, like tomatoes, bell peppers, and cucumbers, are delicious eaten raw or in salads and are often more palatable at first than the cruciferous vegetables or bitter greens. Keep in mind that if you have been eating most of your calories from animal products, processed food, or both, you have been on a diet that is virtually devoid of fiber. So, eating a pound of veggies first thing in the morning may give you gas. You may need to work up to eating that volume of vegetables. So, start out slowly and chew all of your food very well, or as Dr. Michael Klaper says, "to a cream.." Vegetables vary greatly in their ability to produce gas, so if you are prone to hearing a lower GI symphony when you eat them, eat those that are less gas producing at first. You can *Google* which vegetables are the most and least gas producing.

The secret to making vegetables delicious is roasting them. Roasting brings out the natural sweetness and makes food so much more flavorful. Don't believe me? Then simply microwave one sweet potato, roast another, put on a blindfold, taste them both, and see which one you prefer. The first recipe will show you my favorite way to roast vegetables. Remember to take your blindfold off before cooking.

BALSAMIC DIJON GLAZED ROASTED BRUSSELS SPROUTS

I always hated Brussels sprouts, that is, until I tasted this recipe given to me by my very own plant-based physician, Dr. Roy Artal (*www.drartal.com*). The funny thing is that I never liked mustard either, but in this recipe, I absolutely love it! This recipe is a real game changer when it comes to getting people to eat their non-starchy vegetables. The taste will vary depending on which brands of mustard and vinegar you use, so be sure to use brands you love, and always buy the best that you can afford. This marinade is delicious on other vegetables as well. So far, I have used it on broccoli, cauliflower, and white turnips, but the Brussels sprouts are by far my favorite. Make sure to cook as many trays as your oven will hold because two pounds of vegetables yield only about four cups of finished product, and since these taste just like candy, you will have no problem eating them all by yourself. These tasty tidbits are not only heavenly right out of the oven, but also at room temperature and even cold over a salad. This marinade is also delicious on starchy vegetables like cubed sweet potatoes or butternut squash. Always remember to be mindful when roasting vegetables of varying water content together as the ones with the higher water content will be done more quickly and could burn if you leave them in the oven until the denser vegetables are done. I recommend roasting vegetables of varying water content separately, or at least on different trays. You can watch Dr. Artal preparing this recipe on Episode 7 of my television show *Healthy Living with Chef AJ*, which you can find on *Foody TV* and now on *YouTube* as well.

INGREDIENTS:

2 pounds of Brussels sprouts (or any vegetable, for that matter)
4 Tablespoons of salt-free mustard (or your favorite low-sodium Dijon mustard)
4 Tablespoons of your favorite balsamic vinegar

PREPARATION:

Preheat oven to 400 degrees F.

Trim the ends off two pounds of Brussels sprouts and cut in half or fourths (depending on how large they are). The important thing when roasting vegetables is that you make each piece roughly the same size. The smaller you cut them, the faster they will cook.

Place the vegetables in a large bowl and add ¼ cup each of your favorite mustard and balsamic vinegar. Mix well until the veggies are completely coated.

Roast on a large baking tray covered with a non-stick silicone baking mat for at least 30 minutes, stirring every 10-15 minutes. If your Brussels sprouts are quite large or you prefer them crispier or more blackened, roast them up to 30 minutes longer or until they are cooked the way that you like them. The more vegetables that you have on the tray, the longer they will take to roast. If you are cooking more than one tray at a time, which I wholeheartedly recommend that you do, rotate the trays every 15-30 minutes. Make sure you also stir the vegetables every 10-15 minutes.

CHEF'S NOTE:

A thick and syrupy reduced balsamic vinegar that contains only 4% acidity instead of 6%, like *Napa Valley Naturals Grand Reserve*, is preferred. I use a salt-free stoneground mustard made by *Westbrae*. You can cut down on the cooking time of roasted vegetables by cooking them in an Air Fryer.

CHILI FRIES

These are often served at the lunch salad bar at *Rancho La Puerta* where I have had the privilege of presenting many times. You can flavor them any way you like. Here is my favorite way.

INGREDIENTS:

Jicama
Lime Juice
Salt-free chili powder* (I prefer a mild blend)
SMOKED paprika (different than regular paprika)

PREPARATION:

Slice jicama into French fry shapes. It's great to use a crinkle cutter. Or buy pre-sliced jicama. Douse with lime juice and sprinkle with equal amounts of salt-free chili powder and SMOKED paprika. If you like it extra spicy, you can also sprinkle them with a dash of chipotle powder.

CHEF'S NOTE:

*When using any spice blends, in other words, seasonings that contain more than one spice, be sure that you actually like the blend you are using in the recipe. Spice blends like chili powder vary greatly in their heat and intensity, so if yours is particularly strong, you may have to use less. I like the *Whole Foods* brand of chili powder because it is relatively mild and both salt and black pepper free. My friend Shayda, on the other hand, prefers the *Chili 9000* made by *Penzey's* because it has quite a kick. Anytime you are using other spice blends like apple pie spice, curry powder, poultry seasoning (the unfortunate name of a vegan spice blend), or pumpkin pie spice, which are featured in the recipes in this book, please taste them before cooking with them to be sure you like them. No two brands are alike. I was doing a demonstration of my *Almost Instant Apple Pie Rice Pudding* (recipe page 137) at a conference and the Apple

Pie Spice was from a local company I had never heard of. It contained a spice called fenugreek, which has no business being put in a sweet dish. Needless to say, it ruined the recipe and no one would eat it! Lesson learned. Always taste your spice blends before using them in recipes.

Please remember that the taste of individual spices like cinnamon, smoked paprika, and chipotle powder, to name a few, also vary widely by brand, so be sure to use one you really enjoy. All of my recipes that call for smoked paprika taste completely different with regular paprika so please keep that in mind, especially when making recipes that are salt-free. Always make sure that your spices are fresh.

ENLIGHTENED FAUX PARMESAN

If you are struggling to eat your VFB, try this tasty topping. It's really delicious over steamed veggies. I especially love it over broccoli or cauliflower. The *Faux Parmesan* from my book, *Unprocessed*, was made from a cup of walnuts, and while delicious, was very high in fat. Using oats instead of nuts makes this low-fat topping delicious and economical. Be sure to keep some on hand to sprinkle over soups and chili.

INGREDIENTS:

1 cup of gluten-free oats
1 cup of nutritional yeast
1 Tablespoon of *Benson's Table Tasty* (or your favorite salt-free seasoning)

PREPARATION:

Place all ingredients in a blender or food processor fitted with the "S" blade and process into a powder. Store in the refrigerator. You can watch me making this on Episode 11 of *Healthy Living with Chef AJ*.

CHEF'S NOTE:

You can make many different and delicious varieties of this topping by adding ingredients like chipotle powder, jalapeño powder, smoked paprika, or sun-dried tomato powder.

Many of my recipes in *Unprocessed* can be made lower in fat by substituting either beans or grains for all or some of the nuts.

LIP-SMACKING, MOUTHWATERING KALE

Someone who is clearly unfamiliar with my *Ultimate Weight Loss Program* once said that I force people to eat steamed kale for breakfast and drink the water. While I do recommend saving the water from your steamed greens for making broth, and drinking it if you enjoy it (it is called pot liquor in the South and is actually quite delicious), you never have to eat plain steamed veggies unless you want to and enjoy them that way. Dr. Esselstyn recommends that his cardiac patients eat greens six times a day, and this dish may make a kale lover out of you yet!

INGREDIENTS:

10 ounces of chopped onions (approximately 3 cups)
10 ounces of sliced mushrooms (approximately 5 cups)
10 ounces of Tuscan kale, shredded or chopped into bite-sized pieces (approximately 12 cups)
4 cloves of fresh garlic, minced or put through a garlic press, more or less to taste

PREPARATION:

In a large sauté pan, water sauté or dry sauté your onion, depending on your cookware, until translucent and nicely browned. I prefer to take my time so that the onion becomes caramelized and becomes very sweet. Add the garlic and then the mushrooms and cook until they become limp and nicely browned and all the water has evaporated. Depending on your cookware, you may need to add some liquid (water or no-sodium veggie broth) a tablespoon at a time so that your ingredients don't stick to the pan. Remember to stir frequently. Add the kale and cook until it reaches your desired level of doneness. I prefer it less cooked so it retains some of its crispness and its bright green color. If your sauté pan has a lid, you can cover it after you add the kale and cook it that way. Enjoy immediately.

CHEF'S NOTE:

This dish is so flavorful from the onions and garlic that, in my opinion, it requires no further seasonings. That said, please always feel free to make every dish your own, and season it according to your mood and palate. A squeeze of fresh lemon or lime juice is always a wonderful way to finish any dish that contains greens, as is a drizzle of a good quality reduced balsamic vinegar like *Bema and Pa's Smoke Infused, Garlic Cilantro or White Garlic*. I actually prefer mixing equal amounts of lime juice and balsamic vinegar. Dried oregano is very tasty sprinkled over this dish, and for those of you who enjoy spicy foods, some crushed red pepper flakes make a nice addition. This also makes a delicious filling for the *Mexican Stuffed Potato* (recipe page 174).

OVEN ROASTED RATATOUILLE

If you watched the presentation (available on *YouTube*), *From Fat Vegan to Skinny Bitch*, that I gave at *The McDougall Advanced Study Weekend*, you may remember that I grew up living with my aunt, whose mother was a graduate of the *Cordon Bleu*. She often made ratatouille, which I loved the taste of, but not the texture. This recipe captures all of the flavors of the traditional French dish with a texture that is more pleasing to my palate and is very versatile. *Ratatouille* is not only my favorite animated movie but is now my favorite breakfast!

INGREDIENTS:

¾ pound zucchini
¾ pound yellow summer squash (Crookneck)
½ pound Chinese eggplant
½ pound cherry tomatoes, halved
1 red bell pepper, diced large
1 red onion, diced large

PREPARATION:

Preheat oven to 400 degrees F.

Slice the squash and eggplant uniformly, about ¼ inch thick. Place on a large baking tray covered with a non-stick silicone baking mat. Sprinkle bell pepper, tomatoes, and onion over the top. Roast for one hour, stirring every 10-15 minutes, or until your desired level of doneness is reached. Sprinkle with your favorite dried herbs before roasting, if desired. Italian seasoning and Herb de Provence are excellent, but this recipe is so insanely delicious that it doesn't even need any additional seasonings. When using fresh herbs, add them to the dish after cooking. Ribbons of fresh basil or finely chopped Italian parsley are my personal favorites. It is also great with a drizzle of balsamic vinegar over it. This is not only great as a stand-alone dish, but also delicious over Zoodles (spiralized zucchini noodles), brown or wild rice, and chilled over a salad.

CHEF'S NOTE:

You can watch me making this on Episode 8 of *Healthy Living with Chef AJ.*

SALAD SMOOTHIE

As weird as it sounds, this tastes delicious. Truth is, not everyone has time to eat a salad, especially for breakfast. And while we don't recommend fruit smoothies for weight loss and satiety, when made only from non-starchy veggies they are a great way to get all your produce in without all the chewing. Especially handy if you're having dental work!

INGREDIENTS:

2 pounds raw non-starchy salad vegetables
(I like to use 8 ounces of spinach, 8 ounces of tomatoes, 8 ounces of zucchini and 8 ounces of cucumber)
2 Tablespoons lime juice (or your favorite dressing)

PREPARATION: Place all ingredients in a high powered blender and blend until smooth. Leave some texture if desired.

ZOODLES WITH QUICK SUN-DRIED TOMATO MaRAWnara

Did you know that there may be more sugar in a ½ cup serving of pasta sauce from a jar than there is in two *Oreo* Cookies? Please don't buy commercial pasta sauce (or any processed foods for that matter), especially when this sauce is so simple to prepare quickly. It takes just minutes to make yet tastes like it was slowly simmered for hours, and the best part is, there are no pots to clean or anything to cut up! As much as I love roasted vegetables, there are some days, like when it's 100 degrees in the San Fernando Valley, that I just don't want to turn the oven on.

INGREDIENTS:

1 pound zucchini
¾ cup sun-dried tomatoes (oil and salt free), about 3 ounces, soaked in water, to cover
3-4 fresh Roma tomatoes (approximately 12 ounces)
1 red bell pepper, seeded (approximately 8 ounces)
1 - 2 cloves of garlic, peeled (or more to taste)
One shallot (approximately 1 ounce) or red onion equivalent
6-8 fresh basil leaves (or more to taste)
¼ - ½ teaspoon red pepper flakes (optional)

PREPARATION:

You can easily make zoodles (zucchini noodles) by making ribbons from the zucchini, using an inexpensive vegetable peeler, or you can use a vegetable spiralizer.

Cover the sun-dried tomatoes with water and let soak. You will use the soak water in this recipe. In a blender, blend all ingredients until smooth. If you have a high-powered blender, you can make this sauce hot right in the blender; otherwise, you will have to heat it up on the stove on low heat if you prefer it warm. However, this dish is delicious even cold or at room temperature. If you prefer a chunkier consistency, then use a food processor fitted with the "S" blade and process all the ingredients until desired consistency is reached. Serve over zoodles.

CHEF'S NOTE:

When serving this to guests, I always peel the zucchini so that it looks more like real pasta. When making it for myself I leave the peel on as there is lots of fiber in the skin. When the sauce is heated, it softens the zucchini but you could also blanch the zucchini if you like.

My original recipe for this sauce called for 3-4 pitted Deglet Noor dates or 1-2 Medjool dates (approximately one ounce of dates). The dates were used to help balance the acidity of the tomatoes. You could also use a piece of apple, beet, or carrot. Many *UWL* participants make it without the dates and enjoy it. If dates are a trigger food for you and you cannot even have them in the house, please do not use them in this or any recipe. If making this recipe for other people not following *The Ultimate Weight Loss Program*, you can buy a few dates in the bulk bin and use them just for this recipe. (Just blend them in with the sauce.) People vary in how vulnerable they are to food addiction and some are able to use a few dates in a savory recipe without experiencing any cravings, and others are not. Know your personal triggers and always avoid them. This dish tastes incredible topped with the *Oven Roasted Ratatouille* (recipe page 130) and sprinkled with *Enlightened Faux Parmesan* (recipe page 127).

You can watch me make this on Episode 11 of *Healthy Living with Chef AJ.*

"Second Breakfast"

Remember how the Hobbits always ate second breakfast? Well, on the *UWL Program*, you can too! If all you eat is vegetables for breakfast, you will most assuredly be hungry very soon. I simply cannot express how important it is that you eat ample starch, or you will never feel satisfied with your food. While, visually, your plate of food should contain at least ½ to ⅔ vegetables, the majority of your calories must come from unrefined complex carbohydrates like potatoes, rice, and beans. Many people like to eat oatmeal after their veggies but I prefer to eat a roasted Japanese sweet potato. If you do enjoy oats, instead of rolled oats (good), consider trying steel cut (better) or whole oat groats (best). Here are a few second breakfast options that you're sure to enjoy.

ALMOST INSTANT APPLE PIE RICE PUDDING

I love homemade rice pudding but it can take almost an hour for the rice to cook. Using the *Instant Pot* and leftover rice it takes only five minutes!

INGREDIENTS:

4 cups leftover cooked rice (I prefer organic brown *Texmati)*
4 cups finely chopped apples (2-4 depending on their size; use a sweet variety)
3 cups unsweetened non-dairy milk
1 Tablespoon Apple Pie Spice* (or 2.5 teaspoons of cinnamon plus ½ teaspoon nutmeg)
½ teaspoon vanilla powder
¼ teaspoon ground cardamom

PREPARATION:

Place all ingredients in the *Instant Pot* and cook on high pressure for 5 minutes. Release pressure and enjoy hot, or chill for a firmer texture. If you don't have a pressure cooker, then bring the plant milk and spices to a boil. Be careful not to let it boil over. Add the remaining ingredients and return to a boil. Reduce heat and cover. Simmer for about 10 minutes or until most of the liquid is absorbed.

CHEF'S NOTE:

This is delicious served hot, warm, or cold, and is a delightful replacement for your usual oatmeal. If you are making this dish for those not following the *UWL Program,* or if you are at your goal weight and dried fruit is not a trigger for you, add 1 cup of golden raisins.

*concerning spice blends, please read my note under *Chili Fries, p.125.*

ANYTIME OATS

When I travel, which is just about every week, I take these with me. Simply fill a small *Ziploc* bag with the oats and cinnamon and bring a single serving box of unsweetened non-dairy milk with you. Depending on where and how you are traveling, you can't always bring fruit with you, but you can certainly find fruit at your destination. I bring one serving for every day that I am away and it has saved me from being hungry many times.

INGREDIENTS:

½ cup gluten-free oats
½ cup unsweetened non-dairy milk
1 large apple, grated
½ teaspoon cinnamon or more to taste

PREPARATION:

Mix all ingredients in a large bowl. Enjoy immediately or refrigerate and enjoy the next day. This will keep for up to 24 hours. Feel free to substitute another fruit for the apple, such as banana, peach, pear, or pomegranate seeds.

If you are concerned about getting enough Omega 3 fatty acids, add a tablespoon of ground flax seeds or chia seeds. For those not following the *UWL Program*, add 2 table-spoons of currants. If it is still not sweet enough for them, you can add unsweetened apple juice in place of some or all the non-dairy milk.

CHEF'S NOTE:

Any leftovers can be made into *Apple Jack Crackers* (recipe page 271).

APPLE PIE SQUARES

You can slice these into 8 squares or 16 triangles. These are great with a cup of herbal tea. You could even serve them as a dessert with some *Apple Pie Ice Cream* on top (recipe page 259). Hard to believe it's legal!

INGREDIENTS:

4 cups chopped apples (2-4 depending on their size; use a sweet variety)
1 and ½ cups of unsweetened applesauce
6 Tablespoons ground flax seed
½ teaspoon vanilla powder
1 Tablespoon Apple Pie spice* (or 2.5 teaspoons of cinnamon plus ½ teaspoon nutmeg)
2 cups gluten-free oats
½ cup ground millet

PREPARATION:

Preheat oven to 350 degrees F.

Mix all ingredients together and pour into a 9-inch square silicone baking dish and bake for 30-35 minutes. Let cool before slicing and chill for the best texture.

CHEF'S NOTE:

If you do not wish to use ground millet, you can substitute an additional ½ cup of oats instead.

If you are making this dish for those not following the *UWL Program,* or if you are at your goal weight and dried fruit is not a trigger for you, add 2 ounces of dried apples (approximately 1 cup), snipped into small pieces.

You can watch me making this on Episode 11 of *Healthy Living with Chef AJ.*

*concerning spice blends, please read my note under *Chili Fries, p.125.*

BLUEBERRY MILL-OAT MUFFINS

These are so filling that they can be a meal unto themselves. I always take them with me when I travel and they freeze well. I highly recommend you invest in a silicone muffin pan if you are going to make these.

INGREDIENTS:

2 cups Japanese sweet potatoes, roasted and mashed
2 large VERY RIPE bananas
3 cups gluten-free oats, left whole
1 cup millet, ground
½ teaspoon vanilla powder
2 teaspoons cinnamon
½ teaspoon nutmeg
¼ teaspoon cardamom
16 ounces frozen wild blueberries (the small ones)

PREPARATION:

Mix all ingredients together except for frozen blueberries until well combined. Gently fold in the blueberries. Evenly distribute the batter into twelve muffins, using a silicone muffin pan. Bake for 40-45 minutes. Let cool completely before removing from muffin pan.

CHEF'S NOTE:

I prefer to use the Japanese sweet potatoes in this dish because of their color, distinctive flavor, and their denser, starchier texture. I find the orange yams too wet. You can substitute frozen cherries, mango, or pineapple, alone or in combination, for some or all the blueberries. Because cherries are so much larger than blueberries, I chop them with my Ulu blade. I LOVE making these muffins half-pineapple and half-cherry.

If you do not wish to use ground millet, you can substitute an additional cup of oats instead.

CLAFOUTI

As I always say, if you don't want a big booty, skip the donut and eat *Clafouti*!

INGREDIENTS:

1 pound strawberries
1 pound ripe bananas (approximately 3)
1 - 10-ounce jar of fruit-only sweetened jam (or use *Chia Jam* recipe page 213)
2 cups gluten-free oats
1 teaspoon sodium-free baking powder
½ cup unsweetened applesauce
1 cup unsweetened non-dairy milk

PREPARATION:

Preheat oven to 350 degrees F. Slice fruit and mix well with jam. Place in an 8" x 8" silicone pan. Mix remaining ingredients in a bowl and place evenly over fruit. Bake for 45-50 minutes until golden brown.

CHEF'S NOTE:

If this is not sweet enough for family members who are not following the *UWL Program*, substitute unsweetened apple juice for the non-dairy milk.

You can watch me making this on Episode 5 of *Healthy Living with Chef AJ*.

CRAM MUFFINS

These muffins were created as an homage to a dear friend and one of the smartest people I know, Dr. Doug Lisle, who along with Dr. Goldhamer and Dr. McDougall is responsible for teaching me how to become a skinny bitch! He presented some groundbreaking information on bingeing and night eating at the LIVE Vegas *Ultimate Weight Loss* conference in Las Vegas, which he called the Cram Circuit. If people were going to eat at night, I wanted to create something that would be satisfying and wouldn't derail their weight loss effort. And since his favorite dessert is carrot cake, I thought these would help folks who cave to the crave without feeling guilty.

CRAM also stands for Carrot, Raisin, Apple, and Millet.

INGREDIENTS:

3 cups of gluten-free rolled oats
1 cup of unsweetened applesauce
½ cup of ground millet
3 cups of banana purée (made from 4-5 VERY RIPE bananas depending on their size)
4 cups loosely packed raw shredded carrots (about 8 ounces)
4 cups finely chopped apples (about 2-4 apples; use a sweet variety)
1 Tablespoon Apple Pie or Pumpkin Pie Spice* (or 2.5 teaspoons cinnamon and ½ teaspoon ground nutmeg)
½ Tablespoon aluminum-free and sodium-free baking powder
½ Tablespoon sodium-free baking soda
1 Tablespoons apple cider vinegar
1 teaspoon vanilla powder (optional)
½ cup raisins or dried currants (optional)

PREPARATION:

Preheat oven to 350 degrees F.

In a food processor fitted with the "S" blade, purée the ripe bananas. Add the baking powder, baking soda, apple cider vinegar and vanilla powder, if using. Transfer to a large bowl and stir in the remaining ingredients. Mix well until fully incorporated. Divide the mixture among 2 twelve cup silicone muffin pans. Bake for 40-45 minutes until tops are browned. Turn oven off and open the door, allowing the muffins to cool completely in the oven.

CHEF'S NOTE:

If you do not wish to use millet, simply use an additional ½ cups of oats. I prefer to use dried currants over raisins as they are smaller but disperse better. Each muffin will only contain the equivalent of one teaspoon of raisins; however, if dried fruit is a trigger for you, please don't buy it or use it. As there are no dates in this recipe, the sweetness of your muffins will depend on how ripe your bananas are and which variety of apples you use. I always use the sweetest variety of apple available and finely chop them using the food processor fitted with the "S" blade, leaving the peel on, if organic.

concerning spice blends, please read my note under *Chili Fries*, p.125

CRISPY BREAKFAST TATERS

A *Crisp-Ease* tray makes this super crispy without oil and without having to stir them. We love these so much we sometimes have them for dinner.

INGREDIENTS:

Your favorite potato
A red onion
Your favorite seasonings (like *Benson's Table Tasty*, dried parsley, or even no seasoning at all)

PREPARATION:

Preheat oven to 425 degrees F. Cut the potatoes as small as possible and the onion 3-4 times as large as the potatoes because they cook faster and otherwise they will burn. Sprinkle with seasoning, if using. Roast on a *Crisp-Ease* tray or baking tray covered with a non-stick silicone baking mat for at least 30 minutes or until they are as crisp as you like them.

CHEF'S NOTE:

Serve these as part of a kale bowl, with steamed kale, roasted corn, beans, and salsa.

Serve with the *Compliant Ketchup* (recipe page 215) or *Straight up Ketchup* (recipe page 232).

FRUIT COBBLER

Dessert for breakfast? When it's made of just fruit and oats, why not? Right after your vegetables, that is. ☺

INGREDIENTS:

2 pounds of frozen fruit (I like to use mango or sweet cherries or a combination of the two)
2 cups of gluten-free oats (I like to use the extra thick cut)
1 cup of banana purée (made from 10 ounces of very ripe bananas)
2 teaspoons of cinnamon
¼ teaspoon nutmeg
⅛ teaspoon cardamom

PREPARATION:

Preheat oven to 350 degrees F.

In a small bowl, mix the oats and spices. Next, in a blender, purée the bananas. Pour over the two cups of oats and mix until fully incorporated. In a 9" silicone baking pan, place the frozen fruit. Cover with the topping and bake for 40-45 minutes. You can also place this in the dehydrator instead for 4-6 hours.

CHEF'S NOTE:

This is delicious hot right out of the oven, with or without *Cherub Sauce* (recipe page 212). This makes an incredible dessert when served warm with banana "soft serve."

JUST BANANAS MUFFINS

It's bananas that these are just bananas!

INGREDIENTS:

8 VERY RIPE bananas
4 cups oats
1 cup unsweetened non-dairy milk
1 cup unsweetened applesauce
2 teaspoons ground cinnamon
½ teaspoon vanilla powder
1 Tablespoon apple cider vinegar
1 Tablespoon aluminum-free and sodium-free baking powder
1 teaspoon sodium-free baking soda

PREPARATION:

Preheat oven to 350 degrees F.

Place all of the dry ingredients in a large bowl. Purée bananas in a food processor fitted with the "S" blade until smooth. Add the non-dairy milk and applesauce and process again until combined. Pour over dry ingredients and mix until just combined. Do not over mix. Evenly distribute the batter into twelve muffins using a silicone muffin pan. Bake for 40-45 minutes until a toothpick inserted in the center comes out clean.

CHEF'S NOTE:

For blueberry banana muffins, gently fold in 2 cups of wild blueberries. If this is not sweet enough for family members not following the *UWL Program*, substitute 1 cup of unsweetened apple juice for the non-dairy milk.

OATMEAL COOKIES

Cookies for breakfast? With ingredients like these, heck yeah!

INGREDIENTS:

8 very ripe bananas
3.5 cups gluten-free oats
1 Tablespoon cinnamon
½ teaspoon vanilla powder

PREPARATION:

Mash bananas. Stir in the remainder of ingredients. Using a retractable cookie scoop (or a ¼ cup measuring cup) scoop batter and place on a *Silpat* or non-stick silicone baking mat on a cookie sheet. Bake in a preheated 350-degree oven. Bake for 30 minutes or until the tops of the cookies are no longer sticky. Gently flip over and bake for an additional 10 minutes. Let cool. Makes about 24 cookies and 3 cookies are the equivalent of 1 banana and less than ½ cup of oats! You can also prepare these in a food dehydrator.

CHEF'S NOTE:

If making these for family members not following the *UWL Program* or if you are at goal weight and dried fruit is not a trigger for you, add 1 cup of raisins.

RisOATto

I competed in an *Iron Chef* competition and was given instant oats and mushrooms as two of the secret ingredients and came up with this savory oat dish that has the texture of a rice risotto but can be made in a fraction of the time. If you are trying to overcome a sugar addiction, it's best to always start your day in a SAVORY way.

INGREDIENTS:

2 cups of INSTANT Steel Cut Oats
4 cups of no-sodium vegetable broth or water
1 large clove of garlic, pressed (or more to taste)
¾ cup sun-dried tomatoes (oil and salt free), cut into small pieces, about 3 ounces
1 ounce of dried mushrooms, chopped into small pieces
1 ounce of fresh basil, chiffonade cut
1 cup of whole leaf dulse (optional) – I get the smoked *Applewood Dulse* at *www.seaveg.com.*

PREPARATION:

Place all ingredients except for the basil in a medium-sized pot and bring to a boil. Reduce heat to a simmer, cover and cook for approximately 10 minutes until all the liquid is absorbed and oats are cooked. Stir in the fresh basil and dulse, if using, and enjoy!

CHEF'S NOTE:

You can dehydrate this for delicious crunchy *Savory Crackers* (recipe page 277) that are great for travel.

If you are following a strictly salt-free diet, it's a good idea to include sea vegetables, which are high in iodine, in your diet in small amounts a few times a week.

Enticing Entrees

ACORN SQUASH WITH WILD RICE STUFFING

This always appears at my Thanksgiving table to rave reviews.

INGREDIENTS:

4 acorn squashes
Wild rice stuffing with apples (recipe page 152)

PREPARATION:

Cook the acorn squash according to your preferred method. I cook them individually in the *Instant Pot* electric pressure cooker by placing them on the rack with water up to the rack and cook them on high pressure for 10 minutes with a 10-minute natural pressure release. Then cut in half and remove seeds and set aside. You could also cut the squash in half, remove the seeds, and roast them in a preheated 400-degree F oven on a non-stick silicone baking mat, cut side down, for about an hour. Stuff each squash with the *Wild Rice Stuffing with Apples* (recipe page 152), making a rounded mound over the top. Bake in a preheated 400-degree F oven for 30 minutes until rice starts to get a bit crunchy. If there is any filling leftover, place it in a baking dish and bake it at the same time as the squash. Remove the squashes from the oven and drizzle each one with a reduced balsamic vinegar. *Napa Valley Naturals Grand Reserve* and *Bema and Pa's Pumpkin Pie Spice* infused are good choices.

WILD RICE STUFFING WITH APPLES

This would make a delicious stuffing for Thanksgiving even if you weren't making the squash.

INGREDIENTS:

1 cup of finely chopped onion
1 cup of finely chopped celery
1 cup of finely chopped carrots
6 cloves garlic, minced
1 cup of finely chopped Italian parsley
1 teaspoon of poultry seasoning*
4 cups of cooked wild rice (recipe page 241)
2 cups of grated apple (I prefer *Gala* or *Envy*)

PREPARATION:

Water sauté the onions, celery, carrots and garlic until onion is translucent and the carrots are soft. Depending on how small you chop them, this could take 15-20 minutes. Stir in the grated apple and poultry seasoning and cook for another minute or two. Add the parsley and cooked wild rice and stir until well combined. Serve with *CranPEARry Relish* (recipe page 216).

CHEF'S NOTE:

You can buy celery, onion, and carrot together already cut up at many stores such as Trader Joe's. It is called *mirepoix*.

My original recipe called for 1 cup of dried dark sweet cherries, unsweetened and unsulfured (cut in half if large). *Trader Joe's* sells these in 6-ounce bags. If the occasional use of dried fruit is not a trigger for you, or if you are making this recipe for "the others," feel free to add it. If you are not at your goal weight, please remember that dried food is still calorically dense, approximately 1300 calories per pound as opposed to fresh fruit, which is only 300 calories per pound.

*concerning spice blends, please read my note under *Chili Fries, p.125.*

ALL-STAR TOSTADAS

This is made from only vegetables but tastes like chorizo! Guaranteed to be a fiesta in your mouth. Makes approximately 8 cups of filling.

INGREDIENTS:

10 ounces of chopped onions (about 3 cups)

10 ounces of sliced mushrooms (about 5 cups)

16 ounces of riced cauliflower**

6 garlic cloves, minced or pressed in a garlic press, more or less, to taste

2 - 14.5-ounce cans *Muir Glen Salt-Free Fire Roasted Tomatoes*

2 Tablespoons tomato paste

2 Tablespoons salt-free chili powder* (I like the *Whole Foods* brand, it's pepper free and not too spicy)

½ Tablespoon SMOKED paprika (different than regular paprika)

½ Tablespoon ground cumin

1 teaspoon dried oregano

½ teaspoon chipotle powder

¼ teaspoon crushed red pepper flakes

PREPARATION:

In a large sauté pan, water sauté or dry sauté your onion, depending on your cookware, until translucent and nicely browned. I prefer to take my time so that the onion becomes caramelized and becomes very sweet. Add the garlic and then the mushrooms and cook until they become limp and nicely browned and all the water has evaporated. Depending on your cookware, you may need to add some liquid (water or no-sodium veggie broth) a tablespoon at a time so that your ingredients don't stick to the pan. Remember to stir frequently. Break the mushrooms up into smaller pieces with your wooden spoon. Add the remaining ingredients and bring to a boil. Reduce heat and cook over medium heat until the cauliflower is soft. This should take 10-15 minutes, depending on how high of a heat setting you use.

ASSEMBLY:

This healthy "chorizo-like" filling has multiple uses. It can be the base of a tostada, taco, taquito or burrito or eaten over a salad. It is also a delicious filling for a baked potato. We like to serve them as a do-it-yourself-meal and have each person make their own. In addition to the shells and the tortilla filling on the "tostada bar," I also have the *Almost Instant Mexi-Cali Rice* (recipe page 239), *Chili-Lime Slaw* (recipe page 169), *Easy Chipotle Corn Salsa* (recipe page 218) and the *Sweet Pea Guacamole* (from *Unprocessed*) and sliced jalapeño peppers. *Muy sabroso, amigos!*

CHEF'S NOTE:

If you want to make outstanding taquitos, place 2 tablespoons of the *Almost Instant Mexi-Cali Rice* and 2 Tablespoons of the "chorizo-like" filling on a corn tortilla. Roll up and place seam side down on a *Crisp-Ease* tray and bake at 400 degrees for 15-20 minutes until crisp.

You can make baked oil-free tostada shells using my recipe in *Unprocessed*. On *Amazon* you can find molds to make decorative tostada shells or taco shells.

*concerning spice blends, please read my note under *Chili Fries*, p.125.

**riced cauliflower is sold in the refrigerator or freezer section of many stores. If you cannot find it, simply rice the cauliflower yourself using a food processor fitted with the shredding blade.

THE BEST "NO BEAN" BURGERS

I have a dear friend who was born allergic to legumes and really wanted a good bean burger recipe. Using the *Chipotle Bean Burger* recipe (page 161) as my inspiration, I came up with this one. They look and taste virtually identical to the bean version. You may like them even better.

INGREDIENTS:

4 cups cooked BLACK rice
4 cups cooked and mashed sweet potato (the denser Hannah Yams are preferred to the mushy orange ones)
1 - 14.5-ounce can *Muir Glen Salt-Free Fire Roasted Tomatoes*
1 cup red onion, chopped
8 cloves garlic, minced
1 red bell pepper, finely chopped (approximately 1 cup)
1 large carrot, finely chopped (approximately 1 cup)
1 bunch cilantro, finely chopped
12 Tablespoons nutritional yeast
4 Tablespoon no-salt-added chili powder*
1 Tablespoon ground cumin
1 Tablespoon SMOKED paprika (different than regular paprika)
1 teaspoon chipotle powder

PREPARATION:

Preheat the oven to 400 degrees F.

Drain the can of tomatoes and sauté the onion in the liquid from the canned tomatoes until soft. You can purée the tomatoes in a food processor fitted with the "S" blade or leave them whole. Add the chopped carrot, bell pepper, and garlic and sauté until soft and cooked, about 10-15 minutes. Combine all ingredients in a large bowl and stir to mix. I prefer to use latex free food service gloves. Chill several hours or overnight. Make individual patties out of ½ cup of the mixture. Place patties on a baking tray covered with a non-stick silicone baking mat, and bake for 30-45 minutes until you are able to flip them over very easily without them sticking. After you flip them, bake for another 20-30 minutes. Makes 12-16 burgers. These freeze very well.

CHEF'S NOTE:

I like to serve these on *Potato Waffles* (recipe page 179) as "buns" or in large leaves of Bibb lettuce as buns with all the traditional burger fixings like onion, tomato, pickles and mustard. These freeze well.

*concerning spice blends, please read my note under *Chili Fries, p.125.*

BLACK BEAN MUSHROOM CHILI

Adapted from and inspired by a recipe by Jocelyn Graef of the *Low-Fat Herbivore*.

INGREDIENTS:

10 ounces of chopped onions (about 3 cups)
8 cloves garlic, minced or pressed through a garlic press
2 pounds of mushrooms, sliced (I just use 3 - 10-ounce bags of pre-sliced mushrooms from *Trader Joe's*)
2 - 14.5-ounce cans *Muir Glen Salt-Free Fire Roasted Tomatoes*
3 - 15-ounce cans of salt-free black beans (or 4.5 cups of cooked beans)
One pound frozen corn, defrosted
1 Tablespoon ground cumin
1 Tablespoon dried oregano
½ Tablespoon SMOKED paprika (different than regular paprika)
½ teaspoon chipotle powder

PREPARATION:

Place all ingredients except for corn in an electric pressure cooker and cook on high pressure for 6 minutes. Release pressure and stir in corn. If you have the eight-quart *Instant Pot*, you can put all of the ingredients in at once. Sprinkle with *Enlightened Faux Parmesan* (recipe page 127). If you like, you can use the sauté function and sauté the onion, garlic, and mushrooms first.

CHEF'S NOTE:

One can of beans is approximately 1 and ½ cups. If you use cooked beans instead of canned beans, you need to add 2 cups of water.

This is delicious over a baked Yukon Gold potato or brown rice.

BRAVO BURGERS

My friend, Chef Ramses Bravo, Executive Chef at *TrueNorth Health Center* and author of *BRAVO!*, created these during the Iron Chef competition at *Healthy Taste of LA 5*. Given beans and cooked sweet potato as the secret ingredients, he came up with these tasty little gems.

INGREDIENTS:

1 large Hannah Yam (the light yellow ones, not the orange yams)
1 - 15-ounce can of salt-free cannellini beans (or 1.5 cups of cooked beans)
1 shallot
1 bunch of Italian flat leaf parsley, stems removed

PREPARATION:

Preheat oven to 400 degrees F.

Cook sweet potato using your preferred method. Let cool and remove skin. In a food processor fitted with the "S" blade or by hand, finely chop the shallot and parsley. Mix all ingredients together in a large bowl, using your hands, until the mixture is fully incorporated, leaving some texture in the beans. Divide evenly into 4 patties and bake on a non-stick silicone baking mat for 30 minutes. Flip the burgers and bake for another 20 minutes until golden brown.

CHEF'S NOTE:

Enjoy them as is, with your favorite sauce, or in lettuce "buns" with all the fixings. Use these burgers as a template, adding any spices you wish to make them your own. My favorite addition is smoked paprika.

BURGERS ITALIANO

If Mexican flavored burgers aren't your thing, you are sure to say *grazie* for this recipe.

INGREDIENTS:

4 cups cooked BLACK rice
4 cups cooked and mashed sweet potato (the denser Hannah Yams are preferred to the mushy orange ones)
1 cup red bell pepper, finely chopped
1 cup red onion, chopped
3 cups chopped artichoke hearts (one 12-ounce bag)
8 cloves garlic, minced
1 cup of nutritional yeast
1 Tablespoon dried Italian seasoning
¾ cup sun-dried tomatoes (oil and salt free), about 3 ounces
½ cup fresh basil, chiffonade cut

PREPARATION:

Preheat the oven to 400 degrees F.

Line a baking tray with a *Silpat* or a non-stick silicone baking mat. Water sauté the onion until it begins to become soft and caramelized. Add the red bell pepper and minced garlic and continue to sauté until soft. Combine all ingredients in a large bowl and stir to mix. Chill. Make a patty out of ½ cup of the mixture. Place the patties on the baking tray and bake for 30-45 minutes or until they flip over easily without coming apart. Flip and bake for another 20-30 minutes. Makes 12 burgers.

CHEF'S NOTE:

You can roll these into "meatballs" before baking and serve with the *Zoodles with Quick Sun-Dried Tomato MaRAWnara* (recipe page 133). If using canned artichoke hearts, soak first to remove the salt.

CHIPOTLE BEAN BURGERS

Adapted from and inspired by a recipe from the *Whole Foods Market* website. Everyone who tastes these, even hard-core carnivores, say that these are the best bean burgers they have ever tasted. I'm sure you will want them as part of your weekly rotation.

INGREDIENTS:

4 cans salt-free black beans rinsed & drained (or 6 cups cooked beans)
4 cups cooked brown rice
4 cups cooked and mashed sweet potato (I prefer to use the starchier Hannah Yams rather than mushy orange ones)
1 - 14.5-ounce can *Muir Glen Salt-Free Fire Roasted Tomatoes*
1 cup red onion, chopped
8 cloves garlic, minced or put through a garlic press
1 red bell pepper finely chopped (approximately 1 cup)
1 large carrot finely chopped (approximately 1 cup)
1 bunch cilantro finely minced
12 Tablespoons nutritional yeast
4 Tablespoon salt-free chili powder*
1 Tablespoon SMOKED paprika (different than regular paprika)
1 Tablespoon ground cumin
1 teaspoon chipotle powder

PREPARATION:

Preheat the oven to 400 degrees F.

Drain the can of tomatoes and sauté the onion in the liquid from the canned tomatoes until soft. You can purée the tomatoes in a food processor fitted with the "S" blade or leave them whole. Add the chopped carrot, bell pepper, and garlic and sauté until soft and cooked, about 10-15 minutes. Combine all ingredients in a large bowl and stir to mix. I prefer to use latex free food service gloves. Chill several hours or overnight. Make individual patties out of ½ cup of the mixture. Place patties on a baking tray and bake for 30-45 minutes until you are able to flip them over very easily without them sticking. After you flip them, bake for another 20-30 minutes. Makes 24 burgers. These freeze very well.

CHEF'S NOTE:

Serve these flavorful, filling burgers with all the fixings such as sliced tomatoes and onions and salt-free condiments and use large butter lettuce leaves or *Potato Waffles* (recipe page 179) as "buns". They can also be crumbled and served over a salad or used as a delicious filling for a baked potato.

You can watch me make these on Episode 6 of *Healthy Living with Chef AJ.*

*Concerning spice blends, please read my note under *Chili Fries*, p. 125.

ENCHILADA STRATA

There really is not a dish that can't be improved by the addition of kale, which not only makes it more nutritious but even more delicious. If you can't find frozen kale, you can substitute frozen spinach. We often serve this dish at the graduation of the LIVE *Ultimate Weight Loss Program* and slather the *Nacho Cheeze Sauce* (recipe page 224) over it. This casserole makes a lot but it freezes well.

For the Sauce:
INGREDIENTS:

1 red onion, chopped (approximately 10 ounces or 3 cups)

2 cloves garlic, crushed

2 - 14.5-ounce cans of *Muir Glen Salt-Free Fire Roasted Tomatoes*

2 Tablespoons salt-free chili powder*

1 teaspoon ground cumin

3 Tablespoons arrowroot powder (optional, if not a trigger)

1 and ½ cups water

PREPARATION:

Place the onion, garlic, and water in a pot and cook 8-10 minutes until soft. Stir in the tomatoes and spices and cook on low heat for 15 minutes. Add the arrowroot powder, if using, to a small amount of cold water and dissolve, then add to sauce and stir until thickened.

For the Filling:
INGREDIENTS:

4 cups of *Chef AJ's Fire-Roasted Salsa* (recipe page 209)

1.5 pounds of sweet potatoes

1-pound bag frozen corn, defrosted

2 - 15-ounce cans of salt-free black beans (or 3 cups of cooked beans)
2 - 16-ounce bags of frozen kale, defrosted with all of the liquid squeezed out.
12 oil-free corn tortillas (made from just corn or corn and lime)
Chopped scallions for garnish

PREPARATION:

Peel sweet potatoes and boil or steam until soft. Process in a food processor fitted with the "S" blade until smooth and creamy. Place into a large bowl and stir in the salsa, corn, beans, and kale. Mix well. I recommend using food service gloves so that everything gets fully incorporated.

ASSEMBLY:

Preheat oven to 350 degrees F.

Cover the bottom of a large baking dish with half of the enchilada sauce. A lasagna pan (10"x14" or 11"x15") is recommended. Place 6 tortillas on top of the enchilada sauce and then gently and evenly place the sweet potato mixture on top of the tortillas. Top with the remaining 6 tortillas. Pour the remaining sauce over the tortillas. Bake for 30 minutes. Sprinkle with scallions and serve with *Sweet Pea Guacamole* from *Unprocessed*.

CHEF'S NOTE:

If you can find frozen roasted corn that is organic, it adds a nice flavor. Use a paint straining bag from the hardware store to easily squeeze out all the liquid from your defrosted frozen greens.

I do not recommend that you eat corn tortillas by themselves if you are trying to lose weight or if they are a trigger food for you and will cause you to overeat. They have a caloric density of about 1,000 calories per pound, which is double that of whole corn.

In this recipe, they practically melt and you would be consuming the equivalent of about one tortilla. When eating them on their own, many people cannot stop at one. In place of the tortillas you can use potatoes, carefully sliced paper-thin on a mandolin and then cooked. (Be sure to always use the safety guard and wear a glove when using a mandolin). This makes the dish even heartier and just as delicious.

*concerning spice blends, please read my note under *Chili Fries, p.125.*

ENLIGHTENED PORTABELLA MUSHROOM STROGANOFF

I have updated and enlightened this classic recipe from *Unprocessed* by swapping the high-fat tofu and tahini for beans, and removing the tamari. This is scrumptious as a topping over a baked potato.

For the Sauce:
INGREDIENTS:

1 - 15-ounce can of salt-free cannellini beans* (or 1.5 cups of cooked beans)
½ cup water
4 Tablespoons fresh lemon juice (include zest from lemon)
2 cloves garlic
1 - inch piece of fresh ginger - approximately ½ of an ounce (more or less, to taste)

PREPARATION:

Place all ingredients in a blender and blend until smooth.

For the Filling:
INGREDIENTS:

1 red onion, minced
1 pound of portabella mushrooms, sliced
1 teaspoon dried oregano
Chopped Italian parsley, for garnish

PREPARATION:

Water sauté the onions until translucent. Add mushrooms and sauté until they become limp and moisture has evaporated. Stir in oregano. Pour the sauce over the vegetables and mix well. Garnish with fresh parsley.

CHEF'S NOTE:

This is delicious served over steamed greens or brown rice or both. It is also a delicious filling for the *Mexican Stuffed Potato* (recipe page 174). Be sure to make extra rice so that you will have it for leftovers. You can freeze cooked rice in individual serving sizes. Save 4 cups of rice for when you make the bean burgers.

My original recipe called for ¾ of an ounce of pitted dates (approximately 3 Deglet Noor) to be added to the sauce before blending. If you are making this for people who are not following the *UWL Program* or if you are at goal weight and dates are not a trigger for you, consider using. You can purchase them individually in the bulk bins just for this recipe.

*For a legume-free option, substitute for the beans 16 ounces of defrosted frozen cauliflower or 12 ounces of cooked cauliflower and 1 – 4-ounce cooked Yukon Gold potato. This is a great way to sneak in even more vegetables.

INSTANT POT-ATOUILLE

This dish has all the great flavor of the *Oven Roasted Ratatouille* (recipe page 130), and you won't even have to turn on the oven!

INGREDIENTS:

½ cup of water
8 ounces of yellow Crookneck Squash
8 ounces of green zucchini
12 ounces of Chinese or Japanese Eggplant
1 red onion
1 orange bell pepper (about 8 ounces)
2-3 portabella mushrooms (about 6 ounces)
24 ounces (1.5 pounds) Yukon Gold Potatoes
2 - 14.5-ounce cans *Muir Glen Salt-Free Fire Roasted Tomatoes*
½ cup fresh basil, finely chopped into threads (chiffonade cut)

PREPARATION:

Slice all vegetables into bite-size pieces and place all ingredients except for the fresh basil in an 8-quart *Instant Pot* electric pressure cooker and cook on high pressure for 10 minutes. Release pressure and stir in the basil. Serve with rice if desired. (I like to add 2-3 cups of cooked rice to the stew before serving). Sprinkle *Enlightened Faux Parmesan* (recipe page 127) on top.

CHEF'S NOTE:

If you don't have the 8-quart *Instant Pot*, cut the recipe in half. Because I like starch with my starch, I still enjoy serving it with brown rice to soak up some of the juice.

LENTIL TACOS WITH CHILI-LIME SLAW

Delicious as a topping for a cold salad or hot baked potato.

INGREDIENTS:

Corn tortillas (made from just corn or corn and lime)

For the Lentil "Taco Meat:"

INGREDIENTS:

1 pound of dried lentils (green or black, not red)
4 cups water
10 ounces of sliced mushrooms (about 3 cups)
!0 ounces of chopped onion (about 3 cups)
4 teaspoons cumin
1 Tablespoon oregano
2 Tablespoons salt-free chili powder*
2 Tablespoons salt-free seasoning (I prefer *Benson's Table Tasty*)
6 cloves garlic, pressed

PREPARATION:

Place all ingredients in the *Instant Pot* electric pressure cooker on high and cook for 8 minutes. Alternately, place all ingredients in a slow cooker and cook on low for 6-8 hours.

For the Chili-Lime Slaw:
INGREDIENTS:

8 ounces of shredded cabbage
½ cup water
½ cup lime juice
½ teaspoon crushed red pepper flakes (more or less, to taste)

PREPARATION:

Mix together water, lime juice, and red pepper flakes. Pour over shredded cabbage and let marinate at least 15 minutes before serving. Drain excess liquid before topping the tostadas.

ASSEMBLY:

Take one tortilla, heap on the lentil "meat" and top with the *Chili-Lime Slaw*, and, if you wish, the *Sweet Pea Guacamole* from *Unprocessed*. Garnish with chopped cilantro or chopped scallions, if desired.

CHEF'S NOTE:

You can watch me make this on Episode 4 of *Healthy Living with Chef AJ*.

*concerning spice blends, please read my note under *Chili Fries, p.125*.

THE MCDOUGALL/GOLDHAMER

CAULIFLOWER RISOTTO SWEET POTATO STACK

For the past seven years, I have had the privilege of working as a guest chef and presenter at the annual *TrueNorth Health Center's* Holiday Extravaganza. For the past three years, I competed in an SOS-free Iron Chef competition against their Executive Chef, Ramses Bravo. Every year, he wins the savory round and I win the dessert round. Well, last year, it was a complete role reversal and renewed my faith in my culinary skills when I actually beat him in the savory round. The three secret ingredients were chosen by the three plant-based celebrity judges: Mary McDougall (who chose sweet potatoes), Dr. Alan Goldhamer (who chose cauliflower), and Cathy Fisher (who chose red bell pepper). Hence, the name of this outstanding dish. This is a low-fat, *UWL-approved* version.

INGREDIENTS:

2 large Garnet yams, roasted and cooled
2 large Hannah yams, roasted and cooled

Risotto Filling:

One shallot, finely minced
12 ounces of riced cauliflower*
8 ounces of zucchini, finely diced
1 teaspoon *Benson's Table Tasty* (or more to taste)
12 ounces of finely diced hearts of palm or water chestnuts, soaked in water to remove the salt (optional), or additional 8 ounces of zucchini if not using hearts of palm or water chestnuts

PREPARATION:

Water sauté the shallot until translucent. Add the cauliflower and sauté until soft, adding water during the cooking process if the pan becomes too dry. Add the zucchini, and the hearts of palm or water chestnuts (if using), and cook briefly. Stir in the red bell pepper sauce (recipe follows) and *Benson's Table Tasty* and cook until uniformly heated.

Red Bell Pepper Sauce:
INGREDIENTS:

1 large red bell pepper (about 8-10 ounces)
3 cloves of garlic
4 ounces of riced cauliflower*
¾ cup sun-dried tomatoes (oil and salt free), about 3 ounces
½ cup of unsweetened non-dairy milk
1 teaspoon SMOKED paprika (different than regular paprika)
½ teaspoon chipotle powder

PREPARATION:

Place all ingredients in a blender and blend until smooth.

ASSEMBLY:

On a pretty white plate, layer the ingredients as follows. Directly on the plate, place a thick slice (about one inch) of the orange sweet potato (peel removed). Place a scoop of the risotto filling on top of it. Then place another thick slice of the Hannah yam (peel removed) and another scoop of the risotto filling. If desired, add a bit of unsweetened non-dairy the milk to the blender to thin any remaining sauce out and pour into a squeeze bottle to decorate the plate.

CHEF'S NOTE:

For an even more spectacular presentation you can uses these molds, available at *www.stackablegourmet.com.*

*riced cauliflower is sold in the refrigerator or freezer section of many stores. If you cannot find it, simply rice the cauliflower yourself using a food processor fitted with the shredding blade.

MEXICAN STUFFED POTATO

This recipe is so easy that my husband Charles can even make it himself and it's his favorite meal that he always has on his birthday. Yes, he celebrates his birthday with a potato!

INGREDIENTS:

2 Potatoes (any kind, I prefer large Russet potatoes)
1 - 15-ounce can of salt-free Pinto beans (or 1.5 cups of your favorite beans)
8 ounces of frozen corn, defrosted (I prefer the fire roasted organic corn)
One-Minute Salsa (recipe page 228) or *Pico de Gallo* (recipe in *Unprocessed*)

PREPARATION:

Cook potato however you normally would (bake, steam, pressure cook, microwave). Heat up the corn and beans and stuff the potato with them and top with salsa. Add jalapeños and cilantro, if desired. Delicious with the *Sweet Pea Guacamole* from *Unprocessed*.

CHEF'S NOTE:

For those not following the *UWL Program*, add sliced olives, avocado, or guacamole.

ORANGE IS THE NEW BLACK SWEET POTATO

If you like the TV show, you'll love this recipe.

INGREDIENTS:

2 large orange sweet potatoes
1 - 15-ounce can of salt-free black beans (or 1.5 cups of your favorite beans)
8 ounces of steamed broccoli or kale (or *Lip Smacking Mouthwatering Kale*, recipe page 128)

PREPARATION:

Cook potato however you normally would (bake, steam, pressure cook, microwave). Steam the vegetable of your choice and heat up the beans. Stuff the potato with the beans and veggies. Add your favorite toppings such as *One-Minute Salsa* (recipe page 228), oil- and tahini-free hummus or *Yummy Sauce* (recipe page 235).

CHEF'S NOTE:

Whenever you bake potatoes, don't just bake one or two. Bake several so that you will have leftovers for this quick meal or snacks. Make a potato bar and let everyone stuff their own potatoes. Even people who don't normally eat healthy food have loved this meal. We eat this a few times a week, varying the type of potato, bean, veggie, and sauce. The possibilities are endless.

POTATO PIZZAS

Pizza or pizzazz? You decide! And you will never miss the crust.

INGREDIENTS:

Orange flesh sweet potatoes, Yukon Gold potatoes or both
Your favorite SOS-free marinara sauce
Your favorite pizza toppings

PREPARATION:

Preheat oven to 400 degrees F.

Slice potatoes to about ⅛ of an inch thick by hand or carefully using a mandolin (with the guard and a glove). Bake on a large baking tray covered with a *Silpat* or non-stick silicone baking mat or a *Crisp-Ease* tray for about 30 minutes. If not using the *Crisp-Ease* tray, flip the potato slices after 15 minutes. These will serve as your pizza crusts. Top with your favorite SOS-free marinara sauce and your favorite toppings and bake in the oven for another 15 minutes.

CHEF'S NOTE:

You can use the recipe for *Quick Sun-Dried Tomato MaRAWnara* (recipe page 133) for the sauce and sprinkle the *Enlightened Faux Parmesan* (recipe page 127) on your personal pizzas before baking. The toppings I love to use are artichoke hearts, chopped broccoli, mushrooms and red onion. You will have to chop them all finely so they will fit. These make great party appetizers and your guests will gobble them up!

For a delicious variation, use *Pizza Hummus* (recipe page 248) in place of the marinara sauce.

POTATO TAQUITOS

This recipe was contributed by my dear friend and sous-chef, Rebecca Martinez-Rocha, who lost over 150 pounds on *The Ultimate Weight Loss Program*, and is a much healthier version of her mother-in-law's fried taquitos.

For the Filling:
INGREDIENTS:

1 large potato, cooked
⅛ teaspoon pepper
½ teaspoon granulated garlic
½ teaspoon salt-free seasoning
½ teaspoon granulated onion
1 Tablespoon water (or more if needed)
2 ounces cooked and chopped kale or spinach

PREPARATION:

In a large bowl, smash potato, add spices and greens and mix well. Set aside.

For the Taquitos:
INGREDIENTS:

12 oil-free corn tortillas (made from only corn or corn and lime)
Heat tortillas and set aside (keep warm).

PREPARATION:

Preheat oven to 350 degrees F.

Spread about ¼ cup of the filling into a tortilla, roll and seal with a toothpick. Place taquitos on a large baking tray covered with a non-stick silicone baking mat or a *Crisp-Ease tray* and bake for 20 minutes. Flip, bake another 20 minutes or until crisp (be sure to watch to ensure they don't start to turn brown). Serve with *Sweet Pea Guacamole* from *Unprocessed*. If you cook them on a Crisp-ease tray, you don't even need to flip them.

POTATO WAFFLES

This genius recipe is the brainchild of blogger Sandy Plüss from *www.VegansEat YummyFoodToo.com.*

INGREDIENTS:

Small Yukon Gold potatoes (3 to 4 ounces each works best) left whole and not peeled

PREPARATION:

Bake or microwave potatoes until soft. I do not recommend wet cooking methods like steaming or pressure cooking for this recipe. Press potato in a preheated non-stick waffle iron for 10-12 minutes until golden brown. If waffle maker doesn't open easily without the potatoes sticking, close and cook a few minutes longer.

CHEF'S NOTE:

I love to eat these with *Easy Applesauce* (recipe page 217) and chopped red onion. When enjoyed that way, it reminds me of the Potato Latkes served at Chanukah but without the oil or guilt.

I don't recommend using sweet potatoes in this recipe, as they always stick in the waffle iron.

RED LENTIL CHILI

I get more thank you emails for this recipe than for just about any other.

INGREDIENTS:

One pound of red lentils
8 cups of water
2 - 14.5-ounce cans of *Muir Glen Salt-Free Fire Roasted Tomatoes*
1 - 6-ounce can of salt-free tomato paste
10 ounces of chopped onion (approximately 3 cups)
One pound of red bell pepper, (approximately 2 large)
8 cloves of garlic, finely minced
4 Tablespoons apple cider vinegar
1.5 Tablespoons parsley flakes
1.5 Tablespoons dried oregano
1.5 Tablespoons salt-free chili powder*
2 teaspoons SMOKED paprika (different than regular paprika)
½ teaspoon chipotle powder (more or less, to taste)
¼ teaspoon crushed red pepper flakes (more or less, to taste)

PREPARATION:

Blend the tomatoes, red bell peppers, garlic, and dates, (if using), in a blender until smooth. Place all remaining ingredients in an *Instant Pot* electric pressure cooker and cook on high for 10 minutes. Or, place all ingredients in a slow cooker and cook on low for 6-8 hours.

Sprinkle with *Enlightened Faux Parmesan* (recipe page 127) and finely chopped scallions before serving.

My original recipe called for 3 ounces of pitted Deglet Noor dates (about 12) to balance the acidity from the tomatoes and the apple cider vinegar and give the chili a mild sweet and sour flavor. Many *UWL* participants make it without the dates and say it still tastes great. If you are at goal weight and dates are not a trigger for you, or you are making this for people not following the *UWL Program*, consider using them. You can buy them individually in the bulk bins just for this recipe.

CHEF'S NOTE:

This is delicious served over a baked Yukon Gold potato or brown or wild rice. Recipe may be halved, but why would you want to?

You can watch me make this on Episode 3 of *Healthy Living with Chef AJ*.

*concerning spice blends, please read my note under Chili Fries, p.125.

STUFFED PORTABELLA MUSHROOMS

Shayda Soleymani, who lost over 100 pounds on *The Ultimate Weight Loss Program*, and has kept it off for over five years now, contributed this outstanding recipe.

INGREDIENTS:

4-5 portabella mushroom caps, (3-4" in size), gills removed
4-5 medium Yukon Gold potatoes, peeled & chopped (You can also use sweet potatoes)
1 medium red onion, diced
2 medium red tomatoes or bell peppers, diced
2 cups baby spinach or kale, (or any greens you like), chopped
½ cup nutritional yeast, (optional)
1 jalapeño pepper, deseeded, finely chopped
2-3 garlic cloves
1 teaspoon black pepper (optional)

PREPARATION:

Preheat the oven to 350 degrees F.

In a large pot, add the chopped potatoes, cover with cold water and bring to a boil. Lower the heat and simmer until the potatoes are tender, about 10-15 min. Drain. In a large bowl, mash the potatoes. Add the chopped onions, tomatoes, kale, nutritional yeast, jalapeños, garlic, and pepper. Mix everything together. Gently remove the gills from the mushroom caps. Fill the mushrooms with potato mixture. Optionally, you can sprinkle some nutritional yeast on top.

Bake the filled mushrooms uncovered for 20-30 minutes or until mushrooms are tender. Once you remove the mushrooms from the oven, drizzle the mushroom caps with your favorite reduced balsamic vinegar.

CHEF'S NOTE:

You can also cook these in an Air Fryer.

SWEET POTATO CHILI WITH KALE

There is no dish that can't be improved by the addition of kale!

INGREDIENTS:

2 pounds of sweet potatoes, diced (no need to peel if organic)
1 large red onion (approximately 10 ounces), finely chopped
2 - 15-ounce cans kidney beans or 3 cups cooked beans
2 red bell peppers, seeded and finely diced
2 - 14.5-ounce cans *Muir Glen Salt-Free Fire Roasted Tomatoes*
1 Tablespoon salt-free chili powder
2 teaspoons SMOKED paprika (different than regular paprika)
¼ teaspoon chipotle powder (or more to taste)
8 ounces of Lacinato kale, finely shredded like cabbage for coleslaw
3 cups orange juice

PREPARATION:

Place all ingredients except for the kale in an *Instant Pot* electric pressure cooker and cook on high pressure for 7 minutes. Release pressure and stir in the kale. Alternately, place all ingredients in a slow cooker and cook on low for 6-8 hours.

You can watch me make this on Episode 1 of *Healthy Living with Chef AJ.*

*concerning spice blends, please read my note under Chili Fries, p.125.

SATISFYING SOUPS

BROCCOLI BISQUE

Adapted from and inspired by a recipe from Mary McDougall, who has created thousands of healthy, delicious, and low-fat recipes available at *www.drmcdougall.com*.

INGREDIENTS:

1 and ½ pounds of broccoli
1 and ½ pounds of Yukon Gold potatoes
6 cups of no-sodium vegetable broth or water
1 large onion
8 cloves of garlic
2 Tablespoon dried dill
2 Tablespoons *Benson's Table Tasty* (or your favorite salt-free seasoning)
3-4 cups unsweetened non-dairy milk (depending on how thick you want it)
4 Tablespoon salt-free stoneground mustard (or your favorite low-sodium Dijon mustard)
4 Tablespoons nutritional yeast, optional

PREPARATION:

Place all ingredients except for the non-dairy milk, mustard, and nutritional yeast, if using, in an *Instant Pot* electric pressure cooker and cook on high pressure for 6 minutes. Release pressure and add the non-dairy milk and mustard (and nutritional yeast, if using) and blend with an immersion blender, or in the blender, until smooth.

CHEF'S NOTE:

This is delicious over brown rice. I have used cauliflower in place of the broccoli and it was still great!

You can watch me make this on Episode 11 *of Healthy Living with Chef AJ.*

BROCCOLIFLOWER CHEESE BISQUE

When people tell me that they have given up and just can't lose weight, I send them for inspiration to the *YouTube* channel of Heather Goodwin, which is called *The Butterfly Effect – Plant Based Weight Loss*. This *UWL* superstar is now down an astonishing 300 pounds, thanks to delicious recipes like this one she created.

INGREDIENTS:

1 head of cauliflower, core removed
4 cups of no-sodium veggie broth
4 cups of broccoli, broken into florets
3 large carrots, grated
1 medium Yukon Gold potato, peeled and cut into chunks
½ cup celery, chopped
½ small yellow onion
½ cup unsweetened non-dairy milk
½ cup nutritional yeast
Juice of 1 lemon
1 teaspoon garlic powder
1 Tablespoon *Benson's Table Tasty* (or your favorite salt-free seasoning)
⅛ teaspoon ground black pepper
¼ teaspoon thyme

PREPARATION:

Place all ingredients (except for non-dairy milk, lemon juice and nutritional yeast) in an *Instant Pot* electric pressure cooker, and cook on high for 6 minutes. Release the pressure and add the non-dairy milk, nutritional yeast and lemon juice. Blend the soup using an immersion blender right in the pot, or blend carefully in a blender. Blend until creamy, but leave a few chunks for texture.

CREAMY CURRIED KABOCHA SQUASH SOUP

I had the pleasure of serving this soup to the authors of *The Pleasure Trap*, Dr. Doug Lisle and Dr. Alan Goldhamer, and they both loved it! If you haven't yet tried Kabocha squash, you simply must.

INGREDIENTS:

8 cups of cooked Kabocha squash
4 cups of water
¼ cup gluten free rolled oats
3 cups of chopped onion (about 10 ounces)
4-6 cloves of garlic
1 Tablespoon *Benson's Table Tasty* (or your favorite salt-free seasoning)
2 teaspoons SMOKED paprika (different than regular paprika)
1 teaspoon mild curry powder
¼ teaspoon ground ginger
¼ teaspoon ground turmeric
4 cups unsweetened plain non-dairy milk

PREPARATION:

Cook the squash according to your preferred method. The easiest way is to place the whole squash in the *Instant Pot* on the rack, filled with water up to the rack, and cook at high pressure for 10 minutes. Remove carefully when cool enough to handle, cut squash in half and remove seeds. Rinse out the pressure cooker insert to use again. Place the seeded squash and all the remaining ingredients, except for the non-dairy milk, back into the insert and cook on high pressure for 5 minutes. Release the pressure and add the non-dairy milk. Using an immersion blender, add the non-dairy milk and purée the soup right in the pot. Alternatively, carefully blend the contents in a blender. This soup thickens as it cools so feel free to thin it out the next day with water or additional plant milk.

CHEF'S NOTE:

If you have time, use the sauté function and brown the onions before adding the remaining ingredients. This is delicious served over black, red, brown, or wild rice. Garnish with fresh chopped chives and sprinkle with smoked paprika before serving.

DREAM OF TOMATO SOUP REVISITED

The original recipe from my book *Unprocessed*, while delicious, was very high in fat from the one cup of hemp seeds. With this updated version, you get all of the flavor with none of the fat.

INGREDIENTS:

One pound of Roma tomatoes
2 red bell peppers, seeded
1 - 15-ounce can of salt-free cannellini beans* (or 1.5 cups of cooked beans)
1 clove garlic
6-8 large basil leaves
Juice of one lemon
¾ cup sun-dried tomatoes (oil and salt free), about 3 ounces
¼ teaspoon chipotle powder (or more, to taste)

PREPARATION:

Place all ingredients in a high-powered blender and blend until smooth. By using a high-powered blender, the soup will become warm without having to heat it. Sprinkle with chopped scallions.

CHEF'S NOTE:

This is delicious over brown rice or a baked potato.

*For a legume-free option, substitute for the beans 16 ounces of defrosted frozen cauliflower or 12 ounces of cooked cauliflower and 1 - 4-ounce cooked Yukon Gold potato. This is a great way to sneak in even more vegetables.

GREEN SPLIT PEA SOUP

WITH SUN-DRIED TOMATOES & DRIED MUSHROOMS

The sun-dried tomatoes and dried mushrooms make this hearty soup even more flavorful and really kicks it up a notch!

INGREDIENTS:

One pound green split peas
One large onion, chopped
One pound carrots, sliced
One celery heart, sliced
2 large potatoes, cubed
8 cups boiling water
1.5 cups chopped sun-dried tomatoes (oil and salt free), about 6 ounces
1 small package dried mushrooms (about 1 ounce)
6-8 cloves garlic, pressed
4 teaspoons dried parsley
2 Tablespoons *Benson's Table Tasty* (or your favorite salt-free seasoning)
1 teaspoon dried basil
1 teaspoon dried rosemary
1 teaspoon dried oregano
1 teaspoon celery seed
1 teaspoon SMOKED paprika (different than regular paprika)
1 bay leaf

PREPARATION:

Place all ingredients in an *Instant Pot* electric pressure cooker. Cook on high for 10 minutes. Alternately, place all ingredients in a slow cooker and cook on low for 6-8 hours.

CHEF'S NOTE:

Serve over brown rice and/or raw or cooked spinach or other greens. Or stir in some greens right after releasing the pressure.

You can watch me make this on Episode 13 of *Healthy Living with Chef AJ.*

NO-SODIUM VEGGIE BROTH

Thank you to JL Fields, author of *Vegan Pressure Cooking,* for allowing me to share this spectacularly easy, time and money saving recipe. What a brilliant use of scraps!

INGREDIENTS:

1-gallon freezer bag full of vegetable scraps
8 cups of water
2 bay leaves
½ teaspoon each of basil, oregano, rosemary, and thyme

PREPARATION:

Place all ingredients in an *Instant Pot* electric pressure cooker and cook on high pressure for 15 minutes and allow for a natural release. Strain the broth through a fine mesh strainer or cheesecloth. Store in an airtight glass jar or container for 3-5 days or freeze in a heavy-duty freezer bag for 3-6 months.

CHEF'S NOTE:

When I interviewed JL on my teleclass, she said almost anything can go into the scrap bag, even the cores of apples and pears. What is fun about this broth is that it is delicious and different every time you make it. And even if you make a batch you don't care for, hey, it was basically free. Those boxed broths usually have added salt or oil and get expensive. You can use this homemade veggie broth for sautéing or in any of the savory recipes calling for water. If you don't have a fine mesh strainer or cheesecloth, a clean bag designed for paint straining is inexpensive and works great.

QUICK NUTRIENT-RICH BLACK BEAN SOUP

The original recipe from my book, *Unprocessed*, is still one of my most popular recipes, but because it makes 32 cups of soup, you can't make it in a pressure cooker. Here is the scaled down version for the *Instant Pot*.

INGREDIENTS:

6 cups of no-sodium vegetable broth or water
3 - 15-ounce cans of salt-free black beans (or 4.5 cups of cooked beans)
1 red onion, peeled
4 cloves garlic
8 ounces of mushrooms
1 pound frozen spinach or kale, defrosted with the excess water squeezed out
1 large sweet potato, peeled if not organic (about one pound)
1 - 16-ounce bag frozen corn
¾ cup sun-dried tomatoes (oil and salt free), about 3 ounces
1 Tablespoon ground cumin
1 Tablespoon dried oregano
½ Tablespoon SMOKED paprika (different than regular paprika)
½ teaspoon chipotle powder, or more, to taste
4 Tablespoons lime juice, add zest if using fresh

PREPARATION:

Place all ingredients except for the defrosted frozen greens in an *Instant Pot* electric pressure cooker and cook on high pressure for 8 minutes. Release pressure and stir in the greens. Blend soup with an immersion blender or blend carefully in a blender. If you like some texture, leave out some of the corn and beans and stir back in after soup is blended.

CHEF'S NOTE:

Garnish with chopped scallions or *Pico de Gallo* (recipe in *Unprocessed*). This is delicious over brown rice.

You can watch me make this on Episode 12 of *Healthy Living with Chef AJ.*

ROASTED PARSNIP AND BUTTERNUT SQUASH SOUP DUO

Contributed by Chef Ramses Bravo, executive chef at *TrueNorth Health Center* and Author of *BRAVO!* Chef Bravo made this unbelievably delicious soup at the dinner honoring Dr. T. Colin Campbell at the 2nd Annual *Healthy Taste of LA*. This is actually a combination of two delicious soups which are great on their own but become a fantastic duo when paired together.

Creamy Roasted Parsnip Soup with Arugula:
INGREDIENTS:

6 cups peeled and coarsely chopped parsnips
2 shallots, sliced
2 leeks, thinly sliced, white and light green part only
1 celery stalk, thinly diced
2 cloves garlic, chopped
8 cups of no-sodium vegetable broth
½ cup shredded arugula

PREPARATION:

Preheat the oven to 350 degrees F.

Put the parsnips, shallots and ½ cup of the broth in a baking pan and cover it with aluminum foil and bake in the oven for 45 minutes. In a large pot, dry sauté the leeks, celery and garlic over medium heat for 3 minutes. Add the roasted parsnips and the vegetable broth. Increase the heat to medium-high and bring to a simmer for 20 minutes.

Transfer the soup to a blender and process on high speed until smooth, or using an immersion blender, blend the soup right in the soup pot. You may need to process the soup in batches, depending on the size of your blender. On its own, this soup should be garnished with the shredded arugula and ground nutmeg.

Butternut Squash Soup:
INGREDIENTS:

1 large butternut squash
2 celery stalks, chopped
1 red onion, diced large
1 tablespoon chopped ginger
1 tablespoon chopped garlic
1 cup unsweetened applesauce
12 cups of no-sodium vegetable broth
2 fresh apples, peeled and diced

PREPARATION:

Preheat your oven to 350 degrees F.

Cut the butternut squash lengthwise and scoop the seeds out. Place the squash skin side up on a baking tray lined with parchment paper and bake it in the oven until soft when pierced with a fork. When cool to the touch, remove the skin and set the squash pulp aside. In a large pot, dry sauté the celery, red onion, and garlic at medium heat. Cook until the mixture begins to brown. Add the butternut squash pulp and the applesauce to the pot and stir with a wooden spoon for one minute. Add the vegetable broth and bring to a simmer. Cook the soup for 20 minutes. Put the soup, ginger, and the apples in a blender and blend at high speed until smooth. Or using an immersion blender, blend the soup right in the soup pot on its own.

ASSEMBLY:

Once both soups are made, pour them at the same time into each bowl. Garnish with shredded arugula and ground nutmeg.

SMOKY BUTTERNUT BISQUE

I really hate to give any of my recipes preferential treatment but this may be my all-time favorite soup recipe. It's so easy to make and so delicious. I always make sure to have all of the ingredients on hand.

INGREDIENTS:

2 pounds peeled butternut squash
10 ounces of chopped onions, about 3 cups
6 cloves of garlic
3 cups of water
4 pear halves
¼ cups gluten-free oats
1 Tablespoon SMOKED paprika (different than regular paprika)
½ Tablespoon *Benson's Table Tasty* (or your favorite salt-free seasoning)
⅛ - 3/16 of a teaspoon chipotle powder
1 cup unsweetened non-dairy milk

PREPARATION:

Place all ingredients except for the non-dairy milk in the *Instant Pot* electric pressure cooker and cook on high pressure for 6 minutes. Release the pressure and add the non-dairy milk and purée. You can use a handheld immersion blender right in the pot or carefully transfer to a blender to blend.

Alternatively, you can use the sauté function on the *Instant Pot* and sauté the onions until browned, adding small amounts of water if necessary before adding the remaining ingredients.

CHEF'S NOTE:

You can buy already peeled butternut squash in many stores now or even use frozen. It can be difficult to cut a squash so an easy way to cook a whole butternut squash is in your *Instant Pot*. (Simply place the whole squash on the rack, with water filled up to the rack, and cook on high pressure for ten minutes with a natural pressure release.) I always keep canned or jarred pear halves in their own juice on hand for this recipe. You can use fresh but please be sure that they are ripe for the best flavor. We love to serve this soup over any kind of grain (brown rice, millet, quinoa or wild rice) and garnish with finely chopped red onions or crumbled *Nacho Cheeze Kaleritos* (recipe page 273).

SWEET POTATO AND ASPARAGUS BISQUE

This is a variation of the *Broccoli Bisque* adapted from and inspired by Mary McDougall. One day I was making it at *TrueNorth Health Center* and all they had was unsweetened vanilla almond milk, and believe it or not, it was delicious!

INGREDIENTS:

1 and ½ pounds of asparagus
2 pounds of orange sweet potatoes
6 cups of no-sodium vegetable broth or water
1 large onion
8 cloves of garlic
2 Tablespoons dried dill
2 Tablespoons *Benson's Table Tasty* (or your favorite salt-free seasoning)
3-4 cups unsweetened non-dairy milk (depending on desired thickness)
4 Tablespoons of salt-free stone ground mustard or low-sodium Dijon mustard
4 Tablespoons of nutritional yeast (optional)

PREPARATION:

Place all ingredients except for the plant milk, mustard, and nutritional yeast, if using, in an *Instant Pot* electric pressure cooker and cook on high pressure for 10 minutes. Release pressure and add the non-dairy milk, mustard, and nutritional yeast (if using). Purée with an immersion blender right in the pot or carefully in a blender until smooth.

CHEF'S NOTE:

Delicious served over black, red, or wild rice. I like to garnish it with *Pico de Gallo* from *Unprocessed*.

When asparagus is out of season or too expensive I have used an entire head of cauliflower instead (with white sweet potatoes instead of orange) and it's just as delicious. You can also use frozen vegetables as well.

SWEET POTATO AND YELLOW SPLIT PEA SOUP

A tasty twist on traditional green split pea soup.

INGREDIENTS:

One pound yellow split peas
One large onion, chopped
One pound carrots, sliced
One celery heart, sliced
2 large sweet potatoes, cubed
8 cups boiling water
6-8 cloves garlic, pressed
4 teaspoons dried parsley
2 Tablespoons *Benson's Table Tasty* (or your favorite salt-free seasoning)
1 teaspoon dried basil
1 teaspoon dried rosemary
1 teaspoon dried oregano
1 teaspoon celery seed
1 teaspoon SMOKED paprika (different than regular paprika)
1 bay leaf

PREPARATION:

Place all ingredients in an *Instant Pot* electric pressure cooker. Cook on high for 10 minutes. Alternately, place all ingredients in a slow cooker and cook on low for 6-8 hours.

CHEF'S NOTE:

Serve over brown rice and/or raw or cooked spinach or other greens. Or stir in some greens right after releasing the pressure.

You can watch me make this on Episode 2 of *Healthy Living with Chef AJ.*

SALADS, SAUCES, AND SPREADS

BAREFOOT DRESSING

Why is this named *Barefoot Dressing*? Because it will knock your socks off! Guaranteed to make you fall in love with your salad. It is my signature dressing and I've even received e-mails from kids who are now finally eating salads because of it.

INGREDIENTS:

1 and ¼ cups low acid* balsamic vinegar
¼ cup unsweetened rice vinegar
¾ cup lime juice, add zest if using fresh
5 unsweetened pear halves (canned or jarred, in their own juice)
1 cup nutritional yeast
½ cup of salt-free stoneground mustard (or your favorite low-sodium Dijon mustard)
¼ cup of shallots (about an ounce
4 cloves of garlic (about ½ an ounce)
½ Tablespoon chia seeds dissolved in ½ cup of water or the unsweetened pear juice from the can or jar.

PREPARATION:

Dissolve chia seeds in the water or unsweetened pear juice. Place remaining ingredients in a blender and blend until smooth. Add chia seed slurry and blend again. Refrigerate.

CHEF'S NOTE:

I prefer using a 4% acidity vinegar like *Napa Valley Naturals Grand Reserve*, which is thick and syrupy, as opposed to a traditional less sweet balsamic which has 6% acidity. Feel free to use fresh pears instead of canned or jarred, but only if they are very ripe.

BODACIOUS BEET SALAD

My dear friend, Shayda, who lost over 100 pounds on *The Ultimate Weight Loss Program*, gave me this incredible recipe. Originally, it called for cilantro, but I switched it to my favorite herb, mint, and added some red onion.

For the Salad:
INGREDIENTS:

8 ounces of steamed or roasted beets
8 ounces of mango
¼ cup finely chopped red onion
Fresh mint - ¼ cup (about ¼ of an ounce, or more, to taste)

PREPARATION:

Dice beets and mango so they are the same size and place in a bowl. Finely chop the mint and red onion and add. Pour ¼ cup of *Barefoot Dressing* (recipe page 205) or *House Dressing 2.0* (recipe page 221) into the bowl and mix evenly. Serve chilled.

CHEF'S NOTE:

You can buy beets already steamed at *Trader Joes* or *Costco*. You can also buy diced organic frozen mango at *Costco* if you don't want to cut your own. Mustards and vinegars vary widely in their taste, so make sure you are using brands you love on their own. If you don't care for mint, substitute another fresh herb like cilantro or Italian parsley.

CAESAR-Y SALAD

Caesar salad is traditionally made with many ingredients that are not health-promoting: eggs, cheese, oil, salt, anchovies, and oil-soaked croutons. This recipe shows that you can still enjoy the tangy, sweet flavors of this beloved salad in good health.

Recipe by Cathy Fisher of *StraightUpFood.com*.

INGREDIENTS:

For the salad:

1 large head romaine lettuce (about ¾ pound), coarsely chopped
1 medium red bell pepper, seeded and chopped (about 1½ cups)
Ground black pepper

For the dressing:

½ cup water
¾ cup cooked white beans (navy, Great Northern, cannellini)
2 Tablespoons lemon juice
2 Tablespoons salt-free mustard (I like Dijon or stone ground)
1 Tablespoon raisins
1 medium clove garlic, sliced
1 teaspoon dried Italian herb seasoning

PREPARATION:

Place the lettuce and bell pepper into a large salad bowl. Place all the dressing ingredients (water, beans, lemon juice, mustard, raisins, garlic, and herbs) into a blender, and blend until smooth. Pour the dressing over the salad and toss well. Season salad with pepper to taste.

CHEF'S NOTE:

Cathy says that when tomatoes are in season, she likes to use 2 cups chopped tomatoes (or halved cherry tomatoes) instead of the bell pepper.

CHEF AJ'S FIRE ROASTED SALSA

Here is my version of a restaurant-style salsa without salt. It makes a lot, so feel free to cut the recipe in half.

INGREDIENTS:

8 - 14-ounce cans *Muir Glen Salt-Free Fire Roasted Tomatoes*
3 full bunches of cilantro, stems removed
1 large bunch of celery
1 large red onion
8 large cloves of garlic
½ cup lime juice, or more to taste
2 teaspoons of SMOKED paprika (different than regular paprika)
½ teaspoon chipotle powder (more, or less, to taste)
½ teaspoon red pepper flakes (more, or less, to taste)

PREPARATION:

In a food processor fitted with the "S" blade, or by hand, finely chop the cilantro leaves. Pour into a large bowl. Give the celery a coarse chop, then process finely in the food processor. Pour into the bowl with the cilantro. Next, finely chop the onion and garlic in the food processor and add it to the bowl with the cilantro and celery. Add the 8 cans of tomato, lime juice, and spices. Stir well and let flavors meld in the refrigerator for a few hours before serving. This recipe may be cut in half.

CHEF'S NOTE:

Using celery in recipes imparts a natural salty flavor. By chopping it very finely, you don't realize it's even in there. You can chop everything by hand if you like, but the food processor saves time and also makes the veggies somewhat liquefied, which actually works well in this recipe. Of course, you could roast your own tomatoes like they do at *Sharky's*, but who has time? When in Los Angeles, make sure you try the *AJ Burrito, AJ Bowl or AJ Plate* at *www.Sharkys.com*.

CHEF AJ'S HOUSE SALAD

If you would like to see me demonstrate making this salad, please check out my *YouTube* video called, *"A Day in the Life of Chef AJ."*

INGREDIENTS:

3 heads of Romaine lettuce, chopped finely
1 pound of arugula
One pound of Persian cucumbers, finely chopped
One pound bag of riced broccoli or riced cauliflower
½ pound of shredded carrots
½ pound of shredded purple cabbage
One pound of purple grapes sliced in half
1 cup of fresh mint, chopped finely
8 cups cooked grain (quinoa, millet, or wild rice)

Shredded beets (I keep these in a separate bowl because otherwise they turn the entire salad pink)
Chopped red onion (I keep this separate also because Charles does not care for them)

PREPARATION:

Using your preferred chopping methods, chop all ingredients as finely as possible. I use a mandolin (wearing a glove and using the guard) to chop the cucumbers and herb scissors to chop the fresh mint. I use my Ulu blade to chop it all into an awesome chopped salad right before I eat it. Place all the ingredients in an airtight bowl. I use a *Tupperware Thatsa Mega Bowl* which holds 42 cups. I find that my food stays fresher longer in *Tupperware* than in any of the knock-off brands or even than in glass. (Don't worry, they are BPA-free!) If this lasts more than a week, then you aren't eating enough salad! If you would like to purchase this product, go here: *http://cassierolle. my.tupperware.com.*

CHEF'S NOTE:

This recipe is just a template to give you ideas for creating gigantic salads. Please only put in ingredients that you like and will actually eat! Feel free to vary the grain or add a different starch (like beans, corn, or cooked sweet potato) instead of, or in addition to, the wild rice. If you don't care for mint, use another herb like fresh basil, cilantro, or Italian parsley. If grapes are not in season, try fresh apples, grapefruit, oranges, pears, or pomegranate seeds. With fresh fruit in a salad you almost don't even need salad dressing. It's really important to include starch in your salad (or eat immediately afterwards) or you will be hungry and not satisfied. Remember: no starch, no satiety.

For the best salad eating experience possible, try to incorporate all the components of my 8 *Secrets to Superior Salad Satisfaction*:

Salad: Romaine or other lettuce

Salty: finely chopped greens like kale, chard, celery, or some dulse

Sauce: *Barefoot Dressing* or *House Dressing 2.0* or your favorite SOS-free dressing

Savory: Arugula, onion

Snap: Something crunchy like celery, jicama, or water chestnuts

Sour: a lime or lemon juice squeezed over the salad or vinegar

Specialty: Optional but good. Leftover *Balsamic Dijon Glazed Brussels Sprouts*

Starchy: Wild rice or other cooked grain like brown rice, millet or quinoa, or any cooked legume, potato or sweet potato or squash. Cooked cubes of Butternut or Kabocha squash are great!

Sweet: grapes or other fruit

CHERUB SAUCE

A cherub is an angelic being and this sauce is heavenly!

INGREDIENTS:

One pound of frozen sweet cherries
6-8 sweet apples, cored (depending on how large they are) I prefer *Gala* or *Envy*
½ cup of liquid (water, unsweetened apple juice, or unsweetened pomegranate juice)

PREPARATION:

Place all ingredients in an *Instant Pot* electric pressure cooker and cook on high pressure for 10 minutes. Release the pressure and purée using an immersion blender or very carefully in a blender. Cool and store in the refrigerator.

CHEF'S NOTE:

This is a very versatile sauce that can be used with either savory or sweet recipes. I like it on the *Potato Waffles* (recipe page 179), and Charles eats it plain or on the *Fruit Cobbler* (recipe page 145). I like to thin it out a bit and place it in a squeeze bottle and drizzle it over the *Apple Pie Square* (recipe page 139). It is also a great sauce for fresh fruit, especially berries.

CHIA JAM

Tastes great in the *Clafouti* (recipe page 141).

INGREDIENTS:

One pound fresh or frozen berries (such as blackberries, blueberries, cherries, strawberries, or raspberries)
2 Tablespoons chia seeds

PREPARATION:

Place fruit in a food processor fitted with the "S" blade and process until smooth. Pour into a bowl and stir in the chia seeds. Place into the refrigerator. This will thicken as it chills.

CHEF'S NOTE:

Your jam will only be as sweet as your fruit, so please taste the fruit and be sure it's sweet. If you are at goal weight and if unsweetened fruit juice or dates are not a trigger for you, you can sweeten your fruit that way. You can also do this with fruits other than berries such as nectarines, peaches, or plums.

CHIPOTLE ROASTED RED PEPPER SAUCE

This is delicious over *Zoodles* (spiralized zucchini noodles), as a topping for baked potatoes, and even as a dip for oil-free French fries.

INGREDIENTS:

1 cup of roasted red bell pepper (about 2)
¼ cup shallot (about an ounce)
¾ cup of sun-dried tomatoes (oil and salt-free), about 3 ounces
½ cup unsweetened non-dairy milk
2 teaspoons SMOKED paprika (different than regular paprika)
½ teaspoon chipotle powder

PREPARATION:

Place all ingredients in a blender and blend until smooth.

CHEF'S NOTE:

You can buy roasted red bell peppers in a jar for convenience but they will contain salt, so please soak them first to remove as much of the salt as possible. Or you can roast them yourself carefully over a gas flame or in your oven or Air Fryer.

COMPLIANT KETCHUP

Mairead Reddy is an Irish expat who has been living and loving a WFPB (Whole Food Plant-Based) lifestyle since 2005. She created this recipe to enjoy guilt-free with oven-baked fries, hash browns, or any potato.

INGREDIENTS:

2 Tablespoons lemon juice
6 Tablespoons plain reduced balsamic vinegar (using a white balsamic will keep the ketchup light in color)
1 - 6-ounce can tomato paste
1 teaspoon onion granules
¼ teaspoon allspice

PREPARATION:

Place all ingredients in a blender and blend until smooth.

CHEF'S NOTE:

I love to add either chipotle powder or crushed red pepper for extra heat.

I also make this with the *Smoke Infused* vinegar from *Bema and Pa's* and it tastes like BBQ sauce!

CranPEARry RELISH

The cranberry sauce from *Unprocessed* was divine but chock full of calorie dense dates. I think you will like this version just as much. Roasting really brings out the sweetness of any fruit or vegetable.

INGREDIENTS:

1 cup of roasted pear halves (this is the yield from one 25-ounce jar of pears in their own juice)
2 large navel oranges plus their zest
12 ounces of unsweetened fresh cranberries

PREPARATION:

Roast the pear halves until golden brown on a *Crisp Ease* tray, piece of parchment paper, *Silpat*, or other non-stick silicone baking mat. This will take about 35-45 minutes in an oven preheated to 400 degrees F. Zest the oranges and then peel them. Place all ingredients in a food processor fitted with the "S" blade and process until a uniform texture is reached. Do not liquefy. Serve with the *Acorn Squash with Wild Rice Stuffing* (recipe page 151). Also delicious over oatmeal or banana "ice cream."

CHEF'S NOTE:

Blood or Cara Cara oranges are also good to use.

EASY APPLESAUCE

Sure, you can buy organic unsweetened applesauce, but this is so much cheaper and oh, so easy!

INGREDIENTS:

10 whole unpeeled apples, seeds and cores removed
⅓ cup water
1 teaspoon cinnamon

PREPARATION:

Place all ingredients in the *Instant Pot* and cook on high pressure for 4-5 minutes. Blend with an immersion blender right in the pot.

CHEF'S NOTE:

Delicious on the *Potato Waffles* (recipe page 179).

If making this for those who are not following *The Ultimate Weight Loss Program* and they want it sweeter, substitute unsweetened fruit juice for the water.

EASY CHIPOTLE CORN SALSA

People love the *Smoky Chipotle Salsa* from my book *Unprocessed* but have written me and said that it is too labor intensive to chop all the tomatoes or that where they live they can't always get fresh tomatoes in season. Here is the answer to enjoying this delicious salsa quickly and easily all year round!

INGREDIENTS:

2 cups of corn kernels (you can use fresh corn right off the cob raw or frozen corn. I like the frozen organic fire roasted corn)
1 - 14.5-ounce can *Muir Glen Salt-Free Fire Roasted Tomatoes*
1 - 15-ounce can of salt-free pinto beans (or 1.5 cups of cooked beans)
4 Tablespoons lime juice (add zest, if using fresh) more, or less to taste
¼ teaspoon chipotle powder (more or less, to taste)
¼ teaspoon ground cumin (more or less, to taste)
2-4 scallions, chopped
Chopped cilantro, to taste (optional)

PREPARATION:

Place all ingredients in a bowl and refrigerate. Taste will improve as the flavors meld. Delicious on the *All-Star Tostadas* (recipe page 154).

EGGPLANT TAPENADE DIP

Melony Jorenson often hosts the graduation of the live *UWL Program* and serves this yummy dip to rave reviews! You can use this as a dip with raw veggies or add it in any steamed veggie dish like spinach or kale. This is also great on *Zoodles* or as a topping for a baked potato.

INGREDIENTS:

1 large eggplant peeled or 3-4 Japanese eggplant unpeeled
2 red bell peppers
2 red onions
6-8 cloves of garlic
2 Tablespoons of salt-free tomato paste
Salt free seasoning, to taste

PREPARATION:

Preheat oven to 425 degrees F.

Rough chop all of the veggies. Spray with water and add salt free seasonings, if using. Roast all veggies and garlic, putting the garlic under the onions so it doesn't burn. Roast on a baking tray covered with a non-stick silicone baking mat. Roast for 20 minutes and turn them for another 10 minutes. Timing will depend on your oven. Once veggies are browned and cooked, put them in a blender or food processor fitted with the "S" blade and blend, adding the tomato paste and more seasonings if needed.

FOUR-BEAN SALAD

In addition to beans, this salad features corn, peas, and red onion. The dressing is a tangy and mildly spicy vinaigrette. This is a colorful, hearty salad, perfect for any of the three P's: potlucks, parties, and picnics! Recipe by Cathy Fisher of *StraightUpFood.com*.

INGREDIENTS:
For the salad:

3 cups cooked green beans (cut into 1-inch pieces)
1 - 15-ounce can salt-free black beans (or 1.5 cups cooked beans, cooled)
1 - 15-ounce can salt-free kidney beans (or 1.5 cups cooked beans, cooled)
1 - 15-ounce can salt-free garbanzo beans (or 1.5 cups cooked beans, cooled)
1½ cups green peas (thaw first if frozen)
1½ cups corn kernels (thaw first if frozen)
½ cup finely chopped red onion

Tomato Vinaigrette:

1 medium tomato, chopped (including seeds; about ¾ cup)
⅓ cup vinegar (I like apple cider)
2 tablespoons salt-free mustard (I like Dijon or stone ground)
1 teaspoon ground cumin
1 medium clove garlic, sliced

PREPARATION:

Drain and rinse beans. Place all of the salad ingredients (green beans, black beans, kidney beans, garbanzo beans, peas, corn, and onion) into a large bowl. Place all the vinaigrette ingredients (tomato, vinegar, mustard, cumin, and garlic) into a blender, and blend until smooth. Stir into the salad.

HOUSE DRESSING 2.0

This is my go-to dressing when I am out of *Barefoot Dressing* (recipe page 205) and too lazy to make more.

INGREDIENTS:

2 Tablespoons balsamic vinegar (4% acidity instead of 6% is preferred).
2 Tablespoons lime juice or lemon juice
1 Tablespoon salt-free mustard

PREPARATION:

Whisk all ingredients together in a bowl or to make a larger batch use a blender.

You can vary the taste simply by using different flavors of balsamic vinegar.

ISRAELI SALAD

This traditional salad is always served at Middle Eastern restaurants but is very easy to make at home. This recipe was contributed by dear friend and *UWL* participant Melony Jorenson.

INGREDIENTS:

8 Persian cucumbers, chopped
2 red bell peppers, chopped
6 tomatoes, chopped
6 green onions, or 1 small red onion, chopped
1 cup chopped parsley
½ cup chopped mint
Juice of 1 large lemon
Salt-free seasoning, to taste (optional)

PREPARATION:

Mix all of the ingredients together.

CHEF'S TIP:

This is great served over a bed of arugula or quinoa or both. If you can't find Persian cucumbers, use regular cucumbers but I would recommend peeling them.

This is very easy to prepare using an Ulu blade or mezzalune.

LAZY MAN'S SPINACH SALAD

It's hard to believe that a salad of such simple ingredients can be so delicious. Recipe contributed by my longtime dear friend, Tim Ray, who is a very lazy man! ☺

INGREDIENTS:

1 pound baby spinach
1 pint blackberries
1 pint blueberries
1 pint raspberries
1 pint strawberries (quartered)
8 ounces pomegranate seeds
Balsamic vinegar (to taste)

PREPARATION:

Place the spinach in a large bowl. Cover with the fruit. Let each person add their own vinegar to their serving.

NACHO CHEEZE SAUCE

Many of the delicious faux cheese sauces use beans or nuts. I wanted to create one just using vegetables. I hope you will enjoy this one as much as I do.

INGREDIENTS:

12 ounces of cauliflower
4 ounces of Yukon Gold potato
½ cup nutritional yeast
3 Tablespoons lemon juice
2 teaspoons SMOKED paprika (different than regular paprika)
½ teaspoon onion powder
½ teaspoon garlic powder
½ teaspoon chipotle powder

PREPARATION:

Place the cauliflower and potato in the *Instant Pot* electric pressure cooker on the rack with about a cup of water. Cook on high pressure for 6 minutes. Release pressure and carefully place hot contents in a blender with remaining ingredients. Blend until smooth. If you don't want to steam your cauliflower or use the potato, just use a 16-ounce bag of frozen cauliflower, defrosted. It will be slightly less thick without the potato.
Smoked paprika is different than the regular variety. Please do not substitute in my recipes that call for it.

CHEF'S NOTE:

This is delicious over a potato stuffed with broccoli or just over steamed broccoli. It is also great over *The Stuffed Potato Meal* and then topped with *One-Minute Salsa* (recipe page 228) and *Sweet Pea Guacamole* from *Unprocessed*.

NO SIESTA FIESTA SALAD

Teresa Knotwell, an awesome *UWL* participant who helps monitor our group page, came up with this winning recipe.

INGREDIENTS:
For the salad:

3 - 15-ounce cans of salt-free black beans (or 4½ cups cooked beans, cooled)
2 cups frozen corn, thawed
1 large green pepper, diced
1 large red or yellow pepper, diced
½ cup chopped red onion
¾ cup cilantro, or more, to taste

For the dressing:

2 Tablespoons unsweetened seasoned rice vinegar
2 Tablespoons apple cider vinegar
1 lime or lemon, juiced
2 garlic cloves, minced, or more, to taste
2 teaspoons chili powder*
½ teaspoon cumin
¼ - ½ teaspoon crushed red pepper or a pinch of cayenne

PREPARATION:

For the salad, mix all salad ingredients together. Whisk the dressing ingredients together and pour over salad. Toss gently to mix. Best made 4-8 hours in advance. It keeps well for several days.

*concerning spice blends, please read my note under Chili Fries, p.125.

OMG! WATERMELON SALAD

This is a favorite of the world-renowned photographer Henry Grossman.

INGREDIENTS:

Watermelon
Cucumber
Fresh Mint, chopped
Lime juice and zest

PREPARATION:

Cube and seed the watermelon and cucumber. Add fresh mint and lime, to taste. Chill before serving.

CHEF'S NOTE:

I like to use twice as much watermelon as cucumbers. If using the Persian cucumbers, I do not peel or seed, but if using regular cucumbers, I do peel and seed. The amount of lime juice and mint is to taste. If you keep this more than a day or two and it gets soggy, try blending it with ice for a refreshing slushy.

OMG! WATERMELON SALSA

A great use of any leftover *OMG Watermelon Salad*.

INGREDIENTS:

6 cups of OMG Watermelon Salad, finely chopped
One jalapeño pepper, seeded and diced (more or less to taste)

PREPARATION:

Mix all ingredients together and chill before serving.

ONE-MINUTE SALSA

I love salsa on just about everything but there are simply no commercial brands that are free of all the components of the Evil Trinity: Sugar, Oil and Salt. It is so much cheaper and tastier to make your own, and with this recipe, what could be easier? You could even use it as a salad dressing.

INGREDIENTS:

½ of a red onion — small onion
2 cloves of garlic
1 bunch cilantro (more or less to taste)
Juice from one lime (more to taste)
½ jalapeño pepper, seeds removed
1 - 14.5-ounce can *Muir Glen Salt-Free Fire Roasted Tomatoes*

PREPARATION:

Place all ingredients in a food processor fitted with an "S" blade and process until desired texture is reached. *Tupperware* makes a great tool called the *Power Chef*, which makes short work of this. It doesn't use electricity, so you can even take it camping to make fresh salsa.

ROASTED EGGPLANT AND WHITE BEAN PATE

This delicious recipe was contributed by *PCRM* cooking instructor and Texas hottie Kathryn La Russo. Here is what she says about this winning recipe: *This is an oil-free Mediterranean view of the traditional appetizer "baba ganoush." I am constantly grazing during the day to keep my energy up while teaching Bikram yoga, Inferno Hot Pilates, and running a vegan snack business. This spread is great with brown rice crackers or on top of a scoop of brown rice or quinoa. I'll also spoon it over a salad or stuff it into a baked Yukon or sweet potato. Inevitably, I'll have one of my omnivore yoga teacher friends craning their heads into the kitchen for a taste!*

INGREDIENTS:

1 medium eggplant
½ cup chopped red onion
2 or 3 garlic cloves, minced
2 plum tomatoes (seeded and diced)
1 - 15-ounce can salt-free cannellini beans (or 1.5 cups of cooked beans)
¼ cup lemon juice
3 Tablespoons fresh chopped Italian parsley
2 Tablespoons fresh chopped basil
Freshly ground pepper to taste

PREPARATION:

Preheat oven to 425 degrees F.

Wash the eggplant thoroughly and place on a baking tray covered with a non-stick silicone baking mat. Roast until the top of the eggplant is dry and the inside looks ready to cave in. This should take 45 minutes to 1 hour. Let cool and then cut in half and scoop out the flesh, keeping the seeds. Place the eggplant flesh in a food processor fitted with the "S" blade. Add remaining ingredients and process until smooth. Refrigerate. It tastes even better the next day.

ROASTED ONION AND GARLIC RANCH DRESSING

Thank you, Kathy Hester, author of *The Ultimate Vegan Cookbook for Your Instant Pot* and *Vegan Cooking in Your Air Fryer*, for creating this unbelievably delicious recipe just for my book. The first time I made it I practically drank the entire recipe! I am forever grateful and in awe of your talent. Here is what Kathy had to say about the culinary challenge I gave her: *Chef AJ asked me to make an SOS ranch dressing and, of course, I said yes. I love being a mad scientist in the kitchen and helping people eat flavorful food that fits into their diet. The base of this dressing is puréed roasted onion and garlic. It's surprising, but their flavors mellow out so much that you still need to add in a little onion powder and granulated garlic to give it the right bite. Enjoy this on salads, baked potatoes, and as a fun topping on steamed veggies.*

INGREDIENTS:

1 medium sweet onion (will make about 1 cup roasted onion)
1 small head garlic (will make about 1 tablespoon roasted)
½ cup plain unsweetened nondairy milk
1 tablespoon apple cider vinegar
1 ½ teaspoon dried dill (or 1 tablespoon fresh dill)
1 teaspoon dried basil (or 2 teaspoons fresh basil)
¼ teaspoon granulated garlic
¼ teaspoon onion powder
⅛ teaspoon ground black pepper

PREPARATION:

First you are going to roast the onion. Place the whole unpeeled onion on a baking tray covered with a non-stick silicone baking mat to make clean-up easier. Place in a 400-degree oven for 25 minutes and if it isn't soft in the middle, cook for another 25 minutes. (If you have an air fryer, cook for 30 minutes at 400 degrees, check and cook another 20 if it's not soft.)

Cut off the top third of a small whole head of garlic and wrap the remaining ⅔ whole in foil or place in a small covered baking dish. Place in a 400-degree oven for 30 minutes. (If you have an air fryer cook for 30 minutes at 400 degrees, check and cook another 10 minutes if it's not soft.)

Once the onion and garlic have cooled, remove the outer peel layers of the onion, cut in chunks and add to your small blender or food processor. Blend until smooth. At this point, it will look a little like applesauce.

Squeeze the cloves of garlic out and add them to the onion and purée again. Then, add in the plain unsweetened nondairy milk, apple cider vinegar, dill, basil, granulated garlic, onion powder, and black pepper. Blend until smooth.

STRAIGHT UP KETCHUP

Ketchup is a straightforward condiment, mainly calling for tomatoes, vinegar, salt, and sugar. For this recipe, the sugar will come from an apple and the salty flavor from the concentrated tomato paste. Recipe by Cathy Fisher of *StraightUpFood.com*.

INGREDIENTS:

¾ cup water
½ medium apple, peeled, cored, and chopped (about ½ cup)
1 - 6-ounce can salt-free tomato paste
1 tablespoon apple cider vinegar
½ teaspoon dried oregano
¼ teaspoon granulated garlic

PREPARATION:

Place all the ingredients into a blender, and blend until smooth. Refrigerate for two to three hours for the best flavor. Keeps for one to two weeks refrigerated.

CHEF'S NOTE:

You can substitute ½ cup of apple juice for the apple (and decrease the water to ½ cup).
You can substitute 1 tablespoon of lemon juice for the apple cider vinegar.

STRAWBERRY FIESTA DRESSING

I was inspired to create this recipe when visiting the beautiful organic garden at *Rancho La Puerta*, where I have had the privilege of lecturing and teaching cooking classes.

INGREDIENTS:

One pound fresh strawberries (about 4 cups)
2 Tablespoons chopped red onion
½ of 1 jalapeño pepper (seeds removed unless you want it hotter)
¼ cup lime juice (add zest if using fresh)
1-2 Tablespoons chia seeds (optional)

PREPARATION:

Place all ingredients except for the chia seeds in a blender and blend until smooth. Taste and adjust if necessary. Add chia seeds if you would like it thicker.

CHEF'S NOTE:

To make a ROOTIN' TOOTIN' RASPBERRY DRESSING, use a 1-pound bag of frozen raspberries, defrosted, in place of the strawberries. Raspberries tend to be less sweet than strawberries, so you may want to add a pitted date or two, to taste, or a pear to sweeten.

TRIFECTA

Three great tastes that taste great together!

INGREDIENTS:

Bananas
Purple grapes
Strawberries

PREPARATION:

Using equal amounts of all three fruits, slice bananas and strawberries so they are the same size. I like to use a designated banana slicer for this. Cut grapes in half and mix everything together and chill. Serve in a beautiful parfait glass and garnish with a sprig of fresh mint, if desired.

CHEF'S NOTE:

This was a favorite dessert at the LIVE *Ultimate Weight Loss Program*. When making this for others not following the program, sprinkle unsweetened dried flaked coconut over the top. You can actually buy reduced fat coconut that has much less fat.

YUMMY SAUCE

And is it ever.

INGREDIENTS:

1 - 15-ounce can of salt-free cannellini beans* (or 1.5 cups of cooked beans)
Juice and zest of one organic lemon (if the lemon does not yield ¼ of a cup of juice, then add more lemon juice)
½ cup of water
2 Tablespoon of salt-free mustard (I use *Westbrae Stoneground*)
1 clove of garlic

PREPARATION:

Place all ingredients in a blender and blend until smooth. If you are using a high-powered blender, you can make this sauce warm to serve over rice and veggies. It is also delicious cold massaged into shredded cabbage for "Yummy Slaw."

CHEF'S NOTE:

My original recipe called for ¾ ounce of pitted dates (approximately 3 Deglet Noor). If making this for those who are not following the *UWL Program* or if you are at your goal weight and dates are not a trigger for you, feel free to use them in this recipe.

*For a legume-free option, in place of the beans, substitute 16 ounces of defrosted frozen cauliflower or 12 ounces of cooked cauliflower and a 4-ounce cooked Yukon Gold potato. This is a great way to sneak in even more vegetables.

There are endless variations to *Yummy Sauce*. Some of my favorites have been adding fresh ginger, fresh cilantro, scallions, fresh Italian parsley, fresh basil, crushed red pepper flakes, roasted garlic, jalapeño pepper, chipotle pepper, red bell pepper (roasted or raw), nutritional yeast, oil free sun-dried tomatoes, and even wasabi powder!

Spectacular Sides

ALMOST INSTANT MEXI-CALI RICE

This is my version of the "Orange Rice" that my mom used to make when I was a child. Traditionally, Spanish or Mexican rice is made with white rice but I love it with the heartier brown rice. Always make sure you have some cooked rice in your freezer so you can make this easily and often. You can even buy already cooked organic brown rice in the freezer section of most stores.

INGREDIENTS:

6 cups of cooked brown rice (I am partial to the organic brown *Texmati*)
1 - 14.5-ounce can *Muir Glen Salt-Free Fire Roasted Tomatoes*
2 cups of *One-Minute Salsa* (recipe page 228)
4 Tablespoons of tomato paste
10 ounces of chopped onion (about 3 cups)
6 cloves of garlic (more or less to taste) finely minced or pressed through a garlic press
1.5 cups of water

PREPARATION:

Place all the ingredients in an *Instant Pot* electric pressure cooker, and cook on high pressure for 5 minutes. You can either release the pressure immediately or let it come down to pressure naturally. Rice will thicken slightly as it cools. You can stir in some chopped cilantro if you like.

CHEF'S NOTE:

If you have the time, you can use the sauté function and sauté the onions before adding the rest of the ingredients. I love to sprinkle the *Enlightened Faux Parmesan* (recipe page 127) on top. How spicy this rice is will depend on how spicy your salsa is. For a very mild tasting rice, omit the salsa and use another can of fire roasted tomatoes. This makes a delicious side dish or a filling for a burrito. I love eating the hot rice over a cold salad.

ARTICHOKE AND SUN-DRIED TOMATO QUINOA

Many moons ago when I ate pizza, my very favorite toppings were artichokes and sun-dried tomatoes. Now I can have the flavor I loved without the unhealthy ingredients like the bread and cheese.

INGREDIENTS:

1.5 cups of dry quinoa
¾ cup sun-dried tomatoes (oil and salt free), about 3 ounces
2 and ¼ cups water
3 cups of frozen artichoke hearts, defrosted (or one 12 ounce bags) - chopped

PREPARATION:

Place quinoa, water and sun-dried tomatoes in an *Instant Pot* electric pressure cooker and cook on high pressure for 1 minute. After you hear the beeps indicating that it is done, allow the pressure to release naturally. Stir in artichoke hearts and enjoy. Serve immediately warm or cold in a salad.

CHEF'S NOTE:

This is absolutely delicious as it is but you can feel free to add any fresh herbs or salt-free spices that you enjoy, such as roasted garlic and chopped basil.

EASY WILD RICE

Wild rice has a distinctive, nutty flavor and a delicious toothsome texture.

INGREDIENTS:

One pound of wild rice (about 3 cups)
4 cups of water or no-sodium vegetable broth

PREPARATION:

Place all ingredients in an *Instant Pot* electric pressure cooker and press the multigrain button. Allow for a natural pressure release.

CHEF'S NOTE:

Having a pressure cooker can replace your rice cooker and cooks all grains perfectly every time.

HERBED QUINOA TABBOULEH

Tabbouleh is an Arabian vegetarian dish traditionally made of tomatoes, finely chopped parsley, mint, bulgur, and onion, and seasoned with olive oil, lemon juice, and salt. I love the flavors, but not the oil, salt, or gluten. Here is my version. I think you'll find it delicious.

INGREDIENTS:

12 cups cooked quinoa, cooled (made from 3 cups dry quinoa)
3 large cucumbers, peeled, seeded, and diced as small as possible
1 pound of purple grapes, quartered (add even more if you like)
2 ounces fresh mint, finely chopped
2 ounces fresh Italian parsley, finely chopped
2 ounces scallions, finely chopped
1 cup fresh lime juice (add zest if using fresh, or more to taste)

PREPARATION:

Cook quinoa according to the directions on the package and cool. Add remaining ingredients and chill.

CHEF'S NOTE:

This is also delicious with finely chopped apples and quartered cherry tomatoes added to it. It's such a versatile recipe that you really can't mess this one up.

MAGNIFICENT MILLET MEDLEY

After I had finished creating the recipes for this book, I came up with this recipe and served it at a dinner party. The guests, including *Forks Over Knives* producer, Brian Wendel, and Chef Darshana Thacker, really loved the dish, so I simply had to include it. It was inspired by the High Fiber Salad that is served at *The Oaks Spa* in Ojai, where I have had the privilege of speaking many times. Millet is a hearty, spectacular, and, in my opinion, underused, whole grain that I would like to see go mainstream.

INGREDIENTS:

8 cups of cooked millet (made from 2 cups of dry millet)
1 20-ounce can unsweetened crushed pineapple, drained and liquid reserved
½ cup chia seeds
1 cup of lime juice (add zest if using fresh)
8 ounces of finely shredded carrots (about 4 cups)
8 ounces of finely shredded purple cabbage (about 4 cups)
8 ounces of chopped cucumbers (about 2 cups)
1 large green apple, finely chopped
½ cup finely chopped red onion
½ cup fresh mint, finely chopped

PREPARATION:

Cook millet using your preferred cooking method. Toast the millet before cooking, if desired. Cool and measure out 8 cups in a large bowl. Drain the pineapple. You should have at least 1 cup of pineapple juice. Stir the chia seeds into the pineapple juice and allow mixture to thicken as you prepare the rest of the ingredients. Add the remaining ingredients and chill before serving.

CHEF'S NOTE:

Substitute cooked brown rice or cooked quinoa for the millet, if you must.

MUSHROOM WILD RICE

One of the secrets to salt-free cooking is using a variety of interesting flavors and textures. Dried mushrooms impart both.

INGREDIENTS:

One pound of wild rice (about 3 cups)
2 cups of dried mushrooms (about 2 ounces)
4 cups of water or no-sodium vegetable broth

PREPARATION:

Place all ingredients in an *Instant Pot* electric pressure cooker and press the multigrain button. Allow for a natural pressure release.

CHEF'S NOTE:

A pressure cooker can replace your rice cooker and cook all grains perfectly every time.

OVEN BAKED SWEET POTATO FRIES

Try this with the *Chipotle Roasted Red Bell Pepper Sauce* (recipe page 214).

INGREDIENTS:

Sweet potatoes, the bright orange ones

PREPARATION:

Preheat oven to 400 degrees F.

Leaving the skins on, cut sweet potatoes into French fries. Place on a *Crisp-Ease* tray or a baking tray that has been covered with parchment paper or a silicone baking mat such as a *Silpat* and bake for at least 30 minutes or until the desired level of crispiness is reached. How long it takes will depend on how thin you have sliced your potato. Check after 15 minutes and move the fries around to ensure even baking. You can finish these off by carefully placing them under the broiler for a few minutes, if desired.

CHEF'S NOTE:

Many stores sell already sliced sweet potato fries, either in the fresh produce section or frozen. These are fine to use but just make sure that they do not have an oil or salt on them. If you want your fries to cook faster, you can microwave the potato first. You can also make these in an Air Fryer.

You can watch me make this on Episode 10 of *Healthy Living with Chef AJ*.

PAELLA STYLE QUINOA

Another winning recipe contributed by Melony Jorenson.

INGREDIENTS:

8 cups of quinoa, cooked (made from 2 cups of dry quinoa)
No-sodium vegetable broth (recipe page 194) for cooking the quinoa
1-2 pinches of saffron
8 ounces of frozen peas, defrosted
1 - 16-ounce bag of mixed frozen vegetables, defrosted
¼ cup nutritional yeast

PREPARATION:

Cook quinoa according to package using no-sodium vegetable broth instead of water and add 1-2 pinches of saffron to the quinoa. While cooking, defrost the peas and the bag of mixed frozen veggies. Add ¼ cup nutritional yeast and defrosted veggies to cooked quinoa. Mix all the ingredients together.

CHEF'S TIP:

You can cook quinoa very quickly in the *Instant Pot* or buy organic quinoa already cooked in the freezer section in an aseptic package.

PEACHY KEEN-WAH SALAD

This is another outstanding recipe created by *UWL* participant Shayda Soleymani. It's a favorite at potlucks and will be on your table as well.

INGREDIENTS:

8 cups of cooked tri colored quinoa (made from 2 cups of dry quinoa, cooled)
1 - 15-ounce can salt-free kidney beans (or 1.5 cups cooked beans, cooled)
1 - 15-ounce can salt-free black beans (or 1.5 cups cooked beans, cooled)
2-3 medium-sized ripe peaches, diced
1 red bell pepper, diced
1 yellow bell pepper, diced
1 bunch cilantro, chopped
4 Persian cucumbers or English cucumber, diced
1 - 10-ounce bag of frozen corn, thawed
1 small red onion, chopped
8 limes, zest & juice, or more to taste

PREPARATION:

Cook the quinoa using your preferred cooking method and place in a large bowl to cool. Chop up the peaches, bell peppers, cucumber, onion, and cilantro and add remaining ingredients to the quinoa bowl. Add the zest and juice of the lime to everything and toss gently. Refrigerate before serving.

CHEF'S NOTE:

You can buy quinoa already cooked in the freezer section in most stores and even in aseptic packages.

PIZZA HUMMUS

This recipe was contributed by dear friend and *PCRM* cooking instructor and health coach Sharon McRae. You can find out more about her work at *www.Eatwell-Staywell. com.* This is delicious thinned out as a sauce for Zoodles.

INGREDIENTS:

2 - 15-ounce cans of salt-free garbanzo beans (or 3 cups cooked beans)
¾ to 1 cup water or liquid from the can, adjusted for desired thickness
2 cloves garlic
¾ cup sun-dried tomatoes (oil and salt free), about 3 ounces
½ of a medium red onion
4 Tablespoons nutritional yeast
2 teaspoons dried basil
1 teaspoon dried oregano

PREPARATION:

Place all ingredients in a high-powered blender and blend until smooth and creamy.

CHEF'S NOTE:

Try this instead of marinara sauce on your *Potato Pizzas* (recipe page 176).

RAINBOW FIESTA RICE

You can purchase all the ingredients for this festive dish at your local salad bar if you don't want to cook the rice or make the salsa.

INGREDIENTS:

One pound cooked brown rice (approximately 4 cups)
One cup *One-Minute Salsa* (recipe page 228) or more to taste
1 - 15-ounce can salt-free black beans (or 1.5 cups of cooked beans)
2-4 cups of mixed vegetables (or your favorite salad bar fixings) - For a rainbow effect, I like to use shredded carrots (orange), corn (yellow), peas (green), red onions (purple), and salsa (red).

PREPARATION:

Mix all ingredients together in a large bowl and chill.
Hey, if you can't wait, well, then go ahead and eat it warm or at room temperature.

CHEF'S NOTE:

We like to serve this with a large green salad. As plant-based pediatrician Dr. Jay Gordon likes to say, "Every day, eat a salad the size of your head!"

SPICED CARROT & ZUCCHINI QUINOA

This delicious recipe was contributed by my dear friend and *Healthy Taste of LA* demo coordinator extraordinaire, Melanie Hopkins.

INGREDIENTS:

8 cups quinoa, cooked (made from 2 cups of dry quinoa)
2 medium carrots, peeled, cut into small cubes
2 medium zucchinis, trimmed, cut into small cubes
1 Tablespoon Hungarian sweet paprika (different than SMOKED paprika)
1 teaspoon cinnamon

PREPARATION:

In a heavy large skillet over medium heat, sauté carrots in 1 tablespoon water or no-sodium broth until tender, about 5 minutes. Add zucchini and more liquid, if needed. Sauté until tender for about 3 minutes. Mix in paprika and cinnamon. Add quinoa to skillet. Toss to blend.

Delicious Desserts

On *The Ultimate Weight Loss Program*, we recommend fruit for dessert. But every now and then, you may want something a bit more special. So, here are two fruit-sweetened desserts that are mainly starch.

BUTTERSCOTCH PUDDING

Mairead Reddy brought this to an *Ultimate Weight Loss* potluck in Cleveland and I could not believe that it was made from only four ingredients. It is so creamy and delicious and reminds me of the *Snack Pack* butterscotch pudding my mom used to pack in my school lunches. It took me longer to learn how to pronounce Mairead's name (rhymes with parade) than it does to make this butterscotch pudding.

INGREDIENTS:

3 cups of roasted sweet potatoes, the orange flesh variety
2 large, ripe bananas
½ Tablespoon pumpkin pie spice*
½ teaspoon vanilla powder

PREPARATION:

Preheat oven to 400 degrees F.

Poke several holes in the sweet potatoes and roast them on a baking tray covered with a *Silpat* or other non-stick silicone baking mat. Roast for 60-90 minutes, until soft. Let cool and peel. Place all ingredients in a high-powered blender and blend until smooth and creamy. Pour into dessert glasses and chill.

CHEF'S NOTE:

Make sure you roast the sweet potatoes and not steam or microwave them. Slow roasting caramelizes them and brings out the flavor. You can pour the batter into popsicle molds and freeze for a delicious treat. You can also use this as a pie filling with a crust made from 2 cups of oats and 2 cups of pitted dates processed in a food processor fitted with the "S' blade, assuming that dates are not a trigger for you and you are at goal weight.

*concerning spice blends, please read my note under *Chili Fries, p.125.*

SWEET POTATO MOUSSE WITH CARAMELIZED APPLES

At the most recent *Healthy Taste of Sacramento*, I competed in an *Iron Chef.* The secret ingredients were sweet potato and apples, and I won the dessert round. Mary McDougall, Andrew "Spud Fit" Taylor, and Linda Middlesworth were the judges, who apparently all have excellent taste! ☺

For the Sweet Potato Mousse:
INGREDIENTS:

2 cups roasted sweet potatoes
1 cup roasted pears
½ teaspoon apple pie spice* or cinnamon

PREPARATION:

Preheat oven to 400 degrees F.

Roast the pear halves until golden brown on a *Crisp Ease* tray, *Silpat,* or other non-stick silicone baking mat. Poke several holes in the sweet potatoes and roast them on a baking tray covered with a *Silpat* or other non-stick silicone baking mat. Roast for 60-90 minutes, until soft. Place all ingredients in a food processor fitted with the "S" blade and process until smooth.

For the Caramelized Apples:
INGREDIENTS:

2 cups of apple, finely diced
1 cup of water or unsweetened pear juice (from the can or jar, if using)
½ teaspoon apple pie spice* or cinnamon

PREPARATION:

Place all ingredients in a small sauté pan and bring to a boil.
Reduce by continuing to cook until apples are soft and all the liquid is gone. Serve as a parfait on top of the chilled mousse.

CHEF'S NOTE:

The sweeter variety of apple that you use, the sweeter the topping will be. *Opal* and *Envy* are the sweetest to me and the green apples are the least sweet.

*concerning spice blends, please read my note under *Chili Fries, p.125.*

Frozen Fruit Desserts

On *The Ultimate Weight Loss Program*, you don't have to desert dessert, you just need to learn to prepare and enjoy them from natural whole food ingredients and use the fruit, the whole fruit, and nothing but the whole fruit.

APPLE PIE "ICE CREAM"

This is delicious on the *Apple Pie Squares* (recipe page 139).

INGREDIENTS:

1 large sweet apple, sliced and frozen (at least 10 ounces) I like to use *Envy* or *Gala*
2 large ripe bananas, peeled and frozen
1 cup unsweetened non-dairy milk
½ teaspoon vanilla powder
1 teaspoon apple pie spice* or cinnamon

PREPARATION:

In a high-powered blender, blend the apple, non-dairy milk, and spices until smooth. Add the frozen bananas and blend until thick and creamy. Enjoy immediately.

CHEF'S NOTE:

If you are making this for someone not following the *UWL Program* who would like a sweeter ice cream, substitute unsweetened apple juice for half of the almond milk.

*concerning spice blends, please read my note under *Chili Fries, p.125.*

You can watch me make this on Episode 11 of *Healthy Living with Chef AJ.*

BEETSICLES

An uncommon dessert that just can't be beet.

INGREDIENTS:

2 cups frozen cherries
1 frozen ripe banana
1 package of *Beet Boost* (or 1 rounded Tablespoon)
½ cup unsweetened non-dairy milk

PREPARATION:

Place all ingredients in a high-powered blender and blend until smooth. Pour into popsicle molds and freeze or enjoy immediately.

CHEF'S NOTE:

While I don't normally care for supplements, I LOVE this one because it's delicious! Simply made from beets and cherries, you can get it at *www.BeetBoost.com* and use code JP16 for a discount.

I like to use this as one of the layers in the *Layered "Ice Cream" Cake* (recipe page 263). This is my favorite flavor to layer with flavors of contrasting colors such as banana, mango, or pineapple.

BUTTERSCOTCH "ICE CREAM"

If you thought the pudding was creamy, dreamy, and delicious, wait until you taste it frozen!

INGREDIENTS:

3 cups of roasted sweet potatoes, the orange flesh variety
2 large, ripe bananas
½ Tablespoon pumpkin pie spice* or cinnamon
½ teaspoon vanilla powder

PREPARATION:

Preheat oven to 400 degrees F.

Poke several holes in the sweet potatoes and roast them on a baking tray covered with a *Silpat* or other non-stick silicone baking mat. Roast for 60-90 minutes, until soft. Let cool and peel. Place all ingredients in a high-powered blender and blend until smooth and creamy. Pour into ice cube trays and freeze until solid. Remove the frozen cubes from the tray and blend in a high-powered blender using as little unsweetened non-dairy milk as possible to get it to blend. You can also pour the mixture into popsicle molds and freeze for delicious Pumpkin Piesicles!

CHEF'S NOTE:

Make sure you roast the sweet potatoes and not steam or microwave them. Slow roasting caramelizes them and brings out the flavor.

*concerning spice blends, please read my note under *Chili Fries, p.125.*

FRESH HOMEMADE STRAWBERRY "ICE CREAM"

This is great to make when you don't have any frozen fruit on hand.

INGREDIENTS:

2 cups of sliced strawberries (preferably sweet ones)
2 cups of sliced bananas (preferably very ripe ones)

PREPARATION:

Place all ingredients in a *Cuisinart Fruit Scoop* and turn on. Let run for 25 minutes and enjoy! Be sure that the freezer bowl is frozen solid before using.

CHEF'S NOTE:

Keep in mind that the only ingredient in this ice cream is fresh fruit, so it's important that your fruit be as sweet as possible because freezing decreases the sweetness of the fruit. You cannot taste the bananas in this recipe, they are used for sweetness and creaminess, so please be sure they are plenty ripe so that your ice cream will be sweet. If I can find sweet raspberries, sometimes I will use them in place of some or all of the strawberries.

I have the *Yonanas* machine, the *Vitamix*, the *Blendtec* and the *Champion Juicer*. They all make great sorbets. What I like about this machine is that it is the only one that uses fresh fruit that is not frozen. And because it is churning for 25 minutes, it has a very nice texture.

LAYERED "ICE CREAM" CAKE

Recipe by Darshana Thacker, chef and culinary project manager for *Forks Over Knives* (*www.ForksOverKnives.com*). Darshana made this amazing dessert for Brian Wendel's birthday and I was blown away by its beauty, simplicity, and sheer deliciousness!

Makes: 1 9-inch cake
Ready in: 10 hours

The secret to making frozen-fruit ice cream is freezing the fruits when they are at their optimum sweetness. When using bananas, I make sure that they have plenty of dark freckles on them. Mangos should be fragrant and soft to the touch. Bagged frozen fruit works well, too—just try to avoid fruit with too many ice crystals, as they'll make the ice cream more like a slush.

The recipe is completed in stages: Each layer needs to freeze before the next one is added. I recommend using a *Vitamix* or a *Champion Juicer* to get the smoothest, creamiest texture.

INGREDIENTS:

6 ripe bananas (4 for the first layer and 1 each for the other two layers)
3 fresh mangos, or 1 (10-ounce) bag frozen mangos
1 (10-ounce) bag frozen raspberries or mixed berries
2 cups fresh fruit for topping mint leaves for garnish

PREPARATION:

1. Line a baking tray with a silicone mat. Break each banana into three chunks and spread them evenly on prepared tray. Peel and roughly chop mangos (if necessary) into large chunks. Transfer them to the tray with the bananas. Freeze overnight or for at least 4 hours.

2. Prepare first layer: Place 12 banana chunks in the *Vitamix* (or pass through the juicer) and process until smooth. Transfer puréed bananas to a spring-form pan; wrap with plastic and freeze for at least 2 hours.

3. Prepare next layer: Place frozen mangos and 3 banana chunks in the Vitamix (or pass through the juicer) and process until smooth. Remove springform pan from freezer and spread mango mixture over frozen banana layer. Wrap with plastic and freeze for at least 2 hours.

4. Prepare last layer: Place remaining frozen bananas and frozen berries in the Vitamix (or pass through the juicer) and process until smooth. Remove springform pan from freezer and spread berry mixture over frozen mango layer. Wrap with plastic and freeze for at least 2 hours.

5. When ready to serve, remove cake from freezer and let stand for 10 to 15 minutes. Remove the pan sides and place the base on a serving platter.

6. Decorate the top and sides with fresh fruits and mint leaves.

7. Serve immediately.

You can watch me making this cake on the YouTube video called Easy Plant-Based Dinner Party with Chef AJ:

https://www.youtube.com/watch?v=WLRg9pRfLBU&feature=youtu.be

MINT JULEP

This is reminiscent of a drink I used to enjoy at New Orleans Square in Disneyland.

INGREDIENTS:

2 Tablespoons lime juice
6 ounces of fresh baby spinach
1 ounce of fresh mint, about 1 cup
2 frozen bananas
1 cup of ice

PREPARATION:

In a high-powered blender, blend the spinach, mint, and lime juice to a liquid. Add the remaining ingredients and blend until thick and creamy and serve.

PEACHES AND CREAM "ICE CREAM"

When I was a kid, peaches and cream ice cream was one of my favorite flavors. The problem was that it was only seasonal and I was allergic to dairy. Now with frozen peaches being available all year round and thanks to non-dairy milk, I can have this sweet treat all year round!

INGREDIENTS:

8 ounces frozen peaches (approximately 2 cups)
8 ounces frozen bananas (approximately 2)
½ cup unsweetened non-dairy milk
½ teaspoon vanilla powder (optional)

PREPARATION:

Place all ingredients in a high-powered blender and blend until creamy. Enjoy immediately.

CHEF'S NOTE:

Delicious as a sundae with raspberry balsamic vinegar drizzled on top.

You can watch me make this on Episode 8 of *Healthy Living with Chef AJ.*

PUMPKIN PIE "ICE CREAM"

When I was 12 years old, *Baskin Robbins* had a seasonal flavor of ice cream that I loved called *Pumpkin Pie*. Now you can enjoy this delicious, healthy treat all year round without the sugar, dairy, or guilt, even when pumpkin is not in season or you can't find canned pumpkin.

INGREDIENTS:

2 peeled oranges (or ½ cup orange juice)
½ cup unsweetened non-dairy milk
8 ounces of carrots (approximately 1.5 cups), frozen
1 teaspoon pumpkin pie spice* or cinnamon
2 large ripe bananas, frozen

PREPARATION:

Mix all ingredients except for the bananas in a high-powered blender and blend until smooth. Add the bananas and blend until thick and creamy.

*concerning spice blends, please read my note under *Chili Fries, p.125*.

Dehydrated Treats

Dehydrated, crunchy foods are very easy to overeat because the water has been removed. I do not recommend these treats at all if you want to lose weight or if you discover that they are a problem for you, but for many of us at goal weight, they are a godsend when we travel and have a hard time finding enough SOS-free starchy foods to eat. Because they are dehydrated, they have a very long shelf life and do not require refrigeration.

Since I am not a raw foodist, I do not worry about what temperature I dehydrate at, so I crank it all the way up. Many factors affect drying times, especially how full your dehydrator is.

APPLE JACK CRACKERS

This reminds me of one of my favorite cereals from my childhood. You can eat these as crackers or break them up and enjoy as cereal with your favorite non-dairy milk.

INGREDIENTS:

½ cup gluten-free oats
½ cup unsweetened non-dairy milk
1 large apple, grated
½ teaspoon cinnamon or more to taste

PREPARATION:

Mix all ingredients in a large bowl. Spread mixture onto a *Teflex* sheet and dehydrate for a few hours until dry to the touch. Flip over and remove the *Teflex* sheets and continue drying directly on the screen for another 2-8 hours or until desired level of crunchiness is achieved.

CHEF'S NOTE:

If you are concerned about getting enough Omega 3 fatty acids, add a tablespoon of ground flax seeds or chia seeds. For those not following the *UWL Program*, add 2 table-spoons of currants. If it is still not sweet enough for them, you can add unsweetened apple juice in place of some or all the non-dairy milk.

GAME CHANGING gRAWnola

Finally, a *UWL*-approved granola!

INGREDIENTS:

6 cups of gluten-free oats, extra thick cut preferred
8 ounces very ripe bananas (approximately 2)
½ cup unsweetened applesauce
1 Tablespoon cinnamon
½ teaspoon cardamom

PREPARATION:

Purée bananas and applesauce in a blender until smooth. Pour over oats and spices and mix well. Place 4 cups of the wet mixture on a dehydrator tray fitted with a *Teflex* sheet and dehydrate at desired temperature about 2 hours until the top is dry to the touch. Flip over, then break *gRAWnola* into the size pieces you desire, and remove the *Teflex* sheet. Continue drying directly on the screen for another 2-8 hours until the desired level of crunchiness is achieved.

NACHO CHEEZE KALERITO CHIPS

Most kale chips are full of fat and salt, but not these.

If you thought that you would never be able to eat anything that tasted like *Nacho Cheese Doritos*, think again!

INGREDIENTS:

1 - 10-ounce bag of chopped curly kale (about 12 cups)
1 - 16-ounce bag of frozen cauliflower, defrosted
1 roasted red bell pepper (if you use jarred, soak well in water first to remove the salt)
3 Tablespoons lemon juice
2 teaspoons SMOKED paprika (different that regular paprika)
½ teaspoon onion powder
½ teaspoon garlic powder
½ teaspoon chipotle powder
¼ cup water (or just enough to get the batter to blend)
¼ cup nutritional yeast

PREPARATION:

Place the kale in a large bowl. Place remaining ingredients in a blender and blend until smooth. If the ingredients do not blend easily, add a bit more water, a tablespoon at a time, so that you can get a smooth batter. It will be thick. Pour batter over kale and coat well, either using your hands or latex-free food service gloves. If you like extra coating on your kale chips, make one and a half times the batter for the same amount of kale. Place the kale on two dehydrator sheets covered with a *Teflex* sheet and dehydrate at desired temperature until dry to the touch, a few hours. Then flip the chips and remove the *Teflex* sheet and continue dehydrating until dry, which could take another 2-8 hours, depending on the dehydrating temperature, the humidity, how full your dehydrator is, and the surface area exposed. Let cool and store in an airtight container—that is, if there is any left to store, as most people eat them all!

CHEF'S NOTE:

Chipotle peppers are smoked jalapeño peppers. They impart a smoky flavor and are only mildly spicy. If you would like these to be even spicier, substitute crushed red pepper flakes for the chipotle powder. I have not had good luck trying to make kale chips in the oven; they get too brittle and crumbly. If the 9-tray *Excalibur* is out of your budget, you can get the *Nesco* for a more affordable price.

I love using the crumbs as a topping for soups and salads.

PUMPKIN PIE BITES

Unlike cookies made from flour and sugar, these little gems are made up of mostly starch: oats and sweet potatoes. They are terrific for travel.

INGREDIENTS:

6 cups of *Sweet Potato Mousse* (recipe page 254) or *Butterscotch Pudding* (recipe page 253)
2 pounds extra thick cut oats, gluten free

PREPARATION:

Mix all ingredients together until fully incorporated. Using a retractable cookie scoop, place each cookie on the dehydrator tray fitted with a *Teflex* sheet and gently press each cookie down using the palm of your hand which has been moistened. Or, roll the batter into balls. Dehydrate for a few hours until dry to the touch, flip over, remove *Teflex* sheet, and continue dehydrating directly on the screen for 2-8 hours until the desired level of crunchiness is reached. These will further harden as they cool. If you have weak teeth, soak in plant milk before enjoying.

CHEF'S NOTE:

If you want these cookies even sweeter, then use fewer oats.

VANILLA FROSTING

To make a delicious creamy filling for a sandwich cookie, place 2 cups of roasted, peeled Japanese sweet potatoes, ½ teaspoon of vanilla powder, and ¼ cup (4 Tablespoons) date paste (recipe in *Unprocessed*) into a food processor fitted with the "S" blade. Drizzle in some unsweetened non-dairy milk a tablespoon at a time, just to get it to process into a thick but smooth filling. You will probably need about ¼ cup total. Generously spread filling in between two *Pumpkin Pie Bites*. Please only try this if you are at your goal weight and consuming dates is not a trigger for you.

SAVORY CRACKERS

Many participants tell me that one of the most difficult things about being flour free is that they miss crunchy foods like crackers. While it is possible to buy somewhat healthier crackers now, I still haven't found a commercial brand that either wasn't high in fat or didn't have added salt. Get creative making crackers using different cut up veggies and have fun! These are great with any of the soup recipes or crumbled over salads as croutons.

INGREDIENTS:

2 cups of INSTANT Steel Cut Oats
4 cups of no-sodium vegetable broth or water
1 large clove of garlic, pressed (or more to taste)
¾ cup sun-dried tomatoes (oil and salt free), cut into small pieces, about 3 ounces
1 ounce of dried mushrooms, chopped into small pieces
1 ounce of fresh basil, chiffonade cut
1 cup of whole leaf dulse (optional) – I get the smoked *Applewood Dulse* at *www. SeaVeg.com.*

PREPARATION:

Place all ingredients except for the basil in a medium-sized pot and bring to a boil. Reduce heat to a simmer, cover and cook for approximately 10 minutes until all the liquid is absorbed and oats are cooked. Stir in the fresh basil and dulse, if using. Spread mixture onto a *Teflex* sheet and dehydrate for a few hours until dry to the touch. Flip over and remove the *Teflex* sheets and continue drying directly on the screen for another 2-8 hours or until desired level of crunchiness is achieved.

TROPICAL TREATS

For me, these are the perfect cookies. Super crunchy and not too sweet. And because they are dehydrated, they last a really long time.

INGREDIENTS:

One pound of frozen mango, defrosted
One pound of very ripe bananas, weighed after peeling (3-5 depending on the size of the bananas). Please get a food scale. They are inexpensive and useful. They can be used for postage, too!
2 pounds of gluten-free oats (about 8 cups) I like the extra thick cut
Unsweetened coconut for decoration (optional)

PREPARATION:

In a blender, blend the fruit until smooth and pour over oats and mix well. Using a retractable cookie scoop, drop the batter onto a dehydrator sheet covered with a *Teflex*. You should be able to get at least 16 cookies on each tray, so you will need at least 3 trays, as this makes at least 3 dozen cookies. Gently press the scoops down with wet fingertips. Sprinkle with unsweetened coconut, if desired. Dehydrate at desired temperature until the cookies are dry to the touch on top, at least 2 hours, then flip them over, remove the *Teflex* sheet, and dry directly on the screen for another 2-8 hours until completely dry. How long you dehydrate them will depend on what temperature you are using and how crunchy you want them.

CHEF'S NOTE:

When raspberries are sweet and in season, I like to place one in the center of each cookie before dehydrating to make it look pretty.

A FEW OF MY FAVORITE THINGS:
EQUIPMENT AND PRODUCT LIST

The following list of tools and ingredients can assist you in the making of many of these recipes. They are not essential, but recommended. The only piece of equipment that I believe is absolutely essential for healthy eating is the *Instant Pot* electric pressure cooker.

Bema and Pa's Vinegar
www.bemaandpas.com

Use code CHEFAJ for 10% off your order

Chef Terry makes the most delicious vinegars that I've ever tasted and they are available in over thirty flavors. She showcases her vinegars at many conferences that I have been privileged to be a part of. I have tasted all of them and they are all delicious, but my personal favorites are the Cucumber Melon, Garlic Cilantro, Grapefruit, and the Smoke Infused, which tastes like BBQ sauce! They are all sugar-free and all are vegan except for the honey flavor. You can see me use them in Episode 8 of *Healthy Living with Chef AJ*.

Benson's Table Tasty
www.BensonsGourmetSeasonings.com

Use code AJ for 10% off your order

Debbie Benson created an outstanding line of salt-free seasonings for her mother who had heart disease. My personal favorite is the *Table Tasty*. It really does taste like salt! *Table Tasty* is the only one in the seasoning line that is free of both garlic and black pepper, which is good for me as I am allergic to black pepper and that is a key ingredient in most salt-free seasonings. Debbie used to sell her seasonings at a Farmer's Market near me and you could taste them all. Now that she has moved, they are only available online.

Champion Juicer
www.ChampionJuicer.com

When making banana "ice cream" for a large group, this machine can't be beat. While the very affordable *Yonanas* machine is great for one or two servings, it would not be able to make enough "ice cream" for my classes, which have at least twenty people attending. I have had my *Champion Juicer* since 1988 and I have never even used it to make juice! You can see me demonstrate it on Episode 9 of my television show *Healthy Living with Chef AJ* where I make "ice cream" and on Episode 2 where I use it to make peanut butter.

Crisp Ease Trays
Available at *Amazon* and select stores

A gift from my friend and *UWLer* Jackie, the fries that you can make with these clever trays are unparalleled. The best part is that you don't even have to turn them, and cleanup is a breeze.

Cuisinart Fruit Scoop
Available at stores like *Sur La Table* and on *Amazon*

This gadget is more of a luxury than a necessity but what I love about it is that it is the only sorbet maker that uses fresh fruit. Sometimes we just run out of frozen fruit or the bananas are not quite ripe enough for freezing. This machine is lightweight and very simple to use and clean and makes a very creamy frozen dessert. The only drawback is that it only makes enough for three to four people.

Excalibur Dehydrator
Do a *Google* search to find the lowest price

I got my Excalibur dehydrator in 2003 immediately after using one in culinary school. They are much less expensive now. I have seen the nine-tray for as little as $179 with free shipping. What I like about this brand is the shape. The trays are large and I prefer the square shape for making crackers. Please don't buy the five-tray to save money as you won't be able to make kale chips as they are just too voluminous. Many of my students have found these dehydrators at garage sales or on eBay in perfect condition for less than $50. If this is out of your price range, many of my students have told me that the *Nesco* dehydrator, which is often sold at *Costco* or *Walmart* for around $40 works well. If you get the Excalibur, please get the *Teflex* sheets to go with them or you will end up spending a fortune on parchment paper, which also is not great for the environment. I have never had success making any dehydrated recipe in the oven. You can easily make your own sun-dried tomatoes when tomatoes are ripe and in season and the machine will practically pay for itself.

Instant Pot Electric Pressure Cooker
www.Instantpot.com
$10 off at checkout with code AJ

This is a game changer for anyone who wants to eat healthy and save money and time. I have been vegan now for over forty years, and people constantly tell me that they, too, would eat more healthfully if they had more time and money. Well, when you start cooking in a pressure cooker, you will have both. You can cook pounds of beans for less than the price of a single can! And instead of taking two and a half hours, it takes only twenty minutes. You can cook steel-cut oats in only five minutes and quinoa in a minute! The *Instant Pot* is my favorite pressure cooker for many reasons. It has a stainless-steel insert and replaces many of your other appliances like your rice cooker and slow cooker. You can sauté right in the pot like you would right on the stove and you can even make yogurt in it. The company offers great customer service too. If you don't already have one, I recommend you get the 8-quart model. The 3-quart model is a great size for travel! You can see me use the *Instant Pot* on all 13 episodes of *Healthy Living with Chef AJ*.

Napa Valley Naturals Grand Reserve
www.NapaValleyNaturals.com

Use code 25STAR10 for 10% off your order

Some people just do not want to spend the money, especially for the shipping, for the designer flavored balsamic vinegars, so this brand is very affordable for your everyday use. Thick and syrupy and containing only 4% acidity as opposed to the 6% in most vinegar, this sweet vinegar will make you fall in love with your salads. It is pretty much all you need to use for dressing. I like to mix it with equal parts lime juice to cut down on the sweetness a bit and use it for my signature *Barefoot Dressing* (recipe page 205). It's also great for roasting vegetables and over steamed greens. Be sure you get the *Grand Reserve*, which is aged eighteen years. They have other flavors which also have a pink label, so it's easy to pick up the wrong one. I've done it more than once! The company offers discounts if you buy a case online. You can see me use this on Episode 13 of *Healthy Living with Chef AJ*.

Silicone Bakeware and Mats
Available on *Amazon* and many stores

Every time I see a chef use parchment paper, I cringe! We need to start thinking about the environment, people! I have used the same *Silpat* silicone baking mat for over thirty years. You don't have to get a name brand, but you do have to get one if you want to make food without oil. I have had roasted veggies and bean burgers stick to parchment paper, but never to silicone. It will discolor as you use it, but it is very easy to clean. For baking, you can get silicone bakeware in myriad shapes and sizes. I recommend that you at least get a muffin pan and an eight or nine-inch square pan. You can see me use this on Episode 6, 7 and 8 of *Healthy Living with Chef AJ*.

Vitamix
www.Vitamix.com

If you want to make hot soups quickly and creamy sorbets in minutes, a high-powered blender like the *Vitamix* is definitely the way to go. They are more affordable now than ever. I would purchase it wherever you can get the best warranty. What I love most about the *Vitamix* is the tamper. You can make really thick "ice cream" without using much liquid. You can see me use this on Episodes 1, 3, 5, 6, 8, 9, 10 and 11 of *Healthy Living with Chef AJ*.

Yonanas
www.Yonanas.com

If all you want to do is make banana soft serve, this is probably your best machine for the money. Affordable, easy to use and easy to clean, you can watch me make soft serve using it on Episode 1 of *Healthy Living with Chef AJ*.

RECIPE INDEX

ENDNOTES

1. *Statistics show that if one of your parents is obese, you have a forty percent chance of becoming obese.* https://www.ncbi.nlm.nih.gov/pmc/articles/PMC3005642/

2. *While today one out of every five kids under the age of eighteen is obese* https://www.cdc.gov/healthyschools/obesity/facts.htm

3. *... a well-known study by the World Cancer Research Fund, http://www.wcrf.org/sites/default/files/Second-Expert-Report.pdf, p.379*

4. *Those who ate the most vegetables consistently had the lowest body weight and BMI.* https://www.ncbi.nlm.nih.gov/pubmed/26394033

5. *A scientific experiment was conducted with people who were self-professed chocoholics.* http://ajcn.nutrition.org/content/61/6/1206.abstract

6. *The Center for Disease Control (CDC) predicts that in a few short years, over forty percent of Americans will be obese.* http://articles.latimes.com/2012/may/07/news/la-heb-obesity-projection-20120507

7. *...bitter compounds, such as those found in vegetables like broccoli, can turn off the hunger switch.* http://www.ncbi.nlm.nih.gov/pmc/articles/PMC3033292

8. *...it is "significantly more important to worry about not consuming excess fat than it is to worry about consuming sufficient omega-3."* Pulde, Alona, and Lederman, Matthew, *The Forks Over Knives Plan*, N.Y., Simon & Schuster, 2014, p.104

9. *...MRI images showed that as people ate more fruits and vegetables, they exhibited more brain pleasure from them* http://now.tufts.edu/news-releases/training-your-brain-prefer-healthy-foods, Deckersbach T, Das SK, Urban LE, Salinardi T, Batra P, Rodman AM, Arulpragasam AR, Dougherty DD, Roberts SB. "Pilot randomized trial demonstrating reversal of obesity-related abnormalities in reward system responsivity to food cues with a behavioral intervention." Nutrition & Diabetes. Published online ahead of print September 1, 2014. doi:10.1038/nutd.2014.26

10. ...Dr. Pamela Peeke says, "We now know that when you awaken the sleeping dragon of addiction, it becomes stronger, more powerful, and twice as deadly as before."— Peeke, Pamela and van Aalst, Mariska, "The Hunger Fix: The Three-Step Detox and Recovery Plan for Overeating and Food Addiction," N.Y., Rodale, 2012, p.125

ABOUT THE AUTHORS

Chef AJ is the author of the popular book *Unprocessed*, which chronicles her journey from a junk-food vegan faced with a diagnosis of pre-cancerous polyps, to learning how to create foods that nourish and heal the body. She was overweight by age five, obese by age eleven, and nearing 200 pounds in her twenties. Once she discovered *The Secrets to Ultimate Weight Loss*, she began to share that vital information with others.

Chef AJ began her career with a comedy act and appeared on *The Tonight Show* four times. She is the creator of *The Ultimate Weight Loss Program*, and *Healthy Taste of L.A.* She holds a certificate in Plant-Based Nutrition from eCornell & the T. Colin Campbell Center for Nutrition Studies. She dedicates herself to teaching how to create meals to transform health, while dealing with cravings and food addiction. She has practiced a plant exclusive diet for over forty years.

FOR MORE INFORMATION VISIT WWW.EATUNPROCESSED.COM

Glen Merzer is a playwright, screenwriter, and author. He is proud to be the co-author, with Chef AJ, of her first book, *Unprocessed*. He is also co-author, with Howard Lyman, of *Mad Cowboy* and *No More Bull!*; with Pam Popper, of *Food Over Medicine*; with Del Sroufe, of *Better Than Vegan*; and with Benji Kurtz, of *The Plant Advantage*. His first novel, *Off the Reservation*, the story of a vegan congressman from Bloomington, IN, who runs for president, was chosen by *Kirkus Reviews* as one of the Best Indie Novels of 2015, and was selected by *The Progressive Magazine* as one of their Favorite Books of 2015.

Made in the USA
Columbia, SC
27 October 2020